RORSCHACHIANA XXVII

RORSCHACHIANA XXVII

Yearbook of the International Rorschach Society

Edited by

Anne Andronikof

University of Paris 10, France

HOGREFE

Summary translations into Spanish: Pr. Concepcion Sendin
Summary translations into French: Pr. Anne Andronikof

PUBLISHING OFFICES
USA: Hogrefe & Huber Publishers, 875 Massachusetts Avenue, 7th Floor, Cambridge, MA 02139, Tel. (866) 823-4726, Fax (617) 354-6875
E-mail info@hhpub.com
Europe: Hogrefe & Huber Publishers, Rohnsweg 25, 37085 Göttingen, Germany, Tel. +49 551 49609-0, Fax +49 551 49609-88,
E-mail hhpub@hogrefe.de

SALES AND DISTRIBUTION
USA: Hogrefe & Huber Publishers, Customer Service Department, 30 Amberwood Parkway, Ashland, OH 44805,
Tel. (800) 228-3749, Fax (419) 281-6883, E-mail custserv@hhpub.com
Europe: Hogrefe & Huber Publishers, Rohnsweg 25
37085 Göttingen, Germany
Tel. +49 551 49609-0, Fax +49 551 49609-88, E-mail hhpub@hogrefe.de

OTHER OFFICES
Canada: Hogrefe & Huber Publishers, 1543 Bayview Avenue, Toronto, Ontario, M4G 3B5
Switzerland: Hogrefe & Huber Publishers, Länggass-Strasse 76, CH-3000 Bern 9

Hogrefe & Huber Publishers
Incorporated and registered in the State of Washington, USA, and in Göttingen, Lower Saxony, Germany

Printed and bound in Germany
ISSN 1192-5604
ISBN 0-88937-303-5

Table of Contents

Other Topics

Addresses of First Authors

Anne Andronikof
Laboratoire IPSé
Université Paris 10
200, av. de la République
92001-Nanterre
France
andronik@u-paris10.fr

Paul T. Costa, Jr.
Laboratory of Personality and Cognition
Gerontology Research Center
5600 Nathan Shock Drive
Baltimore, MD 21224–6825
USA
paulc@lpc.grc.nia.nih.gov

Antonella De Carolis M.D.
Dept. of Psychiatric Sciences and Psychological Medicine
University of Roma "La Sapienza"
P. le Aldo Moro 5
00185 Rome
Italy
adeca@tin.it

Gregorio E.H. del Pilar
College of Social Sciences and Philosophy
Palma Hall
University of the Philippines, Diliman
Quezon City 1101
Philippines
gregdelpilar@up.edu.ph

Dragana Djurić Jočić
Institute for Psychiatry
Clinical Centre of Serbia
Pasterova 2
11 000 Belgrade
Serbia & Montenegro
midjocic@eunet.yu

John E. Exner
Rorschach Workshops
P.O. Box 9010
Asheville, NC 28815-9010
USA

Carl B. Gacono, Ph.D.
P.O. Box 140633
Austin, TX 78714
USA
DrCarl14@aol.com

Carmen García-Alba
Ronda Delicias 21
Majadahonda
28220 Madrid
Spain
garciaalba@wanadoo.es

Giovanni Marchioro, Ph.D.
Department of Oncology and OncoHematology, U.L.S.S. n°13
Ospedale Civile "P.F. Calvi"
Largo San Giorgio, 3
30033 Noale (Venezia)
Italy
giovanni.marchioro@tin.it

Addresses of First Authors

Dorit Noy-Sharav, M.A.
26, Hechalutz Street,
96222 Jerusalem
Israel
salo@bezeqint.net

Jean-Michel Petot
Laboratoire de Psychologie clinique
des Faits culturels
Université de Paris 10
200, av. de la République
92001-Nanterre
France
Jean-Michel.Petot@u-paris10.fr

Rorschachiana 27, 1–3

Editorial Note

Anne Andronikof

University of Paris 10, France

Science and Soul: Use and Misuse of Computerized Interpretation

Recently, I was contacted by a student who was working on his MA research in psychology: He explained that neither his research director nor he knew anything about the Rorschach but that he wanted to use it in his dissertation about cancer patients. Could I recommend someone who would be willing to score the Rorschach protocols he had collected so that he could process them through "one of these automated interpretation programs"? True, he was "only" a student, but his work was supervised by a colleague and a strident alarm bell went off in my mind.

Indeed, several software programs can be found on the market today, which generate instant interpretive statements for the Rorschach based on statistics mixed with a zest of speculation. The professional (as opposed to amateur) psychologist has to make up his or her mind as to the exact value of these programs and come to a decision: To use or not to use computerized interpretation. Needless to say, the temptation is great, as it substantially reduces the time and energy necessitated by the interpretation process. It also can convey a sense of confidence through the illusory beliefs that a computer cannot be wrong, that statistics make science, and that science determines truth. Whereas these beliefs, which blossomed in the hard (or exact) sciences during most of the past two centuries, are nowadays laughed at by serious scientists, the human sciences seem to be scrambling to acquire the status of "science" by laying claim to these so-called scientific criteria.

But let us for a moment assume there is some truth in those beliefs. Let us assume statistics do help the researcher in separating speculation from facts . . . For the Rorschach interpreter, the snag is that he or she is dealing with human beings, who are known to be complex and unique. Every single clinician has experienced the *fact* that each client to some degree escapes general rules and that identical protocols simply exist no more than identical life behaviors and life histories. Some people do bear a deficient chromosome but will never develop the disease attached to it. Some people display some known "psychotic" feature in the structural summary of their Rorschach protocol but function adaptively in real life, or a specific variable that purports to describe psychopaths but are aeons from delinquency, and so on and so forth.

The discrepancy between computer-produced statements and a custom-made individual interpretation has two reasons. First, a scientific reason: A statistical correlation is not a causal explanation and human behavior does not obey deterministic laws. The second reason has to do with the magic of the Rorschach: A given variable value, a given feature, changes in its interpretive significance as a function of other variable values. This interpretive significance in turn is modified by clinical reality (i.e., the real client).

I personally have put to test various computer interpretation programs and was at first impressed by their thoroughness in scanning the variable clusters but eventually saddened, when not appalled, by the result: A litany of impersonal statements comparing the subject to "most people," sometimes contradictory, and, in some of the programs, wild interpretations apparently based on content features and other non-evidence-based elements. Some programs stray so far as to provide diagnostic statements (clinicians do know that not a single psychiatric diagnosis can be drawn directly from the Rorschach). The whole process and outcome reminded me of a long-standing astrology program which blurts out a complete description of your character and fate when fed with a single entry: Your date and place of birth. How many clinicians pay due attention to the honest and cautionary statements and disclaimers often included in the programs as to their use?

Interpreting a Rorschach protocol is a constantly renewed adventure of the mind, a task that can be earnestly and ethically fulfilled only if the psychologist can draw on all his or her scientific knowledge and go beyond anonymous general statements to reach the uniqueness and complexity of the real person he or she has agreed to assess. If professionals solely rely on computerized programs, then the question is not "what's wrong with the Rorschach?" but "what's wrong with the psychologists?." If psychologists rely exclusively or extensively on computer-generated interpretive statements to formulate their final evaluation, the Rorschach test will be definitively discredited as a valuable tool in personality assessment. Let us remember the profound remark by François Rabelais*: *"Science sans conscience n'est que ruine de l'âme,"* which means "science without conscience is but destruction of the soul."

Comment on "Science and Soul"

John E. Exner, Jr.

Rorschach Workshops, Asheville, NC, USA

Professor Andronikof has focused on an important timely issue in her brief discussion of computerized interpretations of the Rorschach. While computer programs can be of assistance to those using the Rorschach, the outputs from those programs can easily be abused if the user proceeds on the naive assumption that each statement generated by the interpretative segment of the program is valid and complete. Typically, most programs include disclaimers that give emphasis to the fact that interpretative statements are only empirically based hypotheses that must be reviewed and evaluated carefully by the user. These disclaimers are necessary because the computer cannot deviate from its assigned rounds. It cannot think, and it cannot integrate data at a level higher than that for which it has been programmed. The complexity and uniqueness of each human makes it essentially impossible for any program to be developed that would account for all of the idiosyncratic features that mark the individual, but the competent human interpreter can usually do this. As Andronikof points out, excessive reliance on interpretative programs is bad psychology and simply reflects a sort of naivety or carelessness by the program user and ultimately does a grave disservice to clients and the profession.

* French humanist and writer, first half of the 16th century.

Special Section
The Rorschach and the Five-Factor Theory

Rorschachiana 27, 7–10

Introduction to the Special Section on the Rorschach and the Five-Factor Theory

Dragana Djurić Jočić[1] and Jean-Michel Petot[2]

[1]*Institute of Psychiatry, Clinical Center of Serbia, Belgrade, Serbia-Montenegro*
[2]*Département de Psychologie, Université Paris X-Nanterre, France*

Whatever one's judgment is concerning the so-called "Big Five Model" or "Five-Factor Theory" of personality – which is largely accepted, but still vehemently criticized by some researchers (Eysenck, 1992; Block, 1999) – no one can deny that the emergence of this model in the last decade of the 20th century was the main event in the recent history of the academic psychology of personality. Whereas former theories claimed to account for all individual differences either by a set of two or three very broad superfactors (Eysenck), or by a host of more specific factors (Cattell), the Big Five Model, first suggested by Fiske (1949) and later by Norman (1963), implies that five, and only five, factors are needed for explanation of the variance of all personality questionnaires and descriptions of individual differences in human behavior and personality. These factors are: *Neuroticism* or negative emotionality vs emotional stability; *Extraversion* vs introversion; *Openness to Experience* vs closedness, routine-mindedness and down-to-earth attitude; *Agreeableness* vs tough-mindedness; and *Conscientiousness* vs lack of control or Ego weakness. The growing success of this theory was largely due to the high psychometric qualities of the NEO Personality Inventory (NEO-PI) and the NEO Personality Inventory Revised (NEO PI-R), which were developed by Paul T. Costa and Robert R. McCrae (1988, 1992) in order to operationalize the Five-Factor Theory, and the clinical interest of which was soon recognized by practitioners and researchers (Miller, 1991; Widiger & Trull, 1992). Deborah Greenwald (1999) was the first researcher who investigated the relationship of the five broad factors with several selected Rorschach variables, and she obtained very low or confounding results, contrary to the expectations grounded on theory.

During that time, clinical psychologists were faced with a growing revival of criticism against the Rorschach Inkblot Method. While these criticisms had toned down for almost three decades, probably thanks to the methodological improvements brought by the development of the Exner's Comprehensive System, the polemic was revived in the last few years (Garb, 1999; Lilienfield et al., 2000). Among several more or less relevant arguments, one of the most pertinent is that the Rorschach scores and ratios have only poor or no correlations with the dimensions assessed by recognized inventories of personality, the psychometric properties of which are well established. As Drs. Costa and McCrae remind us in their contribution to this special section, this fact really raises question about the validity of Rorschach measures, and must be thoroughly discussed, so that it seemed desirable to sum up the present situation of this issue. Is it possible to find Rorschach correlates or markers of the Big Five? And if not, what are the reasons for that? The present special section is intended to bring some facts and ideas that could clarify this matter. It comprises six papers, four of which are grounded on empirical research, and another two on theoretical reflection.

The empirical contributions were made by psychologists, coming from different countries (France, Italy, Philippines, and Serbia-Montenegro), who recently conducted research on the relationship between the Rorschach and at least one of the "Big Five" dimensions of personality. Dragana Djurić Jočić (Serbia-Montenegro) presents her work, grounded on sophisticated statistical analyses of Rorschach and NEO PI-R data collected with 200 Serbian psychiatric patients, and concluding that there is some structural relation between the five factors and some Rorschach constellations of scores and ratios, even though the magnitude of correlations is low. Jean-Michel Petot (France) proposes an empirical test of the idea proposed by Gregory Meyer, that control of the patients' test taking attitude could enhance the otherwise disappointing correlations between self-report questionnaires and Rorschach data. He investigated the Rorschach correlates of the Big Five dimension Openness on a sample of 96 French psychiatric outpatients, but the findings do not support the test taking attitude hypothesis. Gregorio del Pilar (Philippines) reports his findings on the relationship between self-report markers of Eysenck's extroversion and Five Factor Theory extraversion with Rorschach extratensiveness, and his work confirms that this relation does exist and is statistically significant, even tough it is rather low, in a sample of 129 Philippine college students. The work by Antonella De Carolis and Stefano Ferracuti (Italy), founded on data from a sample of 47 healthy volunteers, demonstrate this fact is not restricted to the Five

Factor Theory and its operationalization by the NEO PI-R: they found some correlation between Eysenck's Big Three model extraversion and neuroticism, which also are present in the Five Factor Theory, and the supposedly related Rorschach variables. The special section is concluded by two more theoretical papers: in the first, Paul T. Costa and Robert R. McCrae (United States), from their point of view of scientists having brought the Five Factor Theory to its present state of sophistication, propose a thorough and provocative reflection on the clinical interest of the Rorschach. As they express some doubt on the validity of this instrument, they view it mainly as a tool facilitating relation and self-expression in a clinical setting. Finally, Petot (France) and Djurić Jočić (Serbia-Montenegro) conclude this series by reviewing several methodological and theoretical points that may contribute to explain the disappointing lack of correlation between the self-report assessment of dimensions recognized by psychology of personality, and the Rorschach assessment of personality.

References

Archer, R.P., & Krishnamurthy, R. (1993). A review of MMPI and Rorschach interrelationships in adult samples. *Journal of Personality Assessment, 61*, 277–293.

Block, J. (1995). A contrarian view of the five-factor approach to personality description. *Psychological Bulletin, 117*, 187–215.

Costa, P.T., & McCrae, R.R. (1992). *The NEO Personality Inventory revised manual.* Odessa, FL: Personality Assessment Resources.

Costa, P.T., & Widiger, T.A. (1994). *Personality disorders and the five-factor model of personality.* Washington, DC: American Psychological Association.

Eysenck, H.J. (1992). Four ways five factors are *not* basic. *Personality and Individual Differences, 13*, 667–673.

Fiske, D.W. (1949). Consistency of the factorial structures of personality rating from different sources. *Journal of Abnormal and Social Psychology, 44*, 329–344.

Garb, H.N. (1999). Call for a moratorium on the use of the Rorschach Inkblots in clinical and forensic settings. *Assessment, 6*, 313–315.

Greenwald, D.F. (1991). Personality dimensions reflected by the Rorschach and the 16PF. *Journal of Clinical Psychology, 47*, 708–715.

Greenwald, D.F. (1999). Relationships between the Rorschach and the NEO-five-factor inventory. *Psychological Reports, 85*, 519–527.

Lilienfeld, S.O., Wood, J.M., & Garb, H.N. (2000). The scientific status of projective techniques. *Psychological Science in the Public Interest, 1*, 25–66.

Meyer, G.J. (1999). The convergent validity of MMPI and Rorschach scales: An extension using profile scores to define response and character styles on both methods and a reexamination of simple Rorschach response frequency. *Journal of Personality Assessment, 72*, 1–35.

Miller, T.R. (1991). The psychotherapeutic utility of the five-factor model of personality. *Journal of Personality Assessment, 57*, 415–433.

Norman, W.T. (1963). Toward an adequate taxonomy of personality attributes: Replicated factor structure in peer nomination personality ratings. *Journal of Abnormal and Social Psychology, 66*, 574–583.

Widiger, T.A., & Trull, T.J. (1992). Personality and Psychopathology: An application of the five-factor model. *Journal of Personality, 60*, 363–393.

Rorschachiana 27, 11–29

Correlation of the Rorschach Method and the NEO PI-R Questionnaire

Dragana Djurić Jočić

Institute for Psychiatry, Clinical Center of Serbia

The problem of convergent validity has been investigated with two clinical instruments that have been the focus of psychologists who specialize in personality assessment. NEO-PI-R is a new generation questionnaire characterized by high metric characteristics, while the Rorschach method has been revitalized and methodologically improved by the Comprehensive System application.

So far, no systematic investigation on the correlation of these two instruments has been published. Nevertheless, the findings obtained by MMPI-2 and Rorschach methods can be taken as referential. Opposite to what we expected, studies have shown that the obtained correlations of MMPI-2 and Rorschach Inkblot Method (RIM) are low or nonexistent (Archer & Krishnamurty, 1993). Although this may imply that either both instruments or one of them are invalid, common practice calls these conclusions into question since clinicians integrating the results of both instruments find them useful in clinical evaluation. Faced with discrepancy in the results, they calmly apply the process of clinical evaluation and integration trying to explain the difference in the light of each particular case. Studies have shown that validity of both instruments in evaluation of objective, external, criteria justify their application since criterion validity (correlation between instruments of evaluation and the psychological constructs they are supposed to measure) is believed to be more important than concurrent validity (correlation between instruments developed for measurement of the same construct).

If the convergent value of the questionnaire and RIM is low, we wanted to know whether the NEO PI-R questionnaire, focusing more on personality traits, would be more correlated with Rorschach indicators than MMPI-2, focusing on the symptomatology level. Second, the correlation of the RIM with the Five-Factor personality Model (Big Five or FFM) has not been studied, so these findings substantiate the correlation of methods and personality theory.

Method

According to the defined problem, the following aims were recognized:

1. Analysis of the relationship between the two instruments for personality evaluation according to an analysis of theoretical concepts and empirical correlation of these indicators.
2. Recognition and investigation of factors influencing the obtained correlation level of the two instruments.
3. Aggregation of data to enable formation of normative database of the Rorschach method for our population.

General Expectations

1. There is some conceptual similarity between some indicators of Rorschach method and NEO-PI-R questionnaire, while some indicators are almost completely uncorrelated.
2. There is a statistically significant correlation between conceptually similar defined indicators of the two instruments.
3. Type and level of the obtained correlation of the two instruments depend on the type of psychopathology of the subjects.

Variables

NEO-PI-R variables are defined as both domains and facets of the scale. There are 5 domains and 30 facets (6 for each domain).

Rorschach variables are included in the form of scores; proportions are expressed as categories (EB). Selection of variables was made in light of conceptual similarities of the crossed variables. The correlation analysis included domains and facets of the questionnaire. In other types of analysis only domains were used since the poor metric properties of facets would yield invalid results on the small sample. The first set of variables was composed of five domains of the NEO-PI-R questionnaire and another set of 32 Rorschach variables was selected in such a way as to have conceptual similarities with domains and show possible correlation with domains in the correlation analysis.

According to operationalization of variables of the two instruments, conceptually similar variables can be recognized and accordingly a table of expected relations was drawn. The problem is that indicators of the same name frequently have differently defined entity territory, so the description of a variable is a better guide for definition of assumed relations than the name itself.

Sample

The study included 200 psychiatric patients (outpatients and inpatients). Half of them were diagnosed as nonpsychotic, mostly with anxious depressive disorder. The other half were diagnosed as psychotic, mostly schizophrenic, and some with schizoaffective or affective disorders. Paranoid cases were excluded. The sample was selected according to psychiatric diagnosis and ICD 10 criteria . The sample was matched for sex (100 men and 100 women), age (range 17–57 years, $M = 33.88$, $SD = 10.87$), and education (mostly high school or university degree).

Instruments

The RIM was applied in the main study and interpreted according to the Comprehensive System (Exner, 1993). The NEO-PI-R questionnaire was also applied (Costa & McCrae, 1992) based on the FFM.

Data Processing Method

The sample was aggregated over a period of 3 years. Ten specialists of clinical psychology applied it. All were experienced in clinical practice ans all were trained in application and interpretation of the RIM. Each protocol was evaluated by 2–3 independent experts and in cases of coding discrepancy the problem was managed by a group of evaluators. Protocols with less than 17 or more than 27 answers were discarded in order to control the influence of number of answers on indicators. The protocols with Lambda values exceeding 0.99 were eliminated. The coded protocols were processed by the RIAP3 program (Exner, 1995). Variables of both instruments were processed by the SPSS program and specially designed software for canonical correlation analysis and canonical analysis of covariance (Momirovic, 1994).

Statistical analysis implied descriptive and psychometric analysis of the instruments. Analysis of the results was performed using correlation analysis in order to determine associations between the individual conceptually similar variables. Relations between variable sets were examined by the means of correlation analysis, factor analysis, canonical correlation analysis, canonical analysis of covariances, and asymmetric redundancy analysis. Identification of aberrant objects was performed in order to obtain qualitative interpretation of the results. Canonical analysis of covariances was applied for separate samples of nonpsychotic and psychotic subjects. Because of the large number of variables and relatively small sample, we believed that correlation analysis was insufficient and that more information on correlations between the two instruments would be obtained by statistical procedures examining the correlations between variable sets in general. In this article we present a part of our results.

Results

1. Descriptive and psychometric analysis of instruments has shown that they can be used for our population. For all the Rorschach variables the examiners achieved (91%) concordance, the maximum for localizations and popular responses (94.4% and 93.6%), and the minimum for Sum Shade and Sum6SpSc (88.4% and 89.6%).
2. Correlation analysis investigated the type of correlation between individual variables. The whole sample ($N = 200$) yielded a small number of low and significant correlations that can be interpreted logically (range between $r = .30–.40$). Most correlations have been obtained for Rorschach variables and the domains of Openness and Extraversion. If the sample was divided according to certain criteria (type of pathology, Erlebnistypus, R, Lambda) larger numbers of significant correlations of a moderate range were obtained.
3. The canonical correlation analysis of the two sets of variables allows selection of five independent levels of correlation, but only one of them is significant (at the level .01). The significant canonical function is moderate (0.58).

Table 1. Correlation of facets and individual Rorschach indicators for the group of anxious depressive patients.

	N		E		O		A		C	
Facets 1			Pure H	.25*	Zf	.32***	An + Xy	.26*	An + Xy	-25.**
					EA	.31***				
					DQ+	.31**				
					FD	.28**				
					Intell	.28**				
					SumC	.27**				
					W	.26***				
Facets 2	MOR	.25**	An + Xy	–.25*	EA	.31**				
			Ego index	.25*	Intell	.30**				
					Sum C	.27**				
					Pure H	.27*				
Facets 3							V	–.25***		
Facets 4			Ego Index	.25*						
Facets 5	EA	.31**	EA	.25*	Intell	.40***				
	Blends	.31**			W	.35***				
	Index res.	.26**			EA	.32***				
	Sum C	.26*			Zf	.32**				
					FD	.30**				
					DQ+	.30**				
					M	.26*				
Facets 6					R	.25*				

$^{*}p < .05$; $^{**}p < .01$; $^{***}p < .001$

Table 4 presents the canonical factors of the left and right sets of variables. The canonical factor of the Rorschach variable set can be interpreted as complexity and responsiveness, i.e., absence of simplification and constriction of the psychic processes. Structural inspection reveals its content: complexity (Blends), aggressiveness (AG), introspection (FD), ideation beyond conscious control (m), introversion (–EB), absence of difficulty in responding to daily requirements (–CDI), absence of motive to simplify stimuli and make problem solutions as simple as possible (–L). Some indicators contribute to the selected functions little or not at all (Afr, Isolate, Ego Index, DEPI, D).

The canonical factors of the NEO-PI-R variables are +N (moderately

Table 2. Correlation of facets and individual Rorschach indicators for the group of psychotic patients.

	N		E		O		A		C	
Facets 1			MOR	–.27**	m	.38***	MOR	–.29**	Index res.	–.25*
					es	.33***			Afr	.25*
					EB	.31**				
Facets 2	m	.28**	S	–26**			Intell	–.27*	S	–.25*
									COP	.25*
Facets 3	m	.36**	Pure H	.25*	M	.26*			FM	–.25*
	AG	.30**			m	.25*			EB	.25*
					Pure H	.25*				
Facets 4	AG	.25*	W:M	.45***			An + Xy	–.25*		
			CF + C	.36***						
			SumC	.34***						
Facets 5	m	.29**	Zd	.26**					m	–.34***
	AG	.29**							AG	–.34***
Facets 6			W	.26*			Y	.30**	AG	–.27**
			Pure H	.25*						

$^{*}p < .05$; $^{**}p < .01$; $^{***}p < .001$

Table 3. Coefficients of canonical correlations and their significance for the whole sample of psychiatric patients ($N = 200$).

	ρ	λ	Hi2	df	sig
1	.583	.322	203.966	160.000	.011
2	.495	.487	129.335	124.000	.011
3	.458	.645	78.797	90.000	.795
4	.316	.817	36.440	58.000	.988
5	.305	.907	17.564	28.000	.937

positive), +O (moderately positive), –C, –E, –A (moderately negative), so that it is composed of introversion, liability to psychopathologic response, and openness to experience as compared to low consciousness (efficacy, success, organization) and lack of collaboration in interpersonal reactions.

Thus, in the closest correlation, these two sets overlap in the fields of openness to experience, which may be positive (healthy interest in environment) and negative (as openness to psychopathological experience). Thus, psychological complexity, responsiveness, and dynamism corre-

Table 4. Canonical factors of the set of Rorschach and NEO-PI-R variables.

Rorschach variables	1	NEO-PI-R variables	1
Pure blend	.466	N	.530
AG	.449	E	–.392
FD	.427	O	.475
m	.399	A	–.259
S	.365	C	–.474
Shade	.352		
Passive	.351		
es	.325		
Active	.286		
Zf	.283		
M	.255		
FM	.232		
Intell	.191		
EA	.184		
X+%	.083		
Zd	.082		
R	.079		
W	.067		
Isolate	.059		
Ego index	.035		
DEPI	.020		
D	–.024		
SumC	–.030		
SCZI	–.081		
Afr	–.100		
Sum 6	–.101		
X–%	–.120		
AdjDScor	–.138		
DScor	–.208		
L	–.244		
CDI	–.282		
EB	–.288		

Table 5. Analysis of overlapping.

Analysis of Rorschach set of variables overlapping			
	var	Red	gen
CV1–1	.061	.021	.504
Analysis of NEO-PI-R set of variables overlapping			
	var	Red	gen
CV2–1	.190	.065	–.063

Table 6. Canonical analysis of covariances, correlation, and significance test for the group of anxious depressive patients.

	Ro	ro2	f-test	df1	df2	sig
1	.443	.196	23.866	1.000	98.000	.000

spond to the concept of Openness, but they are saturated with increased readiness to record unpleasant emotions and experiences and to respond in a psychopathological manner (nonpsychotic). Saturation of the function with inversion, social incompatibility, and low overall efficacy show that this is not necessarily a model of desirable functioning.

Table 5 presents variances, redundancies, and generalizability for Rorschach and NEO-PI-R set variables. The amount of variance explained by the first canonical function of the set of Rorschach variables is low, implying that the canonical factor is not satisfactorily representative for the whole set of measured variables. The factor separated from the NEO-PI-R set is more representative for the specific variable set. Redundancy evidences that separated Rorschach factors explains greater variability within the set of NEO PI-R variables, and more information is obtained from the Rorschach set. Generalizability is greater for the set of Rorschach variables and it shows that the set is more stable than the set of NEO PI-R variables.

4. Canonical analysis of covariance in the group of nonpsychotic (anxious-depressive) patients examined the relation between two groups of variables. It identified a function of .44 significant at the level .00.

Table 7 shows the pattern and structure of the two sets of variables. In the group of nonpsychotic patients two sets of variables were in the closest correlation in the combination of factors that may be interpreted as an overall openness to experience, the personality capacity, and ego strength. Although this factor was visible in the analysis of the whole sample, it is recognized in a more pure form in the group of nonpsychotic patients since it is not contaminated with psychopathology, but results from personal style. The function comprised Rorschach variables that were most closely correlated with the domain of Openness (+EA, +Pure Blend, +Zf, +M, +FD, –CDI).

Analysis of overlap shows that the two sets of variables contribute uniformly in the common quasi-canonical factor even in respect to other results.

Table 7. Pattern and structure of Rorschach and NEO-PI-R variables for the group of anxious depressive patients.

Rorschach variables	X	F	NEO-PI-R variables	X	F
EA	.375	.890	N	.294	.045
Pure Blend	.283	.744	E	.200	.572
Zf	.245	.732	O	.896	.899
M	.268	.725	A	–.227	–.191
FD	.237	.646	C	–.137	.002
a	.192	.642			
W	.204	.612			
Sum Shade	.238	.604			
Intell	.288	.585			
AG	.132	.511			
D Score	.165	.501			
AdjDScore	.197	.486			
Sum6SpSc	.175	.444			
Sum C	.219	.400			
S Score	.208	.389			
p	.104	.367			
SCZI	.101	.288			
Isolate	.110	.249			
m	.045	.226			
DEPI	.074	.221			
Ego Index	.138	.210			
es	–.037	.145			
R	.083	.131			
X–%	.052	.055			
FM	–.013	.099			
S	.085	.054			
Zd	.030	–.028			
EB	–.073	–.123			
X+%	–.056	–.131			
Afr	–.141	–.277			
D	–.116	–.360			
Lambda	–.173	–.535			
CDI	–.212	–.541			

Table 8. Canonical analysis of covariance on sample of nonpsychotic patients, variance, redundancy, and generalizability.

Analysis of Rorschach set of variables overlapping			
	var	red	gen
CV1–1	.207	.038	.876
Analysis of NEO-PI-R set of variables overlapping			
	var	red	gen
CV2–1	.235	.037	.186

Table 9. Canonical analysis of covariance in the group of psychotic patients, correlations, and tests of significance.

	Ro	ro2	f-test	sig
1	.476	.227	28.786	.000

Table 10. Pattern and structure of sets of Rorschach and NEO-PI-R variables for the group of psychotic patients.

Rorschach variables			NEO-PI-R variables		
	X	F		X	F
es	.795	.711	N	.727	.781
AG	.645	.700	E	–.162	–.345
FM	.749	.648	O	.567	.395
Pure Blends	.585	.611	A	–.343	–.340
a	.473	.610	C	–.761	–.818
p	.674	.596			
Sum Shade	.501	.549			
m	.518	.529			
M	.347	.518			
Zf	.323	.396			
Ego Index	.325	.367			
EA	.186	.359			
Zd	.220	.283			
R	.282	.271			
FD	.268	.243			
S	.183	.176			
D	.237	.152			
SCZI	.016	.149			
Sum6SpSc	.113	.199			
Intell	–.053	.106			
X–%	–.014	.081			
Isolate	.134	.079			
W	–.057	.055			
X+%	.169	.044			
DEPI	–.096	–.068			
SUMC	–.140	–.108			
Afr	–.109	–.112			
CDI	–.149	–.298			
EB	–.362	–.425			
AdjDScor	–.386	–.190			
Lambda	–.468	–.528			
DScor	–.502	–.332			

5. Canonical analysis of covariance in the group of psychotic patients identified a function value of .48 significant at the level .000.

Table 10 shows the pattern and structure of two sets of variables. The quasi-canonical factors of the set of Rorschach variables may be interpreted as a state of vulnerability and loss of control. The set combines a set of undesirable indicators related to states of irritation, agitation (es), aggression (AG), forceful needs (FM), and psychological complexity induced by unpleasant affective conditions (Blends) with indicators of overall destabilization (–D score, –AdjD) and introversion (–EB) as well as inability to use defensive simplification tactics for excessively complex problem situations (–Lambda).

A quasi-canonical factor of the NEO-PI-R set of variables makes projections of highly positive +N domain and highly negative –C domain with moderately low introversion and collaboration and moderately high openness. It can be interpreted as a condition of polyvalent destabilization; openness to mainly intrapsychic experience that enables volitional direction of activity associated with introvert behavior and absence of collaboration with the surroundings.

The separated quasi-canonical function can be interpreted as generally high readiness for psychopathological reaction. This constellation corresponds to the condition of psychopathological and affective destabilization, vulnerability, and inability of an individual to be effective, organized, and to direct actions volitionally. The NEO-PI-R questionnaire is not intended for recognition of productive psychotic symptomatology, but the factor selected here probably comprises indicators of two sets of variables related to psychotic anxiety or agitation.

Table 11 illustrates the analysis of the overlap of two sets of variables. The factor separated from the NEO PI-R set is more representative than the factor separated from the Rorschach set. Redundancy shows that the factor separated from the Rorschach set explains a greater part of the

Table 11. Canonical analysis of covariance on sample of psychotic patients, variance, redundancy, and generalizability.

Analysis of Rorschach set of variables overlapping			
	var	red	gen
CV1–1	.152	.028	.820
Analysis of NEO-PI-R set of variables overlapping			
	var	red	gen
CV2–1	.334	.068	.501

variance than the NEO PI-R set. The Rorschach set is more stable than the NEO PI-R set, as in other methods.

To sum up, the obtained results allow the following conclusions:

1. There is a conceptual similarity of certain indicators of the RIM and the NEO-PI-R questionnaire, while some indicators are conceptually independent.
2. The obtained correlations between individual indicators of the two instruments are low (range between $r = 30–40$), significant, and can be interpreted in a logical manner. The convergent validity is low, and the redundancy of the two sets of variables represented by the projective instrument and the questionnaire is low. Rorschach indicators highly correlate with the domains of Openness (accompanied with positive Extraversion) and Neuroticism (associated with markedly negative Conscientiousness). The lowest correlation is with the domain of Agreeableness. If we consider the questionnaire a valid representation of the FFM, the studied relation provides indirect information on the correlation of the RIM and the FFM. Based on our results, we may conclude that the RIM cannot be interpreted by the FFM, i.e., it can explain only a low percentage of variance of the projective method itself.
3. Type and degree of obtained correlation between the sets of variables of the two instruments depend on the psychopathology of the subjects. There is a difference in the degree and type of the two variable sets in the groups of nonpsychotic and psychotic patients, which confirmed the hypothesis that nature of the psychopathology influences the relation between the two instruments. In the group of nonpsychotic patients, overlap of the two instruments was more specifically related to the personality capacity and ego strength, while in the groups of psychotic subjects it was related to vulnerability and the readiness for polyvalent psychopathological response.
4. The two psychodiagnostic instruments overlap to a minor degree. The results consistently confirm low redundancy between the two instruments while the relations of both individual variables and sets show low and significant relations.

Discussion

The problem of convergent validity of psychological instruments is complex in itself, especially when two instruments that are diverse in their nature are compared: a projective instrument vs self-reporting instrument, atheoretical vs theoretical concepts. Application of the RIM for research purposes differs significantly from idiographic application and requires good knowledge of the indicator and its methodological features, and reveals the problem of the nature of the variables involved, their selection, and selection of the analytical method applicable for the instrument with such a large number of indicators in relation to the size of the sample.

In clinical applications, discrepancy in results obtained by two instruments does not trouble the diagnostician. In fact, they believe that the presence of larger numbers of data from multiple sources is logical and needed. The tests are interpreted after selection of information in accordance with the clinical presentation or symptomatology. Some data are discarded as irrelevant, while others are pronounced crucial in the process of clinical evaluation. When the same problem is discussed in clinical practice within convergent validity, this discrepancy is a reason for concern since it questions the validity of each instrument and, thus, the validity of clinical evaluation, as well. In cases of similar conceptual determination of indicators and their validity in respect to behavioral criteria (subject behavior), the investigator should examine the cause of poor overlap.

Published studies, including our findings, have shown that the problem of convergent validity is greater with diverse instruments, so that the overlap of two questionnaires is always higher than the redundancy of the projective instrument and questionnaire. Their different epistemological positions increases the number of factors that influence personality measurement so much that it is difficult to recognize and measure all the influences important for this relation. When an investigator asks "What is it that influences the relation of two instruments and how can we recognize these factors and control them?" instead of asking "How much and in what manner are these two instruments correlated?" (which was the object of this study), the problem becomes even more complex.

The low convergent validity may result from differences in the object of measurement, i.e., the fact that the instruments may cover and measure different aspects of personality. The second hypothesis is that the discrepancy results from differences in the style of response and that the style should be recognized according to especially indicative indicators of the two instruments. Available findings have shown that inasmuch as the response style is complexly defined, it is very difficult to reduce all test-related influences to one function, which would enable us to recognize subjects who yield discrepant results when different techniques are used (Meyer, 1999). Fortunately, although these influences appear to be difficult to explain on the group level, on the individual level, when cases are analyzed individually, the pattern of motivational factors that influence responses appear more understandable and logical.

If we consider the questionnaire a valid representative of the Five-Factor personality model, the studied relation provides indirect information on the correlation of the RIM and the Five-Factor personality model. If we do consider it true, we can, according to our results, conclude that the RIM cannot be interpreted by the Five-Factor personality model, i.e., it can explain only a low percentage of variance of the projective model itself. If we accept domain naming as in the NEO-PI-R questionnaire, Rorschach indicators highly correlate with the domains of Openness (+O) and Neuroticism (accompanied with markedly negative Conscientiousness +N-C).

Since the set of NEO-PI-R indicators in each of multivariate analyses is associated with greater variance, analysis of the results reveals that the questionnaire domains in the common pattern correlated with characteristic Rorschach indicators. The complexity-simplicity and personality power-generalized destabilization functions are obviously, according to all analyses, the area of largest overlap between these two instruments as well as of the RIM and the Five-Factor model (as elaborated by the applied questionnaire). Indicators included into the analysis in this study have been selected according to conceptual similarity and initial results of correlation analysis, but a question remains whether the selection should be different and how would a different selection influence the nature of the selected function. A large number of Rorschach variables (over 100 of basic and derived) always confront the investigator with this problem. Therefore, the selection should always be guided first by theoretical assumptions and second by available empirical findings.

So far, no RIM-applying studies have been used on a sample of non-psychiatric patients mainly because they are less accessible for this type of long-term testing. This type of data is particularly important for the study of convergent validity for at least two reasons. First, the NEO-PI-R questionnaire is intended for personality evaluation instead of psychopathology evaluation. Second, our study has shown that the obtained relation among instruments in degree and type depends on specificity and homogeneity of the sample (different for nonpsychotic and psychotic). Therefore, further study will be needed to comprise other specific samples and enable better generalizations on the nature of correlation of two instruments.

Accordingly, it can be concluded that the convergent value of the two instruments is not an intrinsic feature but depends on a series of test-related and unrelated influences. One of the most important factors is the sample selection criterion since it defines the level and type of correlation among individual indicators (criteria of psychopathology or some crucial Rorschach variables). The lowest validity measures were found on the protocols of the heterogeneous sample. They tended to rise and showed increased validity with better matching of the sample. Thus, test variables are associated to a different degree according to the specific subgroup that we study. Sample control according to psychopathology has been proved to be an important factor influencing association of variables. Therefore, their pattern is different for groups of nonpsychotic and psychotic (and possibly for the group of "normal") individuals. Other criteria that refer only to selection according to crucial Rorschach variables are not quite insignificant. Nevertheless, drawing safe and unequivocal conclusions on the influence of this type of sample on association of indicators of two instruments is more difficult. According to the available reports, it can be said that it is difficult to identify a single function to serve as the basis for control of all diverse influences important for convergent validity.

The low convergent validity of the RIM and the NEO-PI-R questionnaire was the result of a complex interactive influence of multiple factors. Convergent value of the two instruments is not an intrinsic feature but depends on a series of test-related and test-unrelated influences:

1. Theoretic-conceptual differences among indicators: theoretic vs nontheoretic epistemological position, differences in operationalization of indicators on different instruments,
2. Differences in personality facets measured by the two instruments: level of evaluated personality covered by structured and nonstructured tests, levels of conscious and unconscious functioning,
3. Personality: response style, subject psychopathology, motivational factors (manipulation, stimulation, dissimulation, lack of critical insight, psychological confusion, and inconsistency producing test-contradictory answers), and

4. Influences resulting from metric features of the instrument used: the influence of Rorschach variables on other Rorschach indicators (EB, Lambda, number of responses), the problem of variable selection, small sample, selection of appropriate statistical analyses, different sensitivity of instruments for criteria variables, differences in reliability and validity of the psychological instruments compared producing poor correlation of instruments.

References

Archer, R.P., & Krishnamurthy, R. (1993). A review of MMPI and Rorschach interrelationships in adults samples. *Journal of Personality Assessment, 61*, 277–293.

Costa, P.T., Jr., & McCrae, R.R. (1992). *Revised NEO Personality Inventory (NEO-PI-R) and NEO Five-Factor Inventory (NEO-FFI) professional manual.* Odessa, FL: Psychological Assessment Resources.

Exner, J.E. (1993). *The Rorschach: A comprehensive system* (Vol. 1). New York: Wiley.

Exner, J.E. (1995). *Issues and methods in Rorschach research.* Mahwah, NJ: Erlbaum.

Ganellen, R. (1996). *Integrating the Rorschach and MMPI-2 in personality assessment.* Mahwah, NJ: Erlbaum.

Krishnamurthy, R., Archer, R.P., & House, J.J. (1996). The MMPI-A and Rorschach: A failure to establish convergent validity. *Assessment, 3*, 179–191.

Meyer, G.J. (1999). The convergent validity of MMPI and Rorschach scales: An extension using profile scores to define response and character styles on both methods and reexamination of simple Rorschach response frequency. *Journal of Personality Assessment, 72*(1), 1–35.

Meyer, G.J., Bates, M., & Gacono, C. (1999). The Rorschach rating scale: Item adequacy, scale development, and relations with the Big Five Model of personality. *Journal of Personality Assessment, 73*, 199–244.

Momirovic, K. (1994), Prilog poznavanju stvarnih metrijskih karakteristika aktuelne operacionalizacije modela "Big Five" [Contribution to recognition of real metric characteristics of the actual operationalization of the Big Five Personality Model]. *Psihologija, 1–2*, 41–48.

Summary

The aim of the study was to determine the convergent value of two instruments for personality evaluation. The conceptual and empiric correlation of two indicators of the projective method and self-report questionnaire were studied. The Rorschach method as interpreted by the Comprehensive System is considered atheoretical, while the NEO PI-R questionnaire is based on the Five-Factor Model of personality. Therefore, the correlation between the Rorschach method and Five-Factor personality theory has been investigated indirectly. The sample comprised 200 psychiatric patients, 100 nonpsychotic patients (mostly anxious-depressive) and 100 psychotic patients (mostly schizophrenic). Analysis of the results used correlation analysis, factorial analysis, canonical correlation analysis, canonical analysis of covariance, and asymmetric redundancy analysis. Identification of aberrant objects was applied for qualitative interpretation of the results. The obtained results have shown that, although numerous conceptual similarities between indicators of the two instruments have been recognized, their convergent validity is low. Possible causes of the low convergent validity and recommendations for further studies are proposed.

Résumé

Le but de cette étude est de déterminer la validité convergente de deux instruments d'évaluation de la personnalité. On a étudié la corrélation conceptuelle et empirique entre deux indicateurs provenant de la méthode projective et d'un questionnaire d'auto-évaluation. On part du principe que le Rorschach, interprété selon le Système Intégré, est athéorique, tandis que le questionnaire NEO-PI-R est fondé sur le modèle de personnalité en cinq facteurs. On a par conséquent indirectement exploré la corrélation entre le Rorschach et la théorie des cinq facteurs de personnalité. L'échantillon comprend 200 patients psychiatriques, 100 nonpsychotiques (principalement anxio-dépressifs) et 100 psychotiques (principalement schizophrènes). Les résultats ont été traités par les méthodes suivantes: analyse corrélationnelle, analyse factorielle, analyse canonique, analyse canonique de covariance et analyse d'asymétrie de la redondance. L'identification des sujets aberrants a permis l'analyse qualitative des résultats. Les résultats montrent que, malgré les nombreuses ressemblances conceptuelles entre les indicateurs en provenance des deux instruments, leur validité convergente est basse. On examine les causes possibles de cette faible validité convergente et on fait des recommandations en vue d'études ultérieures.

Resumen

El objetivo de este estudio era determinar la validez convergente de dos instrumentos de evaluación de la personalidad. Se estudió la correlación conceptual y empírica entre dos indicadores de un método proyectivo y un cuestionario de tipo autoinforme. El método de Rorschach interpretado según el Sistema Comprehensivo se considera ateorético, mientras que el cuestionario NEO-PI-R se basa en el modelo de personalidad de los Cinco Factores. Por tanto, también se investigó indirectamente la correlación entre Rorschach y la teoría de los Cinco Factores. La muestra estuvo formada por 200 pacientes psiquiátricos, de los cuales 100 eran no psicóticos (en su mayoría con trastornos ansioso-depresivos) y 100 psicóticos (sobre todo esquizofrénicos). El análisis de los resultados incluyó análisis correlacional, análisis factorial, análisis de correlación canónica, análisis canónico de covarianza y análisis de redundancia asimétrica. Se aplicó también la identificación de objetos aberrantes para la interpretación cualitativa de los datos. Los resultados muestran que, aunque existen numerosas semejanzas conceptuales entre los indicadores de ambos instrumentos, su validez convergente es baja. Se proponen posibles causas de este hallazgo y recomendaciones para futuros estudios.

Sažetak
Relacija Rorschach metoda i NEO PI-R upitnika

Cilj istraživanja je utvrdjivanje konvergentne validnosti dva instrumenta procene licnosti. Ispituje se konceptualna i empirijska povezanost indikatora projektivnog metoda i samoopisnog upitnika. Rorschach metod interpretiran Comprehensive Systemom se smatra ateorijskim, a NEO PI-R upitnik je baziran na petofaktorskom modelu licnosti, pa se indirektno ispituje i veza Rorshach metoda s petofaktorskom teorijom licnosti. uzorak se sastoji od 200 psihijatrijskih pacijenata, 100 nepsihoticnih (vecinom ankiozno-depresivnih) i 100 psihoticnih (vecinom shizofrenih). U analizi rezultata primenjena je korelaciona analiza, faktorska analiza, kanonicka korelaciona analiza, kanonicka analiza kovarijanse i metod asimetricne analize redundance. Identifikacija aberantnih objekata primenjena je radi kvalitativne interpretacije rezultata. Dobijeni rezultati pokazuju da iako postoje brojne konceptualne slicnosti izmedju indikatora dva instrumenta, njihova konvergentna validnost je niska. Diskutuje se o mogucim uzrocima niske konvergentne validnosti i preporukama za dalja istraživanja.

Rorschachiana 27, 30–50

Are the Relationships Between NEO PI-R and Rorschach Markers of Openness to Experience Dependent on the Patient's Test-Taking Attitude?

Jean-Michel Petot

Laboratoire de Psychologie clinique des Faits culturels, Université de Paris X-Nanterre, France

The problem of the relationship between the self-report measures and the Rorschach assessment of personality is particularly perplexing and puzzling. On the one hand, empirical researchers often question the validity of the Rorschach Inkblot Method by arguing that correlations between so-called "objective" measures of personality and Rorschach measures are generally poor. On the other hand, clinicians generally assume, since the seminal work of Rapaport, Gill, and Schafer (1968 [1944]), that, to be comprehensive, the psychological assessment of a person must include cognitive tests and at least two kinds of personality measures – self-report questionnaires and projective methods. This implies that projective methods and self-report questionnaires provide *different* kinds of information and probably measure different things; otherwise, it would not be useful to utilize *both* methods with our patients. According to this viewpoint, it is logical that correlations between self-report measures and Rorschach assessment are rather low. This fact would not speak against the validity of either the Rorschach Inkblot Method or self-report questionnaires (Ganellen, 1996).

The theoretical point is discussed later, in the last paper of this special series, but this paper will be in part the application of an interesting methodological suggestion due to Gregory Meyer (1996, 1997, 1999). According to this researcher, self-report instruments and projective methods do measure the same constructs. Thus, correlations between the two methods of assessment should be fair to excellent. However each class of method measures not only the construct it is aimed to assess, but also the attitude of the patient or subject when taking the test. Thus, it is important to pay attention to the test-taking attitude or, according to Meyer, "response-character style" of the patients or subjects.

Patients' attitudes or "response-character styles" can vary in several ways: from conscious reticence to honest and complete disclosure, and from honest disclosure to conscious exaggeration or simulation of pathology; from unconscious tendency to inhibition and avoidance to recognize pathology or abnormalities to normal uninhibited spontaneity; and from normal spontaneity to unconscious tendency to emphasizing problems and pathology. Both kinds of assessment methods – i.e., self-report questionnaires and projective methods – do not elicit the same test-taking attitude. Certain people will easily complete a questionnaire, but are inhibited when taking the Rorschach or TAT. Others engage themselves completely in taking the Rorschach or TAT but are very reluctant to complete a 240 (like the NEO PI-R) or 565 item (like the MMPI-2) questionnaire.

Meyer (1996, 1997, 1999) hypothesized that the lack of correlation between conventional self-report measures and Rorschach scores and variables is an artifact, due to the failure to control for subjects test-taking attitude. He argues that the convergence vs divergence of test-taking attitude strongly moderates the convergence vs divergence of the assessment. Therefore, he assumes correlation should be high and positive when subjects have the same test-taking attitude toward both methods ("convergent" group), and high and negative when subjects have divergent attitudes when taking the self-report questionnaire and projective test ("divergent group"). Meyer (1996) applied this principle to a comparison between MMPI and Rorschach scales designed to assess similar constructs. He reported that the selected Rorschach and MMPI-2 scales of psychosis, affective distress and interpersonal wariness were uncorrelated (mean $r = .03$) when response-character styles were ignored; positively correlated (mean $r = .58$) when only those patients with similar response-character style were considered; and negatively correlated (mean $r = -.55$) when the analyses were restricted to patients who had opposing response-character styles on each method.

But how is patients' response-character style assessed? The criteria utilized by Meyer are related to factor analysis. The cut-off point between "restricted-inhibited" and "expansive-uninhibited" patients on each test is the median of the first factor. In both instruments (MMPI and Rorschach), the first factor is closely related to neuroticism or negative emotionality. This raises a question: if convergence between two markers of neuroticism is the criteria for "response-character style," it may be tautological to find that scores on the scales of distress (= negative emotionality) are convergent among subjects whose score of neuroticism are convergent across instruments, and divergent among subjects whose score of neuroticism are divergent across instruments (Ganellen, 1996). Another alternative set of criteria for the convergence of test-taking attitudes, later suggested by Meyer (1999), raises the same kind of questions, because the "profile criteria" also are related to the first factor of each method: MMPI F and at a lesser degree K scales, and Rorschach R and at a lesser degree L scores. Supposing that the test-taking attitude, *which is indirectly measured by scales related to distress*, moderates convergence of the MMPI and Rorschach negative emotionality or distress scales, what can be said about the convergence of self-report and Rorschach assessment of other dimensions of personality, unrelated to negative emotionality?

That is the reason why this paper focuses on the relationships between the Rorschach data and self-report measures of a Five-Factor Model (FFM) dimension of Personality *other than negative emotionality* (neuroticism). The target of the analysis will be the dimension "Openness to Experience" and its six facets. This dimension was recently defined and very little is known concerning the Rorschach markers of Openness, so that it is interesting to search whether such markers really exist, and if so what they are. Moreover, this dimension has rather low correlation with Neuroticism, i.e., with the main criterion of response-character style. By choosing this dimension, the tautology previously alluded to can be avoided. This study will present and discuss the influence of the test-taking attitude ("response-character style") on the relations between Big Five Model Openness to Experience and some selected Rorschach variables. The expected aim is to convey a better understanding of the rather disappointing correlations previously reported (Djurić Jočić, 2002; Ignjatević, Djurić Jočić, & Pavlović, 1999; Greenwald, 1999; Petot, 2002, 2004) between on the one hand the Rorschach scores and variables, and on the other one the 35 NEO PI-R scales (five dimensions or domains and 30 facets).

Openness to Experience is a broad dimension of personality which is called, according to different writers, Inquiring Intellect (Fiske, 1949), Culture (Tupes & Christal, 1992), Openness to Absorption (Tellegen & Atkinson, 1974), Intellect (Digman & Takemoto-Chock, 1981), Openness to Experience (Costa & McCrae, 1985), etc. As shown by the plenty of different labels, this domain is rather heterogeneous. Saucier (1992) has interestingly suggested that: "... neither the labels Openness nor

Intellect capture well the central cluster of traits that define Factor V; perhaps a more apt label is Imagination for a factor defined by such traits as creativity and curiosity." It is important to note that, in the Costa and McCrae's version of the Five-Factor Model, the Openness domain comprises six subscales corresponding to six facets tapping six different areas of experience. These facets are: Openness to Fantasy: the open person likes daydreaming and may be deeply involved in fantasy; Openness to Aesthetics: the open person is fond of art and beauty; s/he is sensitive to beauty in nature and art; Openness to Feelings: the open person is in touch with her/his own feelings, s/he feels, perceives and expresses them without inhibition; Openness to Actions: the open person is prone to change her/his habits, behaviors, or environment, to try new hobbies, new foods, and so on; Openness to Ideas: the open person is fond of intellectual exercises; this may apply to play or games (puzzles, checkers, chess, etc.) or to mathematical, logical or philosophical reasoning; Openness to Values: the open person is tolerant; s/he is prone to admit and understand moral, political or religious points of view very different from one's own (McCrae, 1994).

Openness as a whole (= domain) has a moderate positive correlation with Extraversion, a moderate negative correlation with Neuroticism (respectively $r = .37$, and $r = -.32$ in the French normative sample), and low, nonsignificant correlations with the two remaining dimensions of personality. The relationships of correlations between the facets of Openness and those of Neuroticism also are low and nonsignificant, with the exception of that between Openness to Feelings and Impulsiveness ($r = .35$; Costa & McCrae, 1992).

Djurić Jočić (2002), Greenwald (1999), Ignjatović, Djurić Jočić, & Pavlović (1999), and Petot (2002, 2004) have found low to moderate relations between Openness and Rorschach variables. This paper is aimed to (1) deepen the analysis of these relations; (2) test the generalizability to Openness of the hypothesis concerning the moderating role of the test-taking attitude. Whatever the results of these separate analyses may be, it will be good, in order to really understand their meaning, to check whether the separate analyses of the relations between NEO PI-R Neuroticism and Rorschach scores and variables really confirm what was assumed by earlier researchers.

Method

Subjects

96 outpatients were assessed prior to therapy in the unit of hypnotherapy of a Public Mental Health Facility (Paul Sivadon Institute of Psychiatry, Paris). The sample is composed of 61 women and 35 men. The ages range from 18 to 62. They presented mainly depressive disorders (major depression and dysthymia), and about the two thirds had at least one comorbid diagnosis of personality disorder (cluster B or C). The mean IQ was high (performance IQ: m = 121, SD = 11).

Procedure

All subjects were administered a complete assessment battery, including, among several other measures of cognitive functioning, psychopathology and personality, the French version of the NEO-PI-R and the Rorschach psychodiagnostic.

Instruments

The NEO PI-R (Costa & McCrae, 1992) is a 240 item self-report questionnaire intended to measure the "Big Five" domains of personality and their 30 facets. Patients were administered the authorized French version (Costa & McCrae, 1992). The Rorschach was scored and interpreted according to the directives of the so-called "French method" (Anzieu, 1961; Rausch de Traubenberg, 1970). Altogether, some scores and ratios from the Exner (1993) System were utilized, especially the scoring of all determinants of a response (Blends), the organizational Z scores, and the EA ratio (Sum M + Weighted Sum C).

Criteria for Test Taking Attitude

As the NEO PI-R does not contain validity scales which could be equivalent to MMPI-2 F and K scales, it seemed preferable to assess the attitude toward this instrument by utilizing the first factor: the cut-off point was therefore the median of Neuroticism (*M* = 119.5). Concerning the

Rorschach test-taking attitude, the "profile criteria" were those used in previous research (Meyer, 1999): they are defined by the combination of R (number of responses) and F% (a measure of the proportion of responses determined by pure form). The utilization of mixed criteria (factor criterion for the NEO PI-R, and profile criteria for the Rorschach) should not be a problem, as Meyer stated (1999, p. 30) that: "The phenomenon under consideration is strong enough so that substantially different operational definitions of response-character styles produce the same general results." The cut-off points were the median of R (median = 25.5) and F% (median = 53.5, i.e., Lambda = 1.15). A patient is "expansive-uninhibited" if and only if R ≥ 25 and $F \leq 53.5$ (i.e., L ≤ 1.15). S/he is "restricted-inhibited" if and only if R < 25 and F > 53.5 (i.e., L > 1.15). Therefore, only 51 patients (= 53%) could be classified as having a clear-cut test-taking attitude toward the Rorschach. 29 were "convergent" across both instruments, 22 were "divergent," and the remaining 45 (= 47%) were discarded from the separate analyses.

Data Analysis

Thirty-five Rorschach scores and ratios were selected on the basis of their expected relation with Openness. Data were analyzed as follows: Spearman's nonparametric coefficient correlations were first computed for the whole group. In order to ascertain whether the test-taking attitude really moderates the relationships between Openness, Neuroticism, and Rorschach variables, separate analyses were afterward conducted for subjects with convergent and divergent test-taking attitudes. As 490 correlations (35 Rorschach variables × 14 NEO PI-R scales, i.e., 7 Neuroticism and 7 Openness scales) were computed, it could be expected that 20 (= 5%) were significant by chance. Therefore, in order to avoid type I error, Bonferroni's correction was applied: correlations are regarded as significant at $\alpha = .05/490 = .0001$. The corresponding magnitude of the correlation coefficient is of $\rho = .38$ for the whole group (n = 96), $\rho = .65$ for the "convergent" subgroup (n = 29), and $\rho = .73$ for the "divergent" one (n = 22). The differences between the correlation coefficients computed on subgroups were assessed by computing a z score which was utilized like a bilateral Student's t for independent samples (Howell, 1997). As 490 pairs of correlations were computed, the value of z must correspond to the probability $\alpha = .0001$ (= .05/490). The corresponding value of z is 3.89; considering the subgroups sizes, it is reached when the absolute value of the difference between the coefficients is ≥ |1.17|.

Results

Relationships Between Openness and Rorschach Variables

Out of the 245 correlations computed between Openness scales and Rorschach variables on the whole group (Table 1, first number in each cell), sixteen remain significant after Bonferroni's correction. Five of them concern negative relations between Openness and Rorschach variables related to determinants: Openness (domain) and the facets Openness to Action and Openness to Ideas with F% (a variable similar to Lambda); and Openness to Ideas with Sum Shading (sum of responses determined by achromatic color or shading) and Blends (Sum of responses having more than one nonformal determinant). The remaining eleven concern special scores: morbid responses, positively correlated with the Openness domain and facet Openness to Ideas; aggressive movements (AG), correlated to Openness to Aesthetics; responses with inappropriate logic (ALOG), negatively related to Openness to Aesthetics and Openness to feelings; Contamination (CONTAM) positively related with both the domain Openness and the facet Openness to Actions; the raw sum of the six critical special scores (Raw Sum6) positively related with the domain and the facets Openness to Actions and Openness to Ideas; and the weighted sum of critical special scores (Weighted Sum6), positively correlated only to Openness to Action.

Do these figures conceal opposing and stronger tendencies connected to the convergence or divergence between subjects' attitude when taking the Rorschach or NEO PI-R? The relationships of figures in each cell may seem rather erratic, for the coefficients computed on the whole group often are out of the range defined by the coefficients computed on the subgroups (e.g., table I, row 1): it must be remembered that "divergent" and "convergent" subgroups are extreme groups, the size of each being only about a quarter of the whole group. As expected, these extreme subgroups do not reflect the main tendency of the whole sample. However, out of the 229 nonsignificant correlations, *no one fully corresponds to the hypothesis of the moderating role of test-taking attitude:* there are no correlations which were both nonsignificant ($\rho < .38$) in the whole

Table 1. Relationships between selected Rorschach variables and openness (domain and facets).

	Domain	Facets					
Rorschach variables	Openness	O 1: Imagination	O 2: Esthetics	O 3: Feelings	O 4: Action	O 5: Ideas	O 6: Values
R	–08 (38; 49)	–05 (28; 06)	03 (10; 37)	–06 (25; 33)	–16 (37; 33)	08 (50; 32)	–27 (02; –05)
Total time (T)	14 (15; 62)	–03 (–01; –05)	22 (04; 64)	06 (17; 52)	03 (02; 32)	26 (30; 32)	–09 (08; 04)
T/R	31 (–01; 47)	–08 (–21; –45)	32 (03; 58)	20 (08; 63)	28 (–14; 21)	29 (10; 12)	19 (07; 37)
Sum W	22 (38; 27)	22 (39; 14)	00 (16; –12)	–03 (09; 05)	18 (31; 32)	33 (49; 39)	22 (14; 16)
Sum D	–10 (07; 38)	–11 (–11; –03)	06 (01; 46)	08 (15; 33)	–16 (13; 21)	–06 (16; 18)	–27 (–13; –12)
Sum Dd	–11 (16; 31)	–10 (06; 05)	11 (05; 40)	–07 (23; –07)	–17 (28; 26)	05 (10; 13)	–34 (–11; 14)
Sum DS	–09 (–19; 25)	04 (–08; 01)	–02 (–25; 12)	–20 (–10; 14)	–17 (–21; –01)	07 (–26; 19)	–06 (24; 26)
Sum S	00 (21; 57)	01 (28; 32)	02 (04; –01)	–26 (08; –41)	–11 (24; 26)	25 (09; 54)	–01 (31; 37)
F% (= Lambda)	**–44** (–29; –52)	–10 (18; 05)	–26 (–31; –31)	–28 (–19; –38)	**–43** (–50; –28)	**–39** (–42; –40)	–28 (14; –43)
E.A.	37 (60; 42)	14 (32; 02)	26 (30; 37)	28 (42; 18)	24 (50; 19)	30 (**68**; 31)	09 (22; –03)
Sum M	37 (57; 44)	17 (43; 06)	23 (30; 27)	26 (35; 19)	27 (44; 09)	34 (57; 41)	16 (34; 15)
Weighted Sum C	24 (46; 37)	08 (12; –02)	22 (22; 40)	23 (39; 33)	16 (44; 23)	19 (62; 21)	01 (02; 13)
Sum (C' + Shading)	25 (19; 53)	14 (–33; 20)	20 (17; 30)	03 (25; 27)	19 (34; 30)	**39** (31; 40)	–05 (12; 00)
Reflection responses	26 (24; 31)	19 (10; 11)	04 (14; –13)	11 (06; 13)	23 (22; 35)	34 (38; 30)	02 (–04; 21)
Sum Blends	34 (40; 31)	21 (22; 14)	22 (23; 18)	17 (41; 27)	30 (35; 30)	**39** (50; 36)	–03 (02; –02)
No. different determinants	26 (20; 42)	04 (–01; 09)	26 (13; 47)	05 (06; 27)	29 (23; 40)	32 (37; 03)	–02 (–03; 13)
A%	–07 (–08; –06)	–07 (–01; –08)	19 (08; 21)	15 (00; 15)	–23 (–18; –25)	–23 (–19; –34)	–11 (–14; –06)
An%	–04 (–56; 53)	10 (–01; 43)	–13 ***(–54; 89)***	–07 (–51; 28)	20 (–22; 02)	–18 (–53; –11)	–07 (–44; –52)
Sum pure H	24 (54; 22)	14 (24; –02)	08 (39; 35)	15 (43; 12)	07 (26; –17)	27 (55; 18)	20 (39; 02)
Sum P	08 (06; 50)	–14 (–48; 01)	12 (32; 43)	13 (06; 41)	09 (13; 04)	11 (–02; 30)	13 (12; 14)

NEO PI-R and Rorschach Markers of Openness to Experience

	Domain	Facets					
Rorschach variables	Openness	O 1: Imagination	O 2: Esthetics	O 3: Feelings	O 4: Action	O 5: Ideas	O 6: Values
Orig+	–08 (–13; –01)	–14 (–17; 25)	05 (04; 11)	–15 (–22; –11)	–11 (–07; –22)	–04 (–04; –23)	10 (09; 14)
Z d	08 (21; –51)	12 ***(64; –93)***	01 (–19; 16)	24 (21; 48)	01 (04; –07)	03 (27; –42)	–09 (07; –18)
Sum MOR	**48** (50; **84**)	33 (06; **77**)	30 (25; 38)	15 (44; 10)	28 (33; 17)	**47** (63; 57)	22 (32; 20)
Sum AG	28 (33; 31)	25 (45; 12)	**41** (08; **79**)	–01 (07; –12)	16 (42; 41)	15 (42; –30)	03 (14; –41)
Sum DV1	15 (–02; 51)	24 (–20; 02)	–04 (02; –16)	–14 (–28; 28)	29 (10; **87**)	20 (00; 67)	14 (13; 22)
Sum DV2	20 (19; 51)	18 (29; –17)	18 (24; –16)	23 (16; 28)	11 (–12; **82**)	–05 (–02; –32)	08 (34; –18)
Sum DR1	32 (25; 54)	08 (–49; 37)	25 (23; 51)	23 (38; 53)	20 (20; 17)	25 (31; –17)	19 (21; –47)
Sum DR2	20 (13; 59)	–12 (–35; 46)	08 (05; –42)	12 (06; 21)	30 (42; 39)	11 (39; **91**)	03 (–11; 56)
Sum INCOM1	19 (–09; 23)	32 (06; 45)	–09 (–09; –36)	–13 (09; –42)	25 (09; 28)	28 (–25; 49)	07 (–26; 10)
Sum INCOM 2	16 (10; **88**)	31 (16; 66)	05 (–04; **82**)	04 (–13; 67)	08 (–06; 64)	30 (12; 32)	–13 (15; –19)
Sum FABCOM 1	00 (–04; 10)	26 (24; 26)	05 (–05; 35)	–05 (09; –30)	–17 (–19; –10)	–04 (–24; 50)	–08 (10; –38)
Sum FABCOM 2	37 (34; **89**)	18 (41; 71)	31 (06; 38)	27 (26; 31)	34 (13; 16)	24 (50; 65)	08 (02; 18)
Sum ALOG	–15 (–30; 60)	22 (29; 52)	**–49** (–62; –42)	**–40** (–58; 23)	05 (–08; **87**)	07 (–01; **87**)	04 (–02; 57)
Sum CONTAM	**47** (32; **79**)	21 (–25; 46)	25 (39; 49)	26 (13; 08)	**52** (42; 63)	27 (23; 43)	17 (32; 00)
Raw Sum 6	**40** (19; **79**)	24 (07; 26)	16 (–10; 29)	14 (–01; 47)	**45** (26; 50)	**38** (40; 62)	11 (23; 26)
Weighted Sum6	35 (20; **75**)	17 (08; 38)	21 (–10; 36)	19 (–01; 38)	**41** (28; 47)	27 (44; 57)	01 (19; 12)

Note. All numbers are Spearman's nonparametric correlation coefficient; decimal point is omitted; significant correlations are shown in **boldface**. The first coefficient in each cell (upper line) is computed on the whole group (n = 96); the second and third coefficients (second line) are respectively computed on patients with convergent test-taking attitude (n = 29), and patients with divergent test-taking attitude (n = 22). When there is a significant difference between subgroup correlation coefficients computed on the "convergent" and "divergent" subgroups, both are shown in *italics*.

group and significant in opposite directions in both the "convergent" ($\rho \geq .65$ or $\leq -.65$) and "divergent" ($\rho \geq .73$ or $\leq -.73$) subgroups.

But it may happen that some pairs of nonsignificant correlation coefficients are (1) opposite and (2) significantly *different one from another.* Only two pairs of correlations concerning Openness realize this picture. The first one is that between the facet Openness to Aesthetics and the Rorschach percentage of anatomic responses (An%, a ratio roughly similar to An + Xray): these variables are unrelated in the whole group; negatively related among subjects with convergent test-taking attitudes (the more they are open, the less they give anatomic responses); whereas they are positively related among subjects with divergent styles (the more these patients describe themselves as open, the more they give anatomic responses). The second one is that between Openness to Fantasy and the Rorschach Zd, a measure of organizational activity: these variables are unrelated in the whole group, positively related in the "convergent" subgroup, and negatively related (significant rho) in the "divergent" subgroup: the more the "convergent" subjects are open, the more they are active "overincorporators"; the more the "divergent" subjects describe themselves as open, the more they are passive and "underincorporators."

Moreover, some correlations, which are not significant at the whole group level, are significant in one subgroup. This applies to the correlation between Openness to Ideas and Experience Actual (EA), which is significant among "convergent" subjects (the more they are open, the higher is their EA). This also applies to nine pairs of correlations which are significant only among "divergent" subjects, and involve variables related with the special scores: domain Openness with the sum of level 2 incongruous combinations (INCOM 2), the sum of level 2 fabulized combinations (FABCOM 2), and the weighted sum of critical special scores (Weighted Sum 6); Openness to Fantasy with the sum of morbid responses (MOR); Openness to Aesthetics with the sum of level 2 incongruous combinations (INCOM 2); Openness to Actions with level 1 and level 2 deviant verbalizations (DV 1 and DV2), and the sum of responses with of inappropriate logic (ALOG); and Openness to Ideas also with ALOG.

Finally, scarcely more correlations (seventeen) are significant at the subgroup level (one in the "convergent" subgroup, sixteen in the "divergent" one) than in the whole group (fifteen). Therefore, is not possible to assume the response-style character moderates the relations between Openness and Rorschach variables.

Relationships Between Neuroticism and the Rorschach Variables

In order to assess the meaning of this finding concerning Openness, it is useful to examine what happens when the same analyses are conducted concerning the domain and facets of Neuroticism. Out of the 245 correlations computed on the whole group (Table 2, first number in each cell), only eight reach significance after Bonferroni's correction. They are correlations between Angry Hostility and Rorschach total time (TT, a variable discarded by the Comprehensive system: the more the patients are hostile, the longer is the test-taking); between the domain Neuroticism and the sum of frequent detail responses (D; the more they feel negative emotions, the more they interpret frequent details); and between the facet Vulnerability and the percentage of Anatomic responses (the more they feel vulnerable, the less they give anatomic responses). The five remaining correlations all concern the same Rorschach "special score," inappropriate logic (ALOG) which was also related with Openness: the domain Neuroticism and four of its facets do have *negative* correlations with the Sum of responses scored ALOG. It is somewhat counterintuitive that the more they feel stable and quiet, the more they produce odd or queer justifications of their responses.

When separated analyses are conducted on "convergent" and "divergent" subgroups, no one pair of variables fully confirms Meyer's prediction. But this may be a combined effect of both the small sample size of the subgroups and the very stringent Bonferroni's correction. One can check in Table 2 that there is a tendency toward figures compatible with Meyer's assumption. Moreover, there are significant differences between the correlations computed separately on "convergent" and "divergent" subgroups. This applies to twelve pairs of correlations between the domain or facets of Neuroticism, and Rorschach variables. Nine of these pairs of correlations involve Neuroticism and variables closely related to the Lambda (F%) and the "four square": three pairs of correlations between F% and Neuroticism (Domain, and facets Anxiety, and Depression); one involving the facet Anxiety and the Experience actual (EA: sum of human movement responses and weighted sum of color responses); three correlations between the domain and the facets Anxiety and Depression, and sum Shading; two correlations between Neuroticism (domain, and anxiety) and the sum of Blends (responses with more than one nonformal determinant). The remaining three differences only involve pairs of correlations between facets and variables linked to the special scores: Anxiety with sum of morbid responses (MOR); Anxiety

Table 2. Relations between selected Rorschach Variables and Neuroticism (domain and facets).

Rorschach variables	Domain Neuroticism	Facets N 1: anxiety	N 2: irritability	N 3: Depression	N 4: self-consciousness	N 5: impulsiveness	N 6: stress vulnerability
R	21 (35; -60)	18 (35; -66)	30 (24; -27)	08 (39; -57)	21 (38; -34)	13 (-05; -19)	15 (43; -59)
TT (Total time)	29 (46; -43)	24 (48; -44)	**41** (44; -09)	21 (38; -16)	17 (45; -16)	17 (27; -36)	22 (25; -41)
T/R	10 (18; 04)	05 (34; 06)	15 (24; 17)	19 (20; 38)	-04 (28; 03)	11 (23; -33)	09 (13; -13)
Sum W	-08 (20; -59)	-12 (12; -74)	-03 (25; -27)	-10 (17; -67)	-11 (12; -43)	04 (12; 03)	-04 (38; -39)
Sum D	**40** (29; -35)	-12 (12; **-74**)	-03 (25; -27)	-10 (14; -67)	-11 (12; -43)	04 (12; 03)	-04 (38; -39)
Sum Dd	16 (32; -32)	17 (18; -33)	18 (25; -17)	07 (36; -23)	17 (25; -08)	12 (35; -23)	16 (25; -32)
Sum DS	16 (04; -47)	19 (20; -51)	21 (04; -30)	06 (11; 66)	11 (11; -26)	06 (-23; 04)	14 (-17; -33)
Sum S	15 (11; -62)	14 (08; -67)	26 (12; 27)	00 (17; -63)	07 (06; -47)	08 (05; -26)	10 (17; -56)
F% (= Lambda)	01 *(**-65**; 68)*	12 *(-48; **76**)*	11 (-45; 34)	-15 *(**-67**; 62)*	03 (-64; 46)	-11 (-49; 17)	05 (-57; 53)
E.A.	10 (51; -53)	05 *(48; -59)*	10 (25; -32)	16 (52; -46)	07 (48; -27)	10 (28; -20)	02 (47; -43)
Sum M	13 (36; -62)	04 (35; -59)	10 (-01; -26)	22 (41; -36)	01 (31; -16)	09 (05; -19)	18 (57; -29)
Weighted Sum C	04 (52; -56)	05 (47; -52)	06 (48; -36)	07 (48; -49)	11 (52; -32)	08 (47; -20)	-11 (19; -47)
Sum (C' + Shading)	08 *(**68**; -58)*	03 (58; -70*)	12 (**70**; -22)	05 *(**68**; -66)*	04 (63; -30)	08 (51; -12)	02 (44; -47)
Reflection responses	01 (27; -46)	-11 (29; -67)	07 (32; -20)	07 (36; -50)	-10 (24; -35)	08 (-10; 12)	-03 (17; -34)
Sum Blends	04 *(60; -61)*	-06 *(56; -69)*	06 (41; -30)	05 (59; -56)	00 (58; -37)	12 (38; -15)	-02 (42; -50)
No of different determinants	01 (43; -44)	-04 (33; -45)	-07 (43; -39)	02 (45; -63)	00 (40; -38)	13 (39; 19)	-04 (28; -19)
A%	14 (-10; 41)	24 (-02; 51)	06 (04; 25)	07 (-12; 51)	10 (-11; 28)	-12 (-19; -17)	21 (07; 31)
An%	-25 (-18; -49)	-34 (-25; -23)	-07 (-08; -08)	-16 (-14; -52)	-19 (-24; 14)	09 (14; -69)	**-43** (-33; -37)
Sum pure H	13 (43; -14)	17 (47; -24)	06 (25; -28)	13 (34; -09)	10 (54; 11)	-10 (06; -20)	12 (36; 01)
Sum P	-06 (-11; -42)	-02 (-12; -31)	-07 (-13; 13)	-05 (-11; -51)	10 (-02; -18)	-11 (-36; 22)	-14 (03; -63)

Rorschach variables	Domain Neuroticism	Facets N 1: anxiety	N 2: irritability	N 3: Depression	N 4: self-consciousness	N 5: impulsiveness	N 6: stress vulnerability
Orig +	-08 (10; -19)	-17 (00; -21)	-11 (16; -08)	-17 (06; -53)	-03 (09; 01)	13 (19; -06)	-07 (02; -04)
Z d	-16 (-08; 12)	-18 (-04; **89**)	02 (06; **-87**)	-19 (-10; 45)	-14 (-13; -41)	08 (09; -04)	-19 (-34; 35)
Sum MOR	32 (41; -20)	34 *(46; **-80**)*	26 (40; 53)	28 (43; -48)	17 (35; 44)	23 (34; -20)	19 (20; -20)
Sum AG	19 (-03; 40)	11 (-01; -06)	08 (-04; 20)	22 (10; 28)	08 (-08; 69)	13 (-16; 17)	22 (-03; 34)
Sum DV1	03 (-03; 53)	-18 (-06; -16)	-18 (-20; 63)	12 (23; 48)	-15 (-03; 06)	-09 *(-44; 62)*	22 (24; 47)
Sum DV2	-21 (-40; -18)	-10 (-15; -14)	-17 (-35; 00)	-28 (-49; -04)	-27 (-38; -26)	-01 (-26; -01)	-11 (-29; -14)
Sum DR1	04 (07; -44)	09 (28; -37)	-05 (18; -20)	-01 (12; -66)	-02 (06; 68)	04 (18; 73)	-19 (-18; -17)
Sum DR2	00 (30; 03)	-13 (21; -54)	11 (30; **79**)	11 (36; -11)	-15 (23; -11)	16 (37; 24)	-09 (13; 00)
Sum INCOM1	-07 (17; -34)	-20 (16; -42)	-08 (-09; -24)	01 (23; -25)	-18 (23; -37)	04 (28; -19)	03 (04; -05)
Sum INCOM 2	21 (39; -41)	17 (42; -68)	27 (41; 21)	11 (31; -76)	08 (32; 66)	16 (25; -57)	13 (18; -15)
Sum FABCOM 1	13 (17; 08)	08 (08; 06)	26 (19; 51)	04 (10; -41)	12 (31; 22)	-10 (-05; -14)	24 (25; 24)
Sum FABCOM 2	03 (37; -37)	-10 *(38; **-83**)*	06 (43; 36)	12 (42; -59)	-08 (30; 21)	09 (10; -38)	00 (32; -28)
Sum ALOG	**-51** (**-72**; 11)	**-50** (**-81**; -56)	-29 *(-46; **79**)*	**-50** (-61; 15)	**-48** (**-74**; -10)	-37 (-49; 37)	**-38** (**-68**; 06)
Sum CONTAM	-06 (00; 27)	-17 (04; -51)	-07 (-19; 54)	-07 (-03; 07)	-12 (00; 53)	25 (21; 18)	-10 (00; 24)
Raw Sum 6	-11 (-12; -43)	-25 (-06; **-75**)	03 (04; 29)	-05 (-10; -45)	-28 (-25; -22)	11 (08; 02)	-09 (-25; -35)
Weighted Sum6	-06 (-04; -40)	-19 (-03; **-76**)	07 (11; 31)	00 (-04; -42)	-21 (-18; -10)	12 (14; -04)	-10 (-19; -37)

Note. All numbers are Spearman's nonparametric correlation coefficient; decimal point is omitted; significant correlations are shown in **boldface**. The first coefficient in each cell (upper line) is computed on the whole group (n = 96); the second and third coefficients (second line) are respectively computed on patients with convergent test-taking attitude (n = 29), and patients with divergent test-taking attitude (n = 22). When there is a significant difference between subgroup correlation coefficients computed on the "convergent" and "divergent" subgroups, both are shown in *italics*.

with the sum of queer fabulized combinations (FABCOM 2); and finally the correlations between Angry Irritability and responses with inappropriate logic (ALOG).

Discussion

Rorschach Markers of Openness

The results support the assumption there are Rorschach markers of Openness. Even though the correlations between NEO PI-R Openness and Rorschach variables are low to moderate, they are consistent with theory. A first group of markers is related to the characteristic of interest in the task and complexity of approach, expressed by the variety of determinants utilized: low F% (L) and conversely high sum shadings, blends, and a tendency to high EA, M, and sum C. A second group of markers comprises critical special scores, which are usually held as indices of thought disorders, but the picture is rather complex: open patients tend to produce many odd or flippant responses, but there are few ALOG and many combinatory special scores (i.e., incongruous and fabulized combinations, and contaminations) in their records. Two explanations remain possible: it is possible that openness is linked with a certain kind of creativity, which may seem odd or queer; it is also likely that the open persons express their inner life more than the closed ones do; as the present sample is composed of psychiatric patients, the inner life they can express is filled with pathological traits. The fact that the combinatory thought disorders (CONTAM and to a lesser degree FABCOM 2) are positively linked to openness, whereas the more schizophrenic-like inappropriate logic (ALOG) does not, could be used as an argument in favor of the first assumption. A third group of Rorschach Openness markers is composed of special scores related to the affective valence of content: morbid responses, and aggressive movement responses. As shadings often are related to negative emotions, and many blends comprise shading or achromatic color as one of their components, Sum Shading and Sum Blends can be related to the former. The link between Openness and markers of negative emotionality can easily be explained by the fact the subjects are both psychiatric patients with intense negative emotions and open persons with high ability to express their inner experience.

Openness, Neuroticism, and the Moderating Role of the Test-Taking Attitude

Our findings establish that the test-taking attitude, as defined according to the first factor of both instruments, *does not moderate the relationship between Big Five Model Openness and the Rorschach markers of Openness*. Out of the 490 computed correlations, none fully meets the criteria derived from the hypothesis that test-taking attitude could explain the observed discrepancies between the NEO PI-R self-report measures of Openness and the Rorschach. Only two correlations computed in the whole group resolve into two opposing correlations, the difference of which is significant. It is clear that the test-taking attitude hypothesis must be discarded. Low correlations at the whole group level generally do *not* conceal stronger and opposite correlations at the subgroup level.

This fact is all the more important since the findings concerning the relations between Neuroticism and the Rorschach variables bring some partial support to the test-taking attitude hypothesis. Even though the analyses separately computed on each subgroup do not produce exactly the result predicted by the test-taking attitude, the findings exhibit a global trend in this direction, with twelve pairs of correlations showing significant differences between patients with "convergent" and "divergent" test-taking attitudes.

Moreover, the psychological meaning of these differences is easy to understand. High EA, sum M, Weighted sum C, sum Shading, and blends, which all are markers of high involvement in the task, tend to be positively associated with Neuroticism among "convergent" subjects, and negatively or not correlated among "divergent" ones. It is logical that subjects who have the same attitude toward both tests either acknowledge or repress emotions at the same degree in both instruments. With the puzzling exception of ALOG, Rorschach special scores tend to be negatively associated to Neuroticism among "divergent" patients, and positively associated or not associated with it among "convergent" patients. Individuals with convergent test-taking attitude generally present little or no association between self-reported negative emotionality and Rorschach markers of thought disorder. But those with "divergent" styles either report few negative emotions whereas their Rorschach reveals disordered thinking or report high levels of neuroticism whereas their Rorschach does not reveal thought disorder. This may be understood as the result of the defensive distortion of self representation among patients with egodystonic personality disorder, especially those with cluster B disorders.

It was expected that the test-taking hypothesis would apply to these relations, because in its early formulation by Meyer (1996) anxiety, which is a construct highly related to Neuroticism, was taken as a criteria for the definition of "response-character style." Since a similar criterion was used by assessing honest-uninhibited test-taking attitude toward the NEO PI-R on the basis of high score on Neuroticism, it could be expected that Rorschach and NEO PI-R measures of Neuroticism were positively related among "convergent" subjects and negatively related among the "divergent" ones. This conclusion is tautological: it only means that the self-report of negative emotions and Rorschach responses other than purely formal must correlate among subjects presenting either (1) both high score on NEO PI-R Neuroticism and many (R 26) Rorschach non pure-form responses (F% < 53, i.e., L < 1.1), or (2) both low score on NEO PI-R Neuroticism and few non purely formal Rorschach responses.

Therefore, subjects with "convergent" test-taking attitude have necessarily either high Neuroticism with high R and low F% (= low Lambda), or low Neuroticism with low R and high F%: correlation between Neuroticism and F% must automatically be negative and high in the "convergent" subgroup. Conversely, subjects with divergent test-taking attitudes must exhibit a positive high correlation between the same two variables. But this phenomenon is strictly limited to the relations between Neuroticism and the set of variables comprising F% and the Rorschach scores automatically linked with it: EA and its components sum M and sum C, experienced stimulation (es) and its components (Sum FM and m and Sum shadings), and blends. It hardly generalizes to other markers of negative emotionality, like the special scores.

The only surprising finding is that despite this tautology, the results only partially confirm the moderating role of test-taking attitude on markers of negative emotions. This is probably due to fact that the criteria for uninhibited-expansive Rorschach test-taking attitude did not only relate to the Rorschach first factor (the stronger marker of which is the number of responses, R), since F% (= Lambda) has higher saturation in the second factor than in the first one. Because of this, redundancy is not complete.

The test-taking attitude hypothesis, which was first applied to the relations between MMPI and the Rorschach, does not apply to the NEO PI-R precisely because it is an operationalization of the Five-Factor Model of Personality, which assumes the existence of four factors different from Neuroticism, and orthogonal with it. Because Openness has low relation with Neuroticism, test-taking attitude assessed according to the Neuroticism score has low or no influence on the correlations between NEO PI-R scales of Openness and Rorschach variables. It all comes down to saying that the modified formulation of Meyer's hypothesis, although it applies rather well to the relations between Neuroticism and the Rorschach variables, does not apply to relations between self reported Openness and the Rorschach markers of this dimension.

Heterogeneity of "Convergent" and "Divergent" Subgroups

Finally, it must be pointed that each of these subgroups is in fact heterogeneous, and comprises itself two very different subgroups. The "convergent" subgroup merges two very different types of subjects: (1) subjects with convergent expressive and uninhibited attitude toward both tests, and (2) subjects with convergent reluctant and inhibited attitude toward both tests. Similarly, the "divergent" subgroup needs to be divided into (1) subjects who respond sincerely to self-report measures but are inhibited or defensive when taking the Rorschach; (2) subjects who consciously or unconsciously distort their responses to self-report questionnaire, but unconsciously reveal in their Rorschach repressed or denied fantasy contents or modes of functioning. It is likely that these four subgroups are clinically very different, and it would be interesting to reformulate the Meyer's hypothesis taking into account the existence of four different test-taking attitudes: positive toward both measures, negative toward both measures, positive toward the self-report and negative toward the Rorschach, positive toward the Rorschach and restrictive toward the self-report. It would be interesting to undertake separate analyses for each of these subgroups. This task is unfortunately beyond our present possibility, for it would need to do six comparisons between subgroups coefficients for each association between a NEO PI-R scale and a Rorschach variable. Even focusing only on Openness, it would be necessary to compute 1,470 correlation coefficients (35 Rorschach variables × 7 Openness scales × 6 comparisons between subgroups correlations), and as the subgroups would be about a half smaller than "convergent" and "divergent" subgroups in the present research, the Bonferroni's correction would lead to demands almost impossible to meet with when one computes correlations on small groups. Further research, to be conducted on much larger samples, would be needed to test this reformulation of the test-taking attitude hypothesis.

References

Anzieu, D. (1961). *Les méthodes projectives* [Projective methods]. Paris: Presses Universitaires de France.

Archer, R.P., & Krishnamurthy, R. (1993). A review of MMPI and Rorschach interrelationships in adult samples. *Journal of Personality Assessment, 61*, 277–293.

Costa, P.T., & McCrae, R.R. (1985). *The NEO personality inventory manual.* Odessa, FL: Personality Assessment Resources.

Costa, P.T., & McCrae, R.R. (1992). *NEO PI-R Inventaire de personnalité révisé* [The NEO Personality Inventory Revised] (adaptation française: J.P. Rolland). Paris: Center de Psychologie appliquée, 1998.

Digman, J.M., & Takemoto-Chock, N.K. (1981). Factors in the natural language of personality: Re-analysis, comparison, and interpretation of six major studies. *Multivariate Behavioral Research, 16*, 149–170.

Djurić Jočić, D. (2002, September). *Correlations of Rorschach method and NEO-PI-R questionnaire.* Paper presented at the 17th Rorschach International Congress, Rome, September 10–14, 2002.

Exner, J.E. (1993 [1974]). *The Rorschach: A comprehensive system.* New York: Wiley.

Fiske, D.W. (1949). Consistency of the factorial structure of personality ratings from various sources. *Journal of Abnormal and Social Psychology, 44*, 329–344.

Ganellen, R.J. (1996). Exploring MMPI-Rorschach relationships. *Journal of Personality Assessment, 67*, 529–542.

Greenwald, D.F. (1999). Relationships between the Rorschach and the NEO-five-factor inventory. *Psychological Reports, 85*, 519–527.

Howell, D.C. (1997). *Statistical methods for psychology* (4th ed.). New York: Duxburg.

Ignjatović, T.D., Djurić Jočić, D., & Pavlivić, D. (1999, July). *Relation between one of the basic personality domain openness and conceptually similar Rorschach indicators.* Poster presented at the 16th Rorschach International Congress, Amsterdam, July 21, 1999.

McCrae, R.R. (1994). Openness to experience: Expanding the boundaries of factor V. *European Journal of Personality, 8*, 251–272.

Meyer, G.J. (1996). The Rorschach and MMPI: Toward a more scientifically differentiated understanding of cross-method assessment. *Journal of Personality Assessment, 67*, 558–578.

Meyer, G.J. (1997). On the integration of personality assessment methods. *Journal of Personality Assessment, 68*, 297–330.

Meyer, G.J. (1999). The convergent validity of MMPI and Rorschach scales: An extension using profile scores to define response and character styles on both methods and a reexamination of simple Rorschach response frequency. *Journal of Personality Assessment, 72*, 1–35.

Petot, J.M. (2002, September). *Rorschach markers of openness to experience.* Paper presented at the 17th Rorschach International Congress, Rome, September 10–14, 2002.

Petot, J.M. (2004). Le test de Rorschach et le modèle de personnalité en cinq facteurs [The Rorschach and the Big Five model of personality]. *Psychologie française, 49,* 81–94.

Rapaport, D., Gill, M., & Schafer, R. (1968 [1944]). *Diagnostic psychological testing* (revised edition., ed. R.R. Holt). New York: International Universities Press.

Rausch de Traubenberg, N. (1970). *La pratique du Rorschach* [The Rorschach in practice]. Paris: Presses Universitaires de France.

Saucier, G. (1992). Openness vs intellect: Much ado about nothing? *European Journal of Personality, 6,* 381–386.

Tellegen, A., & Atkinson, G. (1974). Openness to absorbing and self-altering experiences ("Absorption"), a trait related to hypnotic susceptibility. *Journal of Abnormal Psychology, 83,* 268–277.

Tupes, E.C., & Christal, R.E. (1992). Recurrent personality factors based on trait ratings. *Journal of Personality, 60,* 225–251 (first publication: 1961).

Summary

The low correlations reported between self-report measures and the Rorschach raise questions about the validity of both kinds of instruments. Meyer (1996) suggested that these low correlations are an artefact, due to the failure to control response style. Correlations would be high and positive when subjects have the same response style on both methods, and high and negative when they have divergent response styles. But response style is assessed according to criteria strongly connected with distress, and the enhancement of correlations may be tautologically limited to distress scales. The objective of this research is to verify whether the response style hypothesis applies to Openness to Experience, a dimension unrelated with distress. Correlations were computed between on the one hand Openness and Neuroticism, and on the second one several selected Rorschach variables. Analyses were conducted on the whole sample (n = 96) and on separate subgroups of patients with convergent (n = 29) or divergent (n = 22) test-taking attitude. The findings establish Openness is related to Rorschach low L, high blends, morbid responses, and combinatory special scores. They also establish that response style moderates correlations between Neuroticism and the Rorschach, but not between Openness and the Rorschach. These results seem to confirm the tautological nature of the present formulation of the response style hypothesis, but further refinement in the analysis of test-taking attitude could help reconsider things.

Résumé

Les faibles corrélations constatées entre les questionnaires d'auto-évaluation et les résultats du test de Rorschach ont suscité des interrogations sur la validité des deux types de méthode. Meyer (1996) a émis l'idée qu'il s'agit d'un artefact dû au fait que les attitudes des sujets ne sont pas prises en compte. Lorsque les patients ont la même attitude pendant la passation des deux tests, les corrélations seraient élevées et positives; lorsqu'ils ont une attitude différente à l'égard de chaque instrument, les corrélations seraient élevées et négatives. Mais Meyer évalue ces attitudes au moyen de critères reposant principalement sur la tendance à s'attribuer des émotions négatives. Il est dès lors inévitable que les indicateurs de détresse soient convergents chez ceux qui présentent dans les deux types de test la même tendance à reconnaître ou à dénier leur souffrance psychologique, et divergents chez ceux qui expriment leur souffrance dans l'un des tests et la dénient dans l'autre. Le but de la présente recherche est de vérifier si le style de réponse peut influencer les corrélations impliquant une dimension de la personnalité sans relation avec la détresse psychique, l'ouverture à l'expérience, qui constitue une des grandes dimensions du modèle de personnalité en cinq facteurs. On a calculé les corrélations entre les échelles d'ouverture et de névrosisme du NEO-PI-R et des variables du test de Rorschach, d'abord sur la totalité d'un groupe de patients psychiatriques (n = 96), puis pour chacun des sous-groupes présentant des attitudes de réponse convergentes (n = 29) ou divergentes (n = 22). L'ouverture est globalement associée à un F% faible, à des réponses comportant plusieurs déterminants, à des réponses à contenu morbide et à des cotations spéciales renvoyant à des troubles du cours de la pensée du type combinatoire. L'attitude de réponse a une certaine influence sur les corrélations entre le névrosisme et les variables du Rorschach, mais n'en a aucune sur les relations entre l'Ouverture et ces variables. Cela confirme la nature tautologique de la formulation actuelle de l'hypothèse de l'influence modératrice des styles de réponse. Mais il n'est pas exclu qu'une amélioration de la définition des attitudes de réponse permette ultérieurement de reconsidérer cette question.

Resumen

Las bajas correlaciones halladas entre medidas procedentes de autoinformes y de Rorschach plantean cuestionamientos acerca de la validez de ambos tipos de instrumentos. Meyer (1996) sugirió que estas bajas correlaciones podrían ser un artefacto debido a la dificultad para controlar los estilos de respuesta. Así, las correlaciones serían altas y positivas si los sujetos presentaran el mismo estilo de respuesta a ambos métodos, o bien, altas y negativas cuando tuvieran estilos de respuesta divergentes. No obstante, el estilo de respuesta se evalúa según criterios estrechamente vinculados al malestar psicológico y el aumento de las correlaciones podría acabar estando tautológicamente limitado a las escalas de malestar.

El objetivo de esta investigación consiste en verificar si la hipótesis del estilo de respuesta puede aplicarse a la Apertura a la Experiencia, una dimensión no relacionada con el malestar. Se valoraron las correlaciones entre, por un lado, Apertura a la Experiencia y Neuroticismo y por otro, un grupo de variables Rorschach seleccionadas. Se llevaron a cabo análisis con los datos de toda la muestra ($n = 96$) y con subgrupos separados de pacientes que presentaban en la administración de las pruebas actitudes convergentes ($n = 29$) o divergentes ($n = 22$). Los resultados muestran que la Apertura a la Experiencia correlaciona en Rorschach con: Lambda bajo, Blend alto, Contenidos Mórbidos y Códigos Especiales combinatorios. También se observa que el estilo de respuesta modera las correlaciones entre Neuroticismo y Rorschach, pero no entre Apertura a la Experiencia y Rorschach. Estos datos parecen confirmar la naturaleza tautológica de la hipótesis del estilo de respuesta en su formulación actual, no obstante, un mayor refinamiento en el análisis de las actitudes en la administración de las pruebas podría ayudar a reconsiderar este tema.

Rorschachiana 27, 51–62

Extraversion in Differential Psychology and Experience Balance in the Rorschach

Gregorio E.H. del Pilar

University of the Philippines, Quezon City, Philippines

The aim of this research was to verify the hypothesis that extraversion in differential psychology and experience balance in the Rorschach are related to one another. The relationship between these two constructs remains to this day an open question, with expert opinion running the entire gamut of possibilities. For example, Klopfer (1954), Bash (1955), and Beck (1960) consider the two constructs to be highly similar, while Loosli-Usteri (1965), Rausch de Traubenberg (1990), Anzieu (1992), and Exner (1993) take the opposite view. Moreover, results from empirical studies are also inconsistent (e.g., Bieri & Blacker, 1956, Singer & Spohn, 1954; Palmer, 1956, Singer & Herman, 1954). Inasmuch as the instruments pertinent to the resolution of this question have considerably evolved since the last studies bearing directly on this question were undertaken more than forty years ago, it was decided to pose the question anew.

Extraversion in Differential Psychology

Consistent with a model first proposed by Eysenck in 1947, extraversion has long been considered a broad trait made up of a number of narrower component traits. The NEO PI-R of Costa and McCrae (1992), currently the best-known personality inventory that measures the so-called Big Five personality traits proposes as narrower traits making up extraversion the following: warmth, gregariousness, assertiveness, sensation-seeking and positive emotions. These components are largely coherent with those found in other well-known but older measures of extraversion such as those of Cattell, Guilford, and Eysenck, as well as the more recently developed extraversion scale of Tellegen (1982). It should be noted nevertheless that while Costa and McCrae put a relatively greater stress on the positive affect component, Eysenck and Guilford emphasize impulsiveness in the broad sense.

Among the authors mentioned, it was Eysenck who went furthest in the effort to explain the coherence of the components of extraversion. Although he had never identified them definitively, it is clear that he considered spontaneity, lack of restraint, sociability, activity and venturesomeness as the most important subtraits of extraversion. A careful reading of his work also suggests, in addition to those just mentioned, the trait of reflectiveness. Eysenck (1967) proposed a theory identifying a particular part of the nervous system, namely, the ascending reticular activating system (ARAS), as the basis of the behavior and other psychological functions manifesting extraversion. An impressive amount of research directed at testing this theory has necessitated its revision to a significant extent, without however calling into question its coherence as a broad trait.

Experience Balance and the Question of its Relationship to Extraversion

Rorschach (1921) does not give an explicit definition of experience balance, but he gives a tabular summary of his own observations of characteristics that he reports having found associated with this construct.

The eight characteristics shown in the table show some resemblance to extraversion in differential psychology (as well as, in fact, to Jungian

Table 1. Summary of Rorschach's observations on the correlates of predominance of movement or color responses.

Movement predominant	*Color predominant*
Awkwardness, clumsiness	Skill and adroitness
Measured, stable motility	Restless, labile motility
More intensive than extensive rapport	More extensive than intensive rapport
Less adaptable to reality	More adaptable to reality
Stable affective reactions	Labile affective reactions
Greater productive ability	More reproductive ability
More individualized intelligence	More stereotyped intelligence
More "inner" life	More "outward" life

extraversion). The first and the second characteristics, which deal with motility, resemble activity in the different models of extraversion. The next three characteristics, as indicated explicitly by the fifth, have to do with affectivity. Rorschach groups under this term positive affectivity (freedom from care, ease of empathizing with another) as well as negative affectivity (impulsiveness). These characteristics seem related to positive affect in the type of model represented by that of Costa & McCrae (1992); and to impulsivity in Eysenck's model. The last three characteristics however, which all have to do with "inner life," contrary to the preceding ones, are hardly represented in the different models of extraversion. Indeed, among imagination, creativity and reflectiveness – the functions represented by the last three characteristics in the table – only the last one is part of an extraversion model (i.e., Eysenck's).

A large number of studies (Del Pilar, 1998) confirms Rorschach's observations regarding the association between extraversion on the one hand and motility and impulsiveness on the other (there were no studies related to positive affect). On the other hand, the studies associated with "inner life" seem to indicate that although reflectiveness could still be retained as a psychological correlate of (introversive) experience balance, this was not the case for creativity and imagination. Thus, as much for what they confirm as components of experience balance – motility, affective expressiveness and possibly reflectiveness – as well as what they seem to indicate as not being so – imagination and creativity – these results go in the direction of a closer relationship between experience balance and extraversion.

These results notwithstanding, the effort to demonstrate the link between experience balance and extraversion was not sufficiently maintained to allow movement toward a resolution of this question. On the one hand, this was due to the results of studies which directly tested the relationship between the two concepts. These studies, although small in number, almost all show negative results (Del Pilar, 1998). On the other hand, Rorschach took a position, followed later by a few influential authors, that minimized the association between EB and extraversion.

According to this position, whereas introversion and extraversion are opposite tendencies, the EB types of introversiveness and extratensiveness are not. Rorschach had advanced as one of the principal arguments in support of this position the fact that ideation and affectivity, the dominant functions respectively characterizing the two types, were not opposed but merely different from one another. We will postpone for later our response to this argument.

Methodology

One-hundred twenty-nine Filipino students (68 males, 61 females) were administered the Rorschach Test and a number of personality scales. Extraversion was measured by the Filipino NEO PI-R and the Eysenck Personality Questionnaire-Revised. These latter two were taken in their entirety so as to provide scores for other scales that were used in demonstrating the validity of the Filipino translation of the NEO PI-R. It will be noted in passing that Eysenck's extraversion scale contains mainly items measuring sociability and activity. He had also constructed scales to measure impulsiveness in the strict sense, that is, lack of restraint; and venturesomeness. The subjects also responded to these scales, as well as to the Thoughtfulness scale of the Guilford-Zimmerman Temperament Survey. It should be noted however that this last scale seems limited as a measure of introverted reflectiveness, appearing to likewise measure the tendency to ruminate more characteristic of neuroticism (Sells, Démarée & Will, 1970, 1971; Del Pilar, 1998). Finally, 888 other students participated in the validation studies for the extraversion scales.

The reliability coefficient of the extraversion scales were .88 (FNEO PI-R) and .84 (Eysenck). The component scales of the first instrument as well as the related scales of the second were adequate, having values ranging from 0.62 to 0.78.

Convergent and discriminant validation evidence, shown in the tables below, seemed satisfactory as well.

Table 2. Reliabilities of the extraversion scales and their component scales.

NEO PI-R: Extraversion	.88
E1 Warmth	.70
E2 Gregariousness	.77
E3 Assertiveness	.75
E4 Activity	.69
E5 Sensation-seeking	.62
E6 Positive emotions	.67
Eysenck	
Extraversion EPQ-R	.84
Venturesomeness (I7Q)	.78
Impulsiveness (I7Q)	.78
Thoughtfulness (GZTS)	.75

The administration of the Rorschach test was done in accordance with the directions of the manual for Exner's Comprehensive System (1990), using essentially Filipino as the language of testing. Inasmuch as it had been noticed in Philippine studies on the Rorschach that Filipino subjects had a tendency to give less color responses than subjects in the west, it had been planned to do pursue the inquiry for C responses as far as possible (but taking care not to influence subject responding). It had likewise been planned to take into account the relative spontaneity of the C responses by assigning a weight of 3 to those given during the free association

Table 3. Eysenck scales.

Convergent correlations			Discriminant correlations	
Venturesomeness (I7Q)	Impulsivity (I7Q)	Thoughtfulness (GZTS)	Neuroticism (EPQ-R)	Psychotism (EPQ-R)
.33***	.25***	–.25***	–.19*	–.02

$p < .05$; ***$p < .001$

Table 4. Filipino NEO PI-R.

Results of factor analysis of the 30 facet scales yielding 5 factors		
Scale	Loading on the extraversion factor	Mean loading (absolute value) on the other 4 factors
E1 Warmth	.69	.18
E2 Gregariousness	.65	.10
E3 Assertiveness	.42	.20
E4 Activity	.51	.18
E5 Sensation-seeking	.51	.20
E6 Positive emotions	.66	.12

phase; of 2 to those made at the beginning of the inquiry phase (i.e., after the examiner read the subject's response); and a weight of 1 to those given after a question. The color scores were thus calculated in two ways, yielding the normal color score and a score weighted for spontaneity.

Here, experience balance (EB) is calculated by the *difference* between ΣC (sum of color scores) and ΣM (sum of movement scores), correlated at higher levels with the scales than either sum by itself.

Results

1. Extraversion and experience balance turned out correlated to each other.

As Table 5 shows, using the normal color score, one obtains a correlation between experience balance and extraversion of .24 and .20 using Ey-

Table 5. Correlation between experience balance and extraversion.

Extraversion scale	Weighted Sum C without coefficients of spontaneity	Weighted Sum C with coefficients of spontaneity
EPQ-R (Eysenck)	.24*	.29**
NEO PI-R (Costa & McCrae)	.20*	.22*

senck's and Costa & McCrae's scales, respectively ($p < .05$ for both). This pattern of results for unweighted and weighted color scores, that is, correlations for both being significant but higher for the weighted color scores, were obtained in all the statistical tests run. Consequently, only the results obtained using the weighted color scores will henceforth be reported.

When correlations are calculated, it is justifiable to eliminate outliers, commonly defined as raw scores with standard score (z) equivalents equal to or greater than 3.30 (see for example Tabachnik & Fidell, 1996). Outliers can exaggerate a modest trend or diminish a strong trend obscured by its presence.

An outlier was found in the sample for this study with a z-score of 4.42 on experience balance. This case had a score of −2.04 on Eysenck's extraversion scale and −1.09 on Costa & McCrae's, thus contributing a high negative z cross-product to the correlation between extraversion and experience balance. With its removal, the correlation between EB

Table 6. Correlation between experience balance and extraversion without the outlier.

Extraversion scale	Sum C	Sum C weighted with coefficients of spontaneity
EPQ-R (Eysenck)	.28**	.41***
NEO PI-R (Costa & McCrae	.22*	.33***

*$p < .05$; **$p < .01$; ***$p < .001$

Table 7.

Scale	Correlation with experience balance (weighted sum C)
NEO PI-R	
E1 Warmth	.33***
E2 Gregariousness	.29**
E3 Assertiveness	.19*
E4 Activity	.22*
E5 Sensation-seeking	.13
E6 Positive emotions	.23*
Eysenck	
Extraversion EPQ-R	.41***
Venturesomeness (I7)	.04
Impulsiveness (I7Q)	.06
Thoughtfulness (GZTS)	.00

*$p < .05$; **$p < .01$; ***$p < .001$

Table 8. Relations between Personality Scales and Sum C, Sum M, and EB.

Scale	Sum C (weighted)	Sum M	Experience Balance
E1 Warmth	.28**	–.10	.33***
E2 Gregariousness	.25**	–.07	.29**
E6 Positive emotions	.16 ($p < 0.09$)	–.10	.23*
E4 Activity	.14 ($p < 0.07$)	–.11	.22*
Extraversion NEO	.27**	–.10	.33***
Extraversion Eysenck	–.12	–.12	–.12

$p < .05$; $^{**}p < .01$; $^{***}p < .001$

and E rises to 0.41 using Eysenck's scale and to .33 using the scale of Costa & McCrae. These two correlations are significant at $p < .001$.

2. The aspects of extraversion that are related most strongly to experience balance, for this sample, seem to be what might be called interpersonal positive affect (warmth, gregariousness, positive emotions) and activity.
3. These aspects of extraversion, as well as the two extraversion scales are all positively correlated with color (C) responses and negatively, although very weakly, with movement (M) responses.

Discussion

Figure 1.

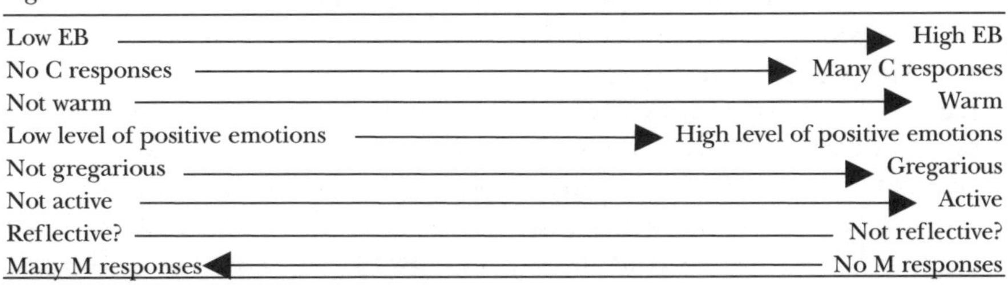

These results tend to confirm the hypothesis of this study that extraversion and experience balance are indeed related to one another. These results thus furnish the empirical support, which for a long time have been lacking, for the apparent similarities between psychological tendencies that reflect extraversion on the one hand, and those that have been found related to experience balance on the other. Figure 1 summarizes the results.

Since the first four components of extraversion shown in the graph correlated positively with color responses, the C continuum near the top is oriented in the same direction as the positive pole of the traits. Since these same traits correlated negatively with movement responses, the M continuum at the bottom is oriented in the opposite direction. These components also correlated positively with experience balance (ΣC – ΣM), thus this relationship is indicated by the continuum EB at the top oriented in the same direction as the positive pole of the traits, as is the case with the C continuum. The fifth component, reflectiveness, is marked with question marks because the scale that operationalized it (the Thoughtfulness scale of the Guilford-Zimmerman Temperament Survey) correlated with neither the color nor the movement responses, nor with their difference, that is, with experience balance. It is nevertheless included in the graph for the following reasons: first, as mentioned earlier, the Guilford scale does not seem a good measure for the reflectiveness associated with introversion, appearing to substantially tap neuroticism (Del Pilar, 1998). Secondly, the scale nevertheless correlated significantly and in the expected direction (i.e., negatively) with the other scales shown in the graph. Thirdly, it seems that this is the only component that seems capable of harmonizing with the theoretical ideas advanced to explain movement responses (Singer, 1960, 1973). It should thus be clear that its inclusion in the graph should be considered as a hypothesis rather than a conclusion.

Assuming that the inclusion of reflectiveness in the above graph is justified, one sees how experience balance (ΣC – ΣM) correlates with extraversion: an extravert – cordial, gregarious, joyous, optimist, active, etc. – has a greater tendency to give color responses than an introvert because of a characteristically higher level of positive affect. At the same time, tending to be less reflective, he has less of a tendency to give movement responses. The opposite of course is likewise proposed: an introvert, less cordial, less gregarious, etc. – will have less of a tendency to give color responses. But having a greater tendency to be reflective, he has a greater tendency to give movement responses. Because of such a configuration of correlations with the two measures in opposite directions, the combination of C and M responses by subtraction gives in principle a difference – experience balance – which correlates even better with extraversion and its components, which was in fact obtained.

Finally, one sees in the graph, by looking at the opposed directions of reflectiveness on the one hand and of positive emotions on the other, how ideation and affectivity, while being different as Rorschach noted, can nevertheless be "opposite" to one another. They are so by virtue of being respectively more associated with opposite poles of a large trait of which they are part.

References

Anzieu, D., & Chabert, C. (1992). *Les méthodes projectives* [Projective methods] (9th ed.). Paris: Presses Universitaires de France.

Bash, K.W. (1955). Einstellungstypus and Erlebnistypus: C.G. Jung und Herman Rorschach [Type of attitude and experience balance: C.G. Jung and Herman Rorschach]. *Journal of Projective Techniques, 19*, 236–242.

Beck, S.J. (1960). *The Rorschach experiment: Ventures in blind diagnosis.* New York: Grune & Stratton.

Bieri, J., & Blacker, E. (1956). External and internal stimulus factors in Rorschach Performance. *Journal of Consulting Psychology, 20,* 1–7.

Costa, P.T., & McCrae, R.R., Jr. (1992). *NEO PI-R professional manual.* Odessa, FL: Psychological Assessment Resources.

Del Pilar, G.E.H. (1998). *"L'extraversion en psychologie différentielle et l'extratension au Test de Rorschach."* [Extraversion in differential psychology and extratension in the Rorschach test]. Unpublished doctoral thesis, Université de Paris X - Nanterre.

Exner, J.E. (1990). *Manuel de cotation du Rorschach pour le système intégré* [Rorschach workbook]. (French trans. A. Andronikof-Sanglade, 1995). Paris: Editions Frison-Roche.

Exner, J.E. (1993). *The Rorschach: A comprehensive system, Vol. 1, 3rd. ed.* (French trans. A. Andronikof-Sanglade, 1995). Paris: Editions Frison-Roche.

Eysenck, H.J. (1947). *Dimensions of personality.* London: Routledge & Kegan Paul.

Eysenck, H.J. (1967). *The biological basis of personality.* Springfield, IL: C.C. Thomas.

Klopfer, B., Ainsworth, M.D., Klopfer, W.G., & Holt, R.R. (1954). *Developments in the Rorschach technique. Vol. I.* Yonkers, NY: World Books.

Loosli-Usteri, M. (1965). *Manuel pratique du test de Rorschach* [Rorschach practical handbook]. Paris: Hermann.

Palmer, J.O. (1956). Attitudinal correlates of Rorschach experience-balance. *Journal of Projective Techniques, 20,* 28–213.

Rausch de Traubenberg, N. (1990). *La pratique du Rorschach* (6th ed.). [The Rorschach in practice]. Paris: Presses Universitaires de France.

Rorschach, H.E. (1921). *Psychodiagnostik* (Psychodiagnostics; English trans. P. Lemkau & B. Kronenberg. Ed. W. Morgenhalter; 2nd edition, 1942. NY: Grune & Stratton). Bern: Ernst Bircher.

Sells, S.B., Démarée, R.G., & Will, D.P. (1970). Dimensions of personality: I. Conjoint factor structure of the Guilford and Cattell trait markers. *Multivariate Behavioral Research, 5,* 391–422.

Sells, S.B., Démarée, R.G., & Will, D.P. (1971). Separate factor structures in Guilford and Cattell trait markers. *Multivariate Behavioral Research, 6*, 135–185.

Singer, J.L., & Herman, J. (1954). Motor and fantasy correlates of Rorschach human movement responses. *Journal of Consulting Psychology, 18*, 325–331.

Singer, J.L., & Spohn, H. (1954). Some behavioral correlates of Rorschach experience-type. *Journal of Consulting Psychology, 18*, 1–9.

Singer, J.L. (1960). The experience type: Some behavioral correlates and theoretical implications. In M. Rickers-Ovsiankina (Ed.), *Rorschach Psychology* (pp. 223–259). New York: Wiley.

Singer, J.L. (Ed.). (1973). *The child's world of make-believe: Experimental studies of imaginative play.* New York: Academic Press.

Tabachnik, B.G., & Fidell, L.S. (1996). *Using multivariate statistics* (3rd ed.). New York: HarperCollins.

Tellegen, A. (1982). *Brief manual of the Differential Personality Questionnaire.* Unpublished manuscript.

Summary

The opinion of Rorschach experts through the years on the link between extraversion (E) and experience balance (EB) have ranged from considering the two as virtually identical to denying any relationship between them. Results of empirical studies have been no less divergent: the studies bearing on the observations made by Rorschach on the psychological correlates of EB seem to have confirmed those which resemble the components of E. On the other hand, studies directly investigating the question of the correlation between the two concepts have nearly unanimously obtained nonsignificant results. To address this question anew, with measures of the two constructs that have evolved since the last empirical studies were done on the question, 129 bilingual Filipino university students were administered Eysenck's (EPQ-R) scale, the Filipino version of the NEO PI-R, and the Rorschach. The obtained correlations with EB of the two E scales were 0.22 ($p < .05$) and 0.29 ($p < .01$). By deleting an outlier, these correlations rise to 0.33 and 0.41, respectively ($p < .001$ for both). The aspects of E most related to EB were warmth, gregariousness, positive emotions and activity. These components of E, as well as total E, correlate positively with the color responses and negatively with the movement responses. The EB formula was found to be generally correlated with E at higher levels compared to the correlations with E of either just the color or just the movement responses. New possibilities for conceptualizing the EB measure, based on its demonstrated relationship with E, are suggested.

Résumé

Au fil des années, l'opinion des experts du Rorschach concernant le lien entre l'extraversion et l'extratension a varié entre deux extrêmes consistant, l'un à les considérer comme pratiquement identiques et l'autre à nier toute relation entre elles. Les résultats des études empiriques ne sont pas moins divergents: les études portant sur les observations faites par Rorschach sur les corrélats psychologiques de l'extratension semblent avoir confirmé ceux qui ressemblent aux composantes de l'extraversion. En revanche, les recherches entreprises directement sur la question de la corrélation entre les deux concepts ont obtenu, presque sans exception, des résultats nonsignificatifs. Afin de renouveler cette question, en utilisant des instruments d'évaluation qui ont évolué depuis les dernières études faites sur la question, on a administré à 129 étudiants philippins bilingues le questionnaire de Eysenck (EPQ-R), la version philippine du questionnaire NEO PI-R, et le test de Rorschach. Des corrélations de 0.22 ($p < .05$) et de 0.29 ($p < .01$) ont été obtenues entre l'extraversion et l'extratension. En supprimant un cas aberrant, ces corrélations s'élèvent respectivement à 0.33 et 0.41 ($p < .001$ pour les deux). Les aspects d'extraversion les plus liés à l'extratension étaient la chaleur, la grégarité, les émotions positives et l'activité. Ces composantes de l'extraversion, ainsi que les notes globales d'extraversion, corrèlent positivement avec les réponses C et négativement avec les réponses K. La corrélation entre la formule d'extratension se montre supérieure aux corrélations de l'extraversion avec les réponses couleur ou les réponses kinesthésiques humaines. On propose de nouvelles possibilités, fondées sur son lien démontré avec l'extraversion, pour conceptualiser la mesure de l'extratension.

Resumen

Durante muchos años, la opinión de expertos en Rorschach sobre las conexiones entre extraversión (E) y tipo vivencial (EB) han presentado un amplio rango, desde la consideración de que ambas variables eran prácticamente idénticas hasta la negación de cualquier relación entre ellas. Los resultados de estudios empíricos no han sido menos divergentes: los trabajos basados en los correlatos psicológicos de EB parecen haber confirmado la semejanza con los componentes de E. Por otro lado, los estudios que han investigado directamente la correlación entre ambos conceptos han obtenidos casi unánimemente resultados no significativos. Se planteó este trabajo para abordar nuevamente el tema administrando a 129 estudiantes universitarios bilingües filipinos la escala de Eysenck (EPQ-R), la versión filipina del NEO-PI-R y el Rorschach. Las correlaciones obtenidas entre EB y las dos escalas E fueron de 0.22 ($p < .05$) y 0.29 ($p < .01$). Descartando un valor extremo, estas correlaciones alcanzan 0.33 y 0.41 respectivamente ($p < .001$ para ambas). Los aspectos de E más relacionados con EB fueron calidez, gregarismo, emociones positivas y actividad. Tanto estos componentes de E como la E total correlacionan positivamente con las respuestas de Color y negativamente con las de Movimiento. Sin embargo, la fórmula EB presenta correlaciones con E a niveles más elevados que solo las respuestas de Color o sólo las de Movimiento. Se sugieren nuevas posibilidades de conceptualización sobre EB basadas en estas correlaciones con E.

Rorschachiana 27, 63–79

Correlation Between the Rorschach Test Coded and Interpreted According to the Comprehensive Exner System and the Eysenck Personality Inventory

Antonella De Carolis and Stefano Ferracuti

Department of Psychiatric Sciences and Psychological Medicine, University of Roma "La Sapienza"

Introduction

The relationships between the Rorschach variables and scores from self-reported questionnaires are still controversial. Many studies suggest a stable relation between the MMPI scales and the Rorschach indices when patients have similar response styles at the two tests (Meyer, 1999; Meyer, 1997; Lindgreen & Carlsson, 2003). Other studies show that the two instruments measure essentially unrelated constructs (Bornstein, 2001; Archer & Krishnamurthy, 1999).

Whether the MMPI scale can prove the clinical validity and reliability of Rorschach variables, but is inadequate to explore the correspondence between the Rorschach and the superfactors of personality structure remains an open question because none of the MMPI scales is in any real sense unifactorial (Eysenck & Eysenck, 1985).

Studies comparing the Rorschach variables and personality superfactors defined by the self-reported questionnaires have also provided inconsistent results. Comparison between Rorschach variables and the Sixteen Personality Factor Questionnaire showed that several findings are inconsistent with the conventional interpretation of some important Rorschach variables (Greenwald, 1991). When scored with the Comprehensive System, the Rorschach has a four-dimensional structure that is independent of self-reported measures; the two dimensions extraversion and neuroticism developed from the MMPI did not correlate with the Rorschach factors (Meyer, 1992). Nor did the Rorschach Rating Scale (RRS), which measures the Rorschach construct from a variety of scoring systems, correspond with the Big Five Model (Meyer, Bates, & Gacono, 1999).

A comparison of the NEO-Five-Factor Inventory (NEO-FFI) with some selected Rorschach variables yielded the opposite results: The Neuroticism scores related significantly to the sum of determinants of Vista (V), Texture (T) and diffuse shading responses (Y) and to the proportion of responses to the chromatic card versus achromatic cards (Afr index), and the scores on Extraversion and Agreeableness related positively to T responses (Greenwald, 1999).

A widely used instrument of personality assessment is the Eysenck Personality Questionnaire (Eysenck & Eysenck, 1975). According to Eysenck model, personality structure is identified by three superfactors or types: Extraversion, Neuroticism, and Psychoticism. According to Eysenck theorization, Psychoticism is opposed to impulse Control, Extraversion is opposed to Introversion, and Neuroticism is opposed to Stability. These types are based on observed correlations between traits. The traits making up the type psychoticism are aggressiveness, coldness, egocentrism, impersonality, impulsiveness, antisociality, unempathy, creativity, and obstinacy. The traits making up the type of extraversion are sociability, liveliness, activeness, assertiveness, sensation-seeking, care freeness, dominance, surgency, and venturesomeness. The traits making up neuroticism are anxiety, depression, feeling of guilt, low self-esteem, tension, irrationality, shyness, moodiness, and emotionality. Psychoticism was considered as a cognitive rather than an affective dimension and the manifestations are related to the ideation (Eysenck & Eysenck, 1985).

The Eysenck model of personality is not the only one considering three dimensions: A model of importance in studies based primarily on self-reported inventories and using factor analytic methods of scale construction and validation is the Tellegen model. The Tellegen model considers the biological perspective of behavior, identifying three major dimensions sustained by supposed neurotransmitter biochemical-behavioral characteristic: Positive Affect, Negative Affect, and Constraint. The first two Tellegen superfactors correspond to emotional dimensions; the last is a nonaffective, behavioral dimension representing the capacity of stimulation control (Watson & Tellegen, 1985; Tellegen & Waller, 1998). An intercorrelation study showed a good correspondence between the concept of Extraversion defined by the Eysenck and the

Tellegen dimension of positive affect, and at the level of underlying factor structure, the broad personality dimensions of extraversion and neuroticism and the broad mood dimensions of positive and negative affect share a common meaning (Tellegen, 1985). A study investigating the relationships between the opposite affective dimensions, defined by the Big Five Model and the Rorschach variables found no correspondence (Meyer et al., 1999).

No research studies have yet investigated the relationships between the Rorschach test, coded according to the Exner Comprehensive System, and the Italian version of the Eysenck Personality Questionnaire (EPI) (Organizzazioni Speciali, 1990). We conducted an exploratory study to investigate the relationships between some Rorschach variables, using the Comprehensive System and the three personality dimensions defined by the EPI.

We first considered the relationships between the Rorschach concept of Erlebnistypus (EB) and Extraversion-Introversion dimension as defined by Eysenck. According to Rorschach's theory, a high ratio of Human Movement responses to color responses reflects an introverted style, whereas a low ratio shows an extraverted tendency (Rorschach, 1921; Exner, 1993). Because some study subjects produced no chromatic responses the ratio was difficult to compute. We therefore considered the difference between movement and color responses as reflecting *EB*. We expected these differences to covariate negatively with the *E* scale, because the greater the index, the more the subject is Introversive. Furthermore, we hypothesized a positive correlation between the weighted sum of chromatic responses *(WSumC)* as a single determinant variable and the *E* scale of the EPI, considering the chromatic responses as expression of positive affectivity. We selected the *WSumC*, a variable that yields a higher correlation test-retest, because the chromatic determinants taken separately have poor temporal stability (Exner, 1993).

The Human Movement responses *(M)*, representing an active form of ideation and reflecting a delayed direct reaction to a stimulus field (Exner, 1993), should be the negative polarity of the *E* scale of the EPI and a negative covariation was expected with the Extraversion scale score.

The Sum of shading determinants *(Sum Shd)* are usually interpreted as an index of negative feelings, indicating painful or dysphoric affects; we hypothesized a positive correlation with the *N* scale of the EPI. We also considered a complex index: the Adjusted Difference score *(AdjD score)*. The *AdjD score* is interpreted as reflecting stable coping adequacy, or the availability of effective coping resources in relation to the level of stress and demands for coping; we hypothesized a negative correlation with the *N* scale, because the more the subject has a neurotic dimension of personality, the more difficulty in coping should be manifest.

We also hypothesized that the *P* scale was associated with oversimplified perception of environmental data, and we expected a negative correlation between the *P* scale and the index of synthetic activity *(Zsum)*. The index *Zsum* is the sum of the weighted *Z* scores that have been assigned. The organizing activity index provides an indication about the extent to which the subject uses cognitive tactics that are more complex than some other mediational approaches (Exner, 1993). We hypothesized that the higher the subjects scored on the *P* scale, the simpler their answers would be and they would avoid blot integration.

Lambda, i.e., the proportion of responses based purely on form F/(R-F), is an index of the extent to which a subject is involved in a new stimulus field (Exner, 1993). When *Lambda* is low the subject may become more involved at a nonadaptive level; conversely, a higher *Lambda* indicates a response style that is oriented toward reducing stimulus situations: the perceptive field is simplified at the input level. We hypothesized that the *P* scale could have a positive correlation with the Lambda index, because it represents reduced dependence on the perceptual field.

Finally, we hypothesized that the Human Movement responses score, representing ideational processes, without considering the formal quality of perception, could be associated with a high *P* value. We hypothesized that the *P* scale would correlate positively with the number of Human Movement responses.

We also grouped the subjects according to the categories defined by the variables *EB*, Difference *(Dscore)*, *AdjDscore*, *Lambda*, and the *Zd*, i.e., the index of response complexity and organizational activity of perceptual data (Exner, 1993), and we compared the EPI score considered in our hypothesis in each of the related subgroups. We expected the EPI *E* scale to yield higher scores in Extratensives than in Introversives and Ambitents. Moreover, we expected the subgroups defined by the Rorschach variables *Dscore* and *AdjDscore*, *Lambda,* and *Zd* to differ in *N* and *P* scale values. We expected *Dminus* and *AdjDminus* subjects, characterized by a manifest, respectively contingent or stable psychological distress, to score higher on the *N* scale of the EPI than the $D = 0$, $AdjD = 0$, *Dplus* and *AdjDplus* subgroups. Finally, we hypothesized that the $L > .99$ subjects, using a narrow focus of attention in perceiving the environment, and the *Zdminus* subjects, who poorly mediate and organize perceptual data, would report higher scores on the *P* scale of the EPI than the other related subgroups defined by *Lambda* and *Zd* scores.

Materials and Method

Subjects

Forty-seven healthy volunteers who had no evident neuropsychiatric problems took part in the study (age: *M* = 29.04 years; *SD* = 5.92, range = 21–52; women: *n* = 29). The education level ranged from 8 to 23 years (*M* = 16.6, *SD* = 2.9).

Procedure

Participants were administered in a single session the Rorschach followed immediately by the EPI (Organizzazioni Speciali, 1990). The EPI is the Italian version of the Eysenck Personality Questionnaire (Eysenck and Eysenck, 1975); the following scales were defined: scale *E* (Extroversion), scale *N* (Neuroticism), and scale *P* (Psychoticism).

Rorschach variables. We selected the following Rorschach indices: *WSumC, M, SumShd, AdjD, Lambda*, and *Zsum*. We also considered the difference between the indices M and WSumC *(M-WSumC)*. Subjects were grouped according to categories defined by the Rorschach variables as follows. The *EB* categories were defined considering the value of the index *Experience Actual (EA)*. The index *EA* was the sum of *M* and *WSumC*. Subjects who had *EA* values of 10 or less and whose *WSumC* or *M* values differed by almost two points were categorized as Extratensive or Introversive rather than Ambitents; and those whose *EA* values exceeded 10 were categorized as Extratensive or Introversive rather than Ambitents only if their *WSum* and *M* values differed by more than two points (Exner, 1993).

The *Dscore* was defined as the difference between *EA* and the index of *Experienced Stimulation (es)*, and the *AdjDscore* as the difference with *Adjusted es*. The *es* index represented the sum of animal movement *(FM)*, inanimate movement *(m)*, achromatic responses *(C')* and shading responses *(Y, T, V);* the *Adjusted es* was obtained by subtracting from the *es* all values except 1 *m* and *Y*. *D* scores were interpreted as the index of contingent anxiety (state anxiety), while the *AdjDscore* as the index of stable anxiety (trait anxiety). The *Dscore* and *AdjDscore* defined the following three categories: *Dminus* and *AdjDminus*, when the demands were greater than the resources of the subject and contingent or stable distress was manifest; $D = 0$ and $AdjD = 0$, when the ability to tolerate negative emotions was sufficient and subjects were free of excessive tension); *Dplus* and *AdjDplus*, when the ability to cope was more than adequate for experienced environmental stimulation.

The *Lambda* categories were determined as follows: $L < .33$, when openness to experience was excessive; $.33 \leq L \leq .99$, when the focus of attention was balanced between internal and external events; and $L > .99$, when the focus of attention was overly narrow and subjects were too simplistic (Exner, 1993; Weiner, 1998).

The index *Zd* was defined according to Exner as the difference between the *Zsum* and the expected value of *Zsum (Zest)*. The *Zdscore* defined three categories: $Zd < -3$, if the subjects took in too little information and consequently tended to examine their experience less thoroughly than would be advisable *(Underincorporation)*; $-3 \leq Zd \leq +3$, if the subjects absorbed just about as much information as they could process adequately (Normal); and $Zd > +3$, if the subjects took in more information than they could organize adequately and tended to examine their experience more thoroughly than was necessary *(Overincorporation)* (Exner, 1994; Weiner, 1998).

Statistical Analysis

We calculated the correlation coefficient (Pearson *r*) between the selected Rorschach indices and the EPI scale; Mann-Whitney *U* test was used to compare the categories defined by the Rorschach variables with the EPI scale.

All the Rorschach protocols were evaluated by two independent raters, neither of whom took part in administering the tests, and a concordance index was calculated between raters.

Results

For all the Rorschach indices the examiners achieved 95% concordance; the maximum concordance was for localizations (98.9%) and the minimum for special scores (95.4%). The mean *R* for the Rorschach was 29.9

Table 1. Values of Rorschach variables *(M* and *SD)* in the whole sample.

R	29.96	(13.92)
Lambda	0.61	(0.45)
EA	9.67	(5.58)
es	13	(6.98)
D score	-1.02	(1.87)
AdjD score	-2.34	(1.96)
WsumC	5.14	(3.33)
M - WSumC	-0.61	(4.00)
Zd score	0.63	(5.77)
SumShd	8.17	(5.16)
ZSum	42.23	(22.46)
Wsum6	4.15	(6.01)
X+%	0.46	(0.14)
X-%	0.13	(0.1)
Xu%	0.38	(0.12)
Intellect. Index	5.26	(4.73)
Egocentricity Index	0.3	(0.14)
Isolation Index	0.22	(0.14)
Affective Ratio	0.56	(0.26)
W	11.94	(6.73)
D	12.38	(8.31)
Dd	5.64	(5.83)
H	3.11	(2.45)

R = Number of Responses; EA = Experience Actual; es = Experienced Stimulation; Dscore = difference between EA and es; AdjDscore = difference between EA and Adjes; M = Human Movement responses; WsumC = Weighted Sum of Chromatic Responses; M-WSumC = difference between human Movement responses and the Weighted Sum of Chromatic Responses; Zd = Processing Efficiency (ZSum – Zest); ZSum = Sum of weighted Z scores; SumShd = Sum Shading; Wsum6 = Weighted Sum of six critical Special Scores; X+% = Ordinary Form; Xu% = Unusual Form; X-% = Distorted Form; W = Responses to the Whole blot; D = Responses to Common Details; Dd = Responses to Unusual Details; H = Human Contents.

(*SD* = 13.9) and the *Lambda* value was .61 (*SD* = .45). The mean value on the *E* scale of the EPI was 13.34 (*SD* = 4.06); for the *N* scale 11.26 (*SD* = 4.87); and for the *P* scale 3.98 (*SD* = 2.27).

Pearson test detected significant correlations between the *Extroversion* scale of the EPI and the variables *WSumC* ($r = .40$; $p < .01$), and *SumShd* ($r = .29$; $p < .05$), and between the calculated difference between Human Movement responses and the Rorschach weighted color responses (*M-WSumC*; $r = .42$, $p < .01$). The *Psychoticism* scale of the EPI correlated significantly with the variable *Zsum* ($r = .22$, $p < .05$)

Table 2. Correlation values (Pearson *r*) between the Rorschach variables and the Eysenck Personality Inventory scales (EPI).

Rorschach variables	EPI E	EPI N	EPI P
M-WSumC	–.42**	–.10	.23
WSumC	–.40**	.12	–.24
M	–.10	–.01	.03
SumShd	.29*	.17	–.07
AdjD score	–.12	.05	–.07
Lambda	.17	–.20	.10
ZSum	.22	–.05	–.33*

*$p < .05$; **$p < .01$

E = Extroversion scale; N = Neuroticism scale; P = Psychoticism scale; M = Human Movement responses; WsumC = Weighted Sum of Chromatic Responses; M-WSumC = difference between Human Movement responses and the Weighted Sum of Chromatic responses; SumShd = Sum Shading responses; AjdD score = difference between Experience Actual and the Adjusted Experienced Stimulation; Lambda = proportion or responses based purely on Form; ZSum = sum of weighted Z scores of organizing activity.

Table 3. Values of the EPI scales in the subgroups defined by the Rorschach indices.

	Categories	*n*	*EPI*	*M*	*SD*
EB	Extratensives	19	E	15.68**	(2.26)
			N	11.84	(5.49)
			P	3.21	(1.96)
	Introversives	10	E	10.60**	(5.34)
			N	10.40	(5.42)
			P	4.40	(1.78)
	Ambitents	18	E	12.39**	(3.56)
			N	11.11	(4.00)
			P	4.56	(2.66)
D	Dminus	23	E	14.52	(3.06)
			N	10.87	(5.24)
			P	3.96	(2.72)
	D = 0	16	E	12.94	(3.96)
			N	12.25	(4.89)
			P	4.38	(1.36)
	Dplus	8	E	10.75	(5.73)
			N	10.38	(3.85)
			P	3.25	(2.38)
AdjD	AdjDminus	16	E	14.38	(3.61)

	Categories	*n*	*EPI*	*M*	*SD*
			N	11.06	(5.46)
			P	4.31	(2.57)
	AdjD = 0	18	E	13.28	(3.69)
			N	11.06	(4.66)
			P	4.06	(2.13)
	AdjDplus	13	E	12.15	(4.96)
			N	11.77	(4.76)
			P	3.46	(2.15)
Lambda	L < .33	15	E	12.53	(4.00)
			N	11.20	(4.59)
			P	4.00	(1.96)
	.33 < L < .99	24	E	13.46	(4.39)
			N	12.29	(4.67)
			P	3.63	(2.55)
	L > .99	8	E	14.50	(3.16)
			N	8.25	(5.34)
			P	5.00	(1.77)
Zd	Zd < –3	12	E	14.50	(3.26)
			N	11.92	(3.48)
			P	3.50	(2.68)
	–3 < Zd < +3	23	E	13.22	(3.41)
			N	11.00	(6.00)
			P	4.13	(2.20)
	Zd > +3	12	E	12.42	(5.71)
			N	11.08	(3.80)
			P	4.17	(2.08)

**Extratensive vs Introversive Mann-Whitney $U = 30.5$, $p = .003$
vs Ambitensive Mann-Whitney $U = 76$, $p = .004$
EB =Erlebnistypus; D =difference between Experience Actual and the Experienced Stimulation; AjdD =difference between Experience Actual and the Adjusted Experienced Stimulation; Lambda = proportion or responses based purely on Form; Zd = Processing Efficiency (ZSum – Zest)

When the subjects were categorized according to the Exner variable *EB*, the mean values for the *Extroversion* scale of the EPI differed significantly, being higher for Extratensive than for Introversive subjects (Mann-Whitney $U = 30.5$, $p = .003$) and Ambitent subjects (Mann-Whitney $U = 76$, $p = .004$), whereas no significant differences were found between the values of the *N* and *P* scales of the EPI obtained from the subjects categorized using the *D*, *AdjD*, and *Zd* scores of the Rorschach.

Discussion

Our data suggest that Rorschach's concept of Erlebnistypus as a holistic dimension corresponds with the Extroversion-Introversion type as defined by the Eysenck questionnaire. The findings only partially confirmed the hypotheses concerning the single determinants. As expected, we found an association between the *E* scale of the EPI and the chromatic determinants, but found no evident relationship with the *M* responses. None of the Rorschach indices were related to the *Neuroticism* scale of the EPI; the hypothesized distinction between the positive and negative dimension of affectivity was not confirmed and the unexpected positive covariation of the *E* scale with the shading determinants disagrees with current interpretations. For the *Psychoticism* dimension, the only result that reached statistical significance was the correlation with the variable *Zsum*. We found none of the other postulated covariations.

In the original description of Rorschach, *EB* closely resembles the concept of Extraversion-Introversion as defined by Eysenck. The behavioral characteristics of Introversives indicate more individualized intelligence, greater creative ability, more ideational processes, stable affective reactions, more intensive than extensive personal relationships, measured motility, awkwardness, and clumsiness. Conversely, Extratensives show stereotyped intelligence, more reproductive ability, labile affective reactions, a more extensive than intensive rapport, restless and labile motility, skill and adroitness (Rorschach, 1921). Introversives respond differently from Extratensives in a variety of behavioral circumstances, such as problem solving, stress situations and environmental responsiveness (Singer, 1960; Molish, 1967), and *EB* is considered also as the consistent style of coping with experience (Weiner, 1998). Introversive subjects prefer to delay formulating decisions or initiating behavior until they have considered all apparent alternative possibilities. Extratensives usually engage in trial-and-error activity and are often influenced by the external feed-back (Exner, 1978). Our results empirically support the descriptive, theoretical correspondences between the Rorschach and Eysenck personality types.

In our study sample, persons who had higher Extroversion levels at the Eysenck also gave a larger number of chromatic responses at the Rorschach. Rorschach originally stated that the responses involving the chromatic colors of the blots were related to affect: the extent to which the use of color merges with form represented the degree of stable affectivity, postulating that color-form determinants *(CF)* and color responses *(C)* were related to action marked by little or no cognitive adaptation (Rorschach, 1921; Exner, 1993).

Another possible interpretation of color determinants considers the degree of cognitive processing in the elaboration of chromatic responses. Chromatic perception has been defined as a "passive process," because color captures the subject's attention and requires little activity from the perceiver (Schachtel, 1943). Color perception is generally considered as a more immediate process than the complex elaborations involved in perception of form; experience is dominated by, and subject to the most immediately manifest and vivid aspects of the environment (Rickers-Ovsiankina, 1943; Rappaport, 1953; Shapiro, 1956). The *E* scale of the EPI predominantly measures social integration (Stone, 1985). Our data indicate that a self-reported high degree of sociability, corresponding to a higher score on the *E* scale of the EPI, is associated with the Rorschach indices interpreted as overt expression of affectivity, openness to the environment and an inclination to react to perceptual data.

The current interpretation of shading determinants differs according to each specific category (i.e., diffuse shading determinants *(Y)* such as helplessness and constraint; texture determinants *(T)* including needs of proximity; and vista determinants *(V)* such as negative feelings, and negative attitudes to the self). Published data on the *Y* variables is contradictory. Some authors reported an association between the diffuse shading responses and the increased level of anxiety (Eichler, 1951; Cox & Sarason, 1945; Levitt & Grosz 1960). Conversely, others found no relationship between scores on the Taylor Manifest Anxiety Scale and diffuse shading answers (Goodstein, 1954; Holtzman, Iscoe, & Calvin, 1954). Evidence concerning the diffuse shading responses is equivocal and, at best, indicates that *Y* answers at times represent some type of tension (Exner, 1993). An important point to remember when interpreting the association between the determinants of shading and the *E* scale of the EPI is that the Rorschach test is primarily a measure of perception. For perceptual analysis, these variables also reveal a higher reactivity to environmental stimuli. This finding again shows that external data have a greater effect on cognitive processes when the subjects have a higher degree of Extroversion as measured by the EPI.

In our study sample, the Psychoticism dimension of the EPI was related to a cognitive-mediational variable, but had no relationship with the affective indices. The *ZSum* Rorschach variable reflects the ability to perceive complex relationships among reality. Hence the correlation indicates that a person who shows ideation associated with suspiciousness, impulsiveness and to some extent irresponsibility, is less inclined to attribute or be aware of associative connections among the various elements in the perceptual field.

Finally, we failed to confirm the hypothesized association between the EPI scale and Human Movement responses. The Human Movement determinants have a complex meaning, encompassing reasoning, imagination, a higher degree of conceptualization, and an ability to delay the action. In our study, we found no relationship between *M* responses and a specific personality dimension.

In conclusion, our data indicate some correspondence between the holistic concept of Erlebnistypus defined by the Rorschach and the personality trait of Extroversion-Introversion as measured by the *E* scale of the EPI. Although we failed to show that the Rorschach indices are a valid method for distinguishing between the opposite polarity of affectivity, as determined by the EPI, we found a relationship between Eysenck's Extroversion and the general tendency to react to external stimuli at perceptual level. Finally, in our study sample the dimension Psychoticism seemed to have some relationship with the cognitive index, thus partially confirming our hypothesis. Despite the need for caution in interpreting results from a small study sample, our data substantially agree with an extended previous research.

References

Archer, R.P., & Krishnamurthy, R. (1999). Reply to Meyer on the convergent validity of the MMPI and Rorschach. *Journal of Personality Assessment, 73,* 319–321.

Bornstein, R.F. (2001). Clinical utility of the Rorschach Inkblot Method: Reframing the debate. *Journal of Personality Assessment,* 77(1), 39–47.

Cox, F.N., & Sarason, S.B. (1954). Test anxiety and Rorschach performance. *Journal of Abnormal and Social Psychology, 49,* 371–377.

Eichler, R.M. (1951). Experimental stress and alleged Rorschach indices of anxiety. *Journal of Abnormal and Social psychology, 46,* 344–356.

Exner, J.E. (1978). *The Rorschach: A comprehensive system, Vol. 2: Current research and advanced interpretation.* New York: Wiley.

Exner, J.E. (1993). *The Rorschach: A comprehensive system, Vol. 1: Basic foundations* (3rd ed.). New York: Wiley.

Eysenck, H.J., & Eysenck, M.W. (1985). *Personality and individual differences.* New York: Plenum.

Eysenck, H.J., & Eysenck, S.B.G. (1975). *Eysenck personality questionnaire.* San Diego: Educational and Industrial Testing Service.

Eysenck, H.J., & Eysenck, S.B.G. (1990). *Eysenck Personality Inventory. Breve manuale dell'adattamento italiano* [Eysenck Personality Inventory. Brief manual of Italian version]. Firenze: Organizzazioni Speciali.

Goodstein, L.D. (1954). Interrelationship among several measures of anxiety and hostility. *Journal of Consulting Psychology, 18,* 35–39.

Greenwald, D. (1991). Personality dimensions reflected by the Rorschach and the 16PF. *Journal of Clinical Psychology, 47,* 708–715.

Greenwald, D.F. (1999). Relationships between the Rorschach and the NEO-Five Factor Inventory. *Psychological Reports, 85,* 519–527.

Holtzman, W.H., Iscoe, I., & Calvin, A.D. (1954). Rorschach color responses and manifest anxiety in college women. *Journal of Consulting Psychology, 18,* 317–324.

Levitt, E.E., & Grosz, H.J. (1960). A comparison of quantifiable Rorschach anxiety indicators in hypnotically induced anxiety and normal states. *Journal of Consulting Psychology, 24,* 31–34.

Lindgreen, T., & Carlsson, A.M. (2003). Correction to "Relationship between the Rorschach and the MMPI-2 in a Swedish population: A replication study of the effects of first factor related test interaction styles." *Journal of Personality Assessment, 80*(1), 113.

Meyer, G.J. (1992). The Rorschach's factor structure: A contemporary investigation and historical review. *Journal of Personality Assessment, 59*(1), 117–136.

Meyer, G.J. (1997). Thinking clearly about reliability: More critical corrections regarding the Rorschach comprehensive system. *Psychological Assessment, 9,* 495–498.

Meyer, G.J., Bates, M., & Gacono, C. (1999). The Rorschach rating scale: Item adequacy, scale development, and relations with the Big Five Model of personality. *Journal of Personality Assessment, 73,* 199–244.

Molish, H.B. (1967). Critique and problems of the Rorschach. A survey. In S.J. Beck & H.B. Molish, *Rorschach's test. II: A variety of personality pictures* (2nd ed.). New York: Grune & Stratton.

Rapaport, D. (1953). *Some metapsychological consideration concerning activity and passivity.* Paper read at the Austen Riggs Center.

Rickers-Ovsiankina, M. (1943). Some theoretical consideration regarding the Rorschach method. *Rorschach Research Exchange, 7,* 41–53.

Rorschach H. (1921). *Psychodiagnostik* [Psychodiagnostics]. Bern, Switzerland: Ernst Bircher.

Schachtel, E. (1943). On color and affect. *Psychiatry, 6,* 393–409.

Shapiro, D. (1956). Color-response and perceptual passivity. *Journal of Projective Techniques, 20*(1), 52–59.

Singer, J.L. (1960). The experience type: Some behavioral correlates and theoretical implications. In M. Rickers-Ovsiankina (Ed.), *Rorschach psychology.* New York: Wiley.

Stone M. (1985). Maudsley personality inventory. In D.J. Keyser & R.C. Sweetland (Eds.), *Test critiques* (Vol. I, pp. 279–283). Kansas City: Test Corporation of America.

Tellegen A. (1985). Structures of mood and personality and their relevance to assessing anxiety, with an emphasis on self-report. In A.H. Tuma & J.D. Maser (Eds.), *Anxiety and the anxiety disorders* (pp. 681–706). Hillsdale, NJ: Erlbaum.

Tellegen, A., & Waller, N.G. (1998). Exploring personality through test construction: Development of the multidimensional personality questionnaire. In S.R. Briggs & J.M. Cheek (Eds.), *Personality measure: Development and evaluation* (Vol. 1). Greenwich: JAI.

Watson, D., & Tellegen, A. (1985). Toward a consensual structure of mood. *Psychological Bulletin, 98*, 219–235.

Weiner, I.B. (1998). *Principles of Rorschach interpretation*. Mahwah, NJ: Erlbaum.

Summary

The relationships between the Rorschach test and the self-reported personality questionnaires are an important and unresolved issue in confirming structural and clinical hypotheses. In a sample of healthy volunteers (n = 47) we conducted a study to investigate the correlation between the Italian version of the Eysenck Personality Questionnaire (Eysenck Personality Inventory, EPI) and some selected Rorschach variables defined according to the Exner Comprehensive System. The results showed that the *Extroversion* Scale of the EPI corresponds with the calculated difference between the Human Movement responses and the Weighted Sum of the Color response (*M-WSumC*, $r = -.42$, $p < .01$), the Weighted Sum of Color responses (WSumC, $r = .40$, $p < .01$) as a single variable, and the Sum of Shading responses (*SumShd*, $r = .29$, $p < .05$), but had no relationship with the Human Movement responses. None of the hypothesized Rorschach variables showed a significant correlation with the Neuroticism scale of the EPI. Furthermore, the Psychoticism scale of the EPI was negatively correlated with the Rorschach index *Zsum* (r –.33, $p < .05$). Finally, the comparison between the subgroups defined by the Erlebnistypus categories showed that Rorschach Extratensive subjects scored higher on the Extroversion scale of the EPI than Introversive (Mann-Whitney $U = 30.5$, $p < .01$) or Ambitent subjects (Mann-Whitney $U = 76$, $p < .01$). These results indicate that Rorschach's concept of Erlebnistypus as a holistic dimension and Eysenck's construct of Extroversion-Introversion are sufficiently homogeneous for psychometric assessment, but the single determinants of Rorschach responses have no correspondence with the EPI scores.

Résumé

La question des relations entre le test de Rorschach et les questionnaires d'auto-évaluation de la personnalité est importante pour la confirmation des hypothèses structurales et cliniques mais demeure sans réponse. Nous avons effectué une étude sur un échantillon de 47 sujets volontaires pour explorer la corrélation entre la version italienne du questionnaire de personnalité d'Eysenck (Eysenck Personality Inventory: EPI) et une sélection de variables du Rorschach définies conformément au système intégré d'Exner. Les résultats montrent que l'échelle d'extraversion de l'EPI corrèle avec la différence entre la somme des réponses de kinesthésie humaine et la somme pondérée des réponses couleur (ΣK – ΣC, $r = 0.42$, $p < .01$), la somme pondérée des couleurs (Σ, $r = 0.40$, $p < .01$), la somme des réponses d'estompage et de valeur achromatique (ΣC + E, $r = 0.29$, $p < .05$) mais n'a pas de relation avec les réponses kinesthésiques humaines. Aucune des variables Rorschach n'a présenté les corrélations significatives attendues avec l'échelle de névrosisme de l'EPI. De plus, l'échelle de "psychoticisme" de l'EPI est corrélée négativement avec l'indice SumZ ($r = -0.33$, $p < .05$). Finalement, la comparaison entre les sous-groupes définis par leur type de résonance intime montre que les sujets extratensifs au Rorschach ont à l'EPI des scores d'extraversion plus élevés que les introversifs (U de Mann-Whitney = 30.5, $p < .01$) ou les ambiéquaux (U de Mann-Whitney = 76, $p < .01$). Ces données indiquent, compte tenu des limitations dues à la taille de l'échantillon, que le concept holistique de type de résonance intime issu du test de Rorschach présente une correspondance psychométrique avec la dimension d'extraversion-introversion définie par le questionnaire d'Eysenck. Les autres variables du Rorschach considérées dans cette étude n'ont que partiellement confirmé les relations attendues avec les échelles de l'EPI.

Resumen

Las relaciones entre Rorschach y cuestionarios de personalidad de tipo autoinforme constituyen un tema de discusión importante y aún sin resolver a la hora de confirmar hipótesis estructurales y clínicas. Este estudio se llevó a cabo con una muestra de voluntarios no pacientes (n = 47) para investigar la correlación entre la versión italiana del cuestionario de Eysenck (Eysenck Personality Inventory, EPI) y algunas variables de Rorschach definidas según en Sistema Comprehensivo de Exner. Los datos muestran que la Escala de Extroversión del EPI correlaciona con la diferencia entre las respuestas de Movimiento Humano y la Suma Ponderada de Color (M – SumPond C; $r = .29$; $p < .01$), con la SumPond C (SumPond C; $r = .40$; $p < .01$) y con la Suma de Sombreados (SumSh; $r = .29$; $p < .05$), consideradas como variables simples. Pero no presenta correlación con las respuestas de Movimiento Humano. Ninguna variable Rorschach seleccionada presentó correlación significativa con la escala de Neuroticismo del EPI. Además, la escala de Psicoticismo del EPI correlacionó negativamente con el índice Rorschach Z Sum ($r = -.33$; $p < .05$). Finalmente, la comparación entre subgrupos divididos según su tipo vivencial mostró que los sujetos Extratensivos en Rorschach obtenían puntuaciones más elevadas en la escala de Extroversión del EPI que los Introversivos (Mann-Whitney U = 30.5; $p < .01$) y los Ambiguales (Mann-Whitney U = 76; $p < .01$). Estos resultados indican que el concepto de tipo vivencial de Rorschach como una dimensión holística y el constructo de Eysenck de Extroversión-Introversión son suficientemente homogéneos para la evaluación psicométrica, pero los determinantes aislados de Rorschach no parecen tener correspondencia con las puntuaciones del EPI.

Sommario

Le relazioni intercorrenti tra il test di Rorschach ed i questionari di autovalutazione della personalità rappresentano un problema non completamente risolto e di notevole importanza per la valutazione di ipotesi psicologiche sia in ambito teorico che clinico. Abbiamo condotto uno studio esplorativo su 47 soggetti per valutare eventuali corrispondenze tra l'Eysenck Personalità Inventory (EPI), la versione italiana dell'Eysenck Personality Questionnaire, ed alcune variabili Rorschach definite secondo il Sistema Comprensivo di Exner. I risultati mostrano una covariazione statisticamente significativa tra la scala dell'Estroversione dell'EPI (Scala *E*) e la differenza calcolata tra le risposte di Movimento Umano e la somma delle determinanti cromatiche (*M-WsumC*; $r = .42$, $p < .01$), la somma delle determinanti cromatiche singolarmente (*WsumC*; $r = .40$, $p < .01$) e la somma delle determinanti di chiaroscuro (*SumShd*; r di Pearson = .29, $p < .05$), mentre non è stata dimostrata nessuna correlazione tra la Scala *E* e le determinanti di Movimento Umano. Nessuna delle variabili selezionate nello studio risultano covariare in modo statisticamente significativo con la scala del *Nevroticismo* dell'EPI. La scala dello Psicoticismo, invece, ha mostrato una correlazione inversa con un indice Rorschach indicativo della tendenza all'organizzazione e all'integrazione dei dati percettivi (*Zsum*; $r = -.33$, $p < .05$). Infine abbiamo diviso i soggetti in sottogruppi corrispondenti alle categorie definite dall'Erlebnistypus *(EB)* e ne abbiamo confrontato i valori medi della scala *E*. Il confronto ha mostrato che i soggetti con *EB* Extratensivo hanno valori della scala *E* dell'EPI significativamente più elevati rispetto ai soggetti con *EB* Introversivo (*U* di Mann-Whitney = 30.5, $p = .003$) ed ai soggetti con *EB* Ambitensivo (*U* di Mann-Whitney = 76, $p = .004$). I dati, pur con le limitazioni legate alla numerosità del campione, suggeriscono che l' *Erlebnistypus*, concetto olistico originario del test di Rorschach, mostra una corrispondenza a livello psicometrico con la dimensione Estroversione-Introversione definita dal questionario di Eysenck. Le altre variabili Rorschach, considerate nello studio, hanno confermato solo parzialmente le relazioni ipotizzate con le scale dell'EPI.

Rorschachiana 27, 80–100

A Five-Factor Theory Perspective on the Rorschach

Paul T. Costa, Jr. and Robert R. McCrae

National Institute on Aging, NIH, Department of Health and Human Services, Baltimore, MD, USA

No psychological instrument is more controversial than the Rorschach. Thousands of practicing psychologists rely on it without reservation in making clinical decisions of the gravest importance (e.g., Archer & Newsom, 2000), whereas many researchers regard it as nearly worthless as a tool for psychological assessment (Lilienfeld, Wood, & Garb, 2000). Historically, perhaps the deepest divisions have been between psychoanalytically-oriented psychologists, who believe that projective techniques are needed to penetrate the defences which cloud conscious awareness of real personality features, and trait psychologists, who rely on self-reports as the most direct and generally most accurate way to find out what a person is like.

Although the first author was trained by Samuel Beck, one of the masters of Rorschach interpretation, and although we have used projective tests including the Holtzman Inkblot Test (HIT; Holtzman, 1961) in our research (Costa & McCrae, 1986; McCrae & Costa, 1980), there is no doubt that we are trait psychologists. In a recent summary we concluded that projective techniques in general "are highly inferential, ignore other factors that contribute to responses, are unreliable over time, and are inadequate as samples of behavior. The bottom line is that they frequently fail to show evidence of external validity; that is, they do not predict the kinds of outcomes they are supposed to" (McCrae & Costa, 2003, p. 153). Our purpose in writing this chapter is not to repeat those criticisms nor to repudiate them, but to consider the Rorschach from the perspective of the trait-based Five-Factor Theory of personality (FFT; McCrae & Costa, 1996, 1999). We hope from that perspective to explain how Rorschach responses might be understood and used, and what research designs would be most useful in testing these hypotheses.

Paul T. Costa, Jr. and Robert R. McCrae

The Rorschach and the Five-Factor Model

The Five-Factor Model (FFM) of personality is a descriptive taxonomy of personality traits into higher-order factors, commonly labeled Neuroticism, Extraversion, Openness to Experience, Agreeableness, and Conscientiousness (McCrae & John, 1992). In the past 20 years, the FFM has become the dominant model of personality trait structure, assessed by a variety of measures (De Raad & Perugini, 2002) that include both self-report and observer rating versions. A large body of research has established the universality of the structure (Rolland, 2002) and the heritability (Bouchard & Loehlin, 2001) and long-term stability (Roberts & DelVecchio, 2000) of the factors. Studies comparing ratings from different observers attest to the consensual validation of traits from all five factors (McCrae et al., in press).

The FFM is intended to be a comprehensive model; it purports to include virtually all the traits that can be measured by self-report or observer rating. A series of studies has shown that it does so with respect to most established personality questionnaires (e.g., Conn & Rieke, 1994; Costa, Busch, Zonderman, & McCrae, 1986; McCrae, Costa, & Piedmont, 1993). But the few studies that have been reported relating the FFM to various scores derived from the Rorschach show little evidence of concordance. Greenwald (1999) proposed a series of hypotheses linking variables from the Comprehensive System (CS; Exner, 1993) to the scales of the NEO Five-Factor Inventory (NEO-FFI; Costa & McCrae, 1992b). For example, she anticipated that Agreeableness would be directly related to *COP* and inversely related to the Isolation Index, *S*, and *AG*. None of her 17 hypotheses was supported. Similar null findings are reported elsewhere in this volume, and all parallel the lack of beyond-chance associations we found when examining HIT variables (Costa & McCrae, 1986).

On the one hand, these results are surprising, because Meyer, Bates, and Gacono (1999) demonstrated substantial overlap in the constructs purportedly measured by the two instruments. Their Rorschach Rating Scale (RRS) consists of a set of items, each summarizing a construct from a variety of Rorschach systems – for example, "This person feels aggressive or combative impulses in his/her interactions" represents the construct measured by *AG*. Meyer and colleagues asked clinicians and lay raters to select an individual they knew well and assess him or her on both the RRS and an adjective measure of the FFM. An RRS factor called

Narcissism, Aggression, and Dominance had a strong negative loading on the Agreeableness factor; *Passive Dependence, Vulnerability, and Inferiority* loaded on the Neuroticism factor. *Social and Emotional Engagement* vs *Constriction* was a definer of the Openness factor. Extraversion and Conscientiousness were not well represented among Rorschach constructs, and *Intellectual Defenses and Obsessive Character* was not well represented in the FFM measure. It appears, then, that there ought to be convergence between Rorschach measures and the FFM dimensions of Neuroticism, Openness, and Agreeableness, because the two instruments are assessing similar constructs in these domains.

On the other hand, the failure to find convergence is not unprecedented. It is well known that there is limited evidence of agreement between Rorschach measures and the Minnesota Multiphasic Personality Inventory (MMPI; Hathaway & McKinley, 1983), a self-report measure of personality and psychopathology (Archer, 1996). The usual interpretation of this discordance is that the two instruments operate on different levels, with the Rorschach tapping deeper aspects of the psyche. We would like to address that idea in the context of a personality theory that was developed to account for findings from research on the FFM, but which has a much broader applicability.

One reason to pursue this issue, and not simply dismiss the Rorschach as a failed psychometric tool, is evidence that some Rorschach variables do measure something. Parker, Hanson, and Hunsley (1988) conducted a meta-analysis which found that Rorschach variables had acceptable reliability and, based on five studies with a clear rationale for the hypothesis tested, an estimated validity of .41. Meyer and Handler (1997) summarized evidence that Klopfer's Rorschach Prognostic Rating Scale predicted treatment outcome. Our own research on the HIT included a two-year longitudinal retest, which showed significant stability for 18 of 22 variables, ranging as high as .73 for Form Definiteness. The HIT apparently measures some enduring psychological features, although they may be cognitive or perceptual styles rather than personality traits per se. Alternatively, they may be representations of trait-relevant characteristics that are missed by self-report measures.

Self-report measures are certainly not perfectly valid. That fact is seen most clearly when self-reports are compared to the ratings of knowledgeable informants. Correlations of .5 or .6 are not uncommon (McCrae et al., in press), but that still leaves a large portion of the variance unaccounted for. Even when multiple raters are combined, there appears to be a ceiling of about .70 for the consensual validity of self-reports. It is possible that the remaining variance might be represented in scores on projective instruments like the Rorschach.

A Five-Factor Theory of Personality

FFT is a model of the personality system that identifies important components and specifies how they are related (see Figure 1). Central to the theory is the distinction between *Basic Tendencies,* which are abstract capacities and dispositions, and *Characteristic Adaptations,* which are developed over time through the interaction of the individual with his or her environment. Perhaps the clearest example of this distinction comes from language. All healthy children are born with the capacity to learn language – a Basic Tendency – but it is their social environment that determines which language they learn. Fluency in French or Serbo-Croatian is a Characteristic Adaptation, as are habits, attitudes, interests, roles, and relationships.

FFT differs from most theories of personality in assuming that personality traits are Basic Tendencies rather than Characteristic Adaptations, and that Basic Tendencies are influenced solely by biological mecha-

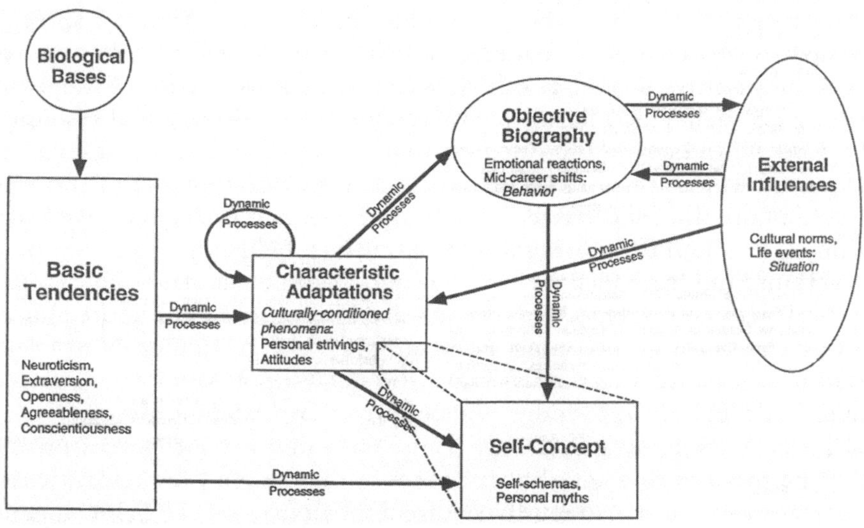

Figure 1. A model of the personality system, showing the major components and the causal pathways that link them. Adapted from McCrae & Costa, 1999.

nism, including not only genes, but also the physiological results of disease, injury, aging, and pharmacological agents. In this view, personality traits are essentially a matter of temperament. Although this postulate is both radical and likely to prove oversimplistic in the long run, it provides a powerful and parsimonious explanation for the heritability, stability, and universality of personality traits (McCrae & Costa, 2003).

Other aspects of the theory are more relevant to the interpretation of personality test scores. According to FFT, personality traits are not directly observable, either to external observers or, through introspection, to the self. This is not because people repress self-knowledge, but simply because traits appear only as they are manifested in Characteristic Adaptations. For example, in the course of life experience, an extravert learns that parties are fun, that there are many opportunities for talking with co-workers during the workday, and that roller-coasters produce a natural high. Faced with the same experiences, an introvert learns that parties are boring, that it is possible to avoid most people at work, and that roller-coasters produce no sensation other than nausea. The interests and aversions that are shaped by such experiences become Characteristic Adaptations, and are registered in the *Self-Concept* as aspects of the individual's identity. Note that the Self-Concept is itself a Characteristic Adaptation, acquired as the person interacts with the environment.

The Self-Concept is a repository of beliefs, attitudes, and narratives (McAdams, 1993) about the self, and as the arrows in Figure 1 show, it is influenced by Basic Tendencies, other Characteristic Adaptations, and the *Objective Biography*, which is the cumulative record of life experience and behavior. Like all Characteristic Adaptations, it is also shaped by *External Influences*, the category that subsumes all environmental influences. The most obvious influences on the development of the Self-Concept are the Objective Biography and External Influences. We learn who we are both from observation of our own behaviors and emotional reactions, and from feedback from others: parents, teachers, peers. Other Characteristic Adaptations are involved because they underlie almost all psychological functioning. For example, in order to conceive of oneself as an extravert one must know the meaning of the word *extravert*, and that semantic knowledge is a Characteristic Adaptation.

Basic Tendencies, specifically traits, have indirect influences on the development of the Self-Concept because they shape Characteristic Adaptations. But they also may have direct influences on the Self-Concept. John and Robins (1994) have shown that narcissism, a trait related to low Agreeableness, distorts the accuracy of self-perceptions. High levels of

Openness are associated with the structural complexity of life narratives (McAdams et al., in press). Neuroticism contributes to low self-esteem (Costa, McCrae, & Dye, 1991).

Self-Reports, Observer Ratings, and the FFT

When individuals complete a self-report inventory like the MMPI or the Revised NEO Personality Inventory (NEO-PI-R; Costa & McCrae, 1992), they draw on their Self-Concept. When asked if they "really like most people they meet," it is unlikely that respondents recall specific instances of meeting people and tally the number of times they really liked them. Instead, they draw on established beliefs about how they relate to others and the affects that are prompted by the idea of meeting people. Self-reports of personality traits are generally accurate because most people's self-concepts have encoded accurate inferences about what they are like. In this sense, FFT holds that people are basically rational (McCrae & Costa, 1999), in contrast to psychoanalytic views that people are governed largely by unconscious and irrational forces that must be inferred from indirect signs.

Ratings from knowledgeable observers are presumably accurate because the informants have observed the target on many occasions and developed what might be called an *Other Concept* that is reasonably accurate.* Why, then do self-reports and observer ratings show correlations that are not only less than 1.0, but consistently lower than the reliability of the measures? There are many possibilities (McCrae, Stone, Fagan, & Costa, 1998)–so many that it is remarkable that agreement is as strong as it is (Funder, 1989). Although there are also limitations on observer ratings, most attention has been paid to problems with self-reports, especially problems of self-deception and impression management (cf. Paulhus, 1984). There is no doubt that self-reports can be deliberately falsified (Paulhus, Bruce, & Trapnell, 1995), and it is likely that people

* By "accurate" we mean relatively, not absolutely, accurate. Most people may claim they are "above average" in altruism, a claim that cannot be literally true for all of them. But those respondents who say they are much above average are in fact likely to be more generous than those who claim only to be somewhat above average. It is for this reason that self-report (and observer rating) scores are always interpreted with reference to norms.

are sometimes deceived about their own personality traits. Much of the appeal of projective methods lies in their apparent immunity to these two sources of bias. But it must be recalled that self-reports are generally valid, in both normal (Piedmont, McCrae, Riemann, & Angleitner, 2000) and clinical (Bagby et al., 1998; Mutén, 1991) samples. Information from projective tests may perhaps usefully complement self-reports, but there is no scientific justification for replacing self-reports by projectives.

Projective Measures and Five-Factor Theory

All projective measures – sentence completions, TATs, inkblots – present the respondent with ambiguous stimuli and analyze the responses. The fundamental projective hypothesis, stated by Rapaport (1942, cited in Wiggins, 2003) is the belief that "all behavior manifestations of the human being, including the least and most significant, are revealing and expressive of his personality." That view is entirely consistent with FFT, which sees the Objective Biography as the result of the interaction of External Influences on Characteristic Adaptations, which themselves reflect Basic Tendencies. Not all behavior manifestations are equally revealing, however. We learn more about a person by taking a life history than by watching her walk down the street. From the perspective of FFT, the question is not whether the Rorschach can tell us about personality; the question is how well it does so.

Some projective techniques, like the Twenty Statements Test (Kuhn & McPartland, 1954) draw on the Self-Concept, and, perhaps not surprisingly, show convergence with self-reports and observer ratings of personality traits in the FFM (McCrae & Costa, 1988). Other projectives, including especially the Rorschach, do not require any reference to the Self-Concept. Instead, they evoke responses guided by the respondent's Characteristic Adaptations, and these responses are thought to reveal psychologically important aspects of the person.

Rorschach responses inevitably tell us something about the respondent. They are made in a particular language, and they draw upon the constructs available in a particular culture; indeed, one of the criticisms of the use of the Rorschach in anthropological field work was the claim that most scoring systems disregarded cultural context (Rabin & Limuaca, 1967). Like the recognition of objects in daily life, Rorschach responses require basic perceptual and cognitive processes – represented as *Dynamic Processes* in Figure 1 – and Rorschach diagnosis is perhaps most successful in detecting cognitive and perceptual aberrations that distinguish psychotic patients from normals or nonpsychotic patients (Jorgensen, Andersen, & Dam, 2000).

But how might normal personality traits be reflected in Rorschach responses? There are several possibilities:

1) The manifest content might suggest the conscious concerns of the individual. For example, responses depicting violent actions might suggest the fearfulness of respondents high in Neuroticism or the hostility of respondents low in Agreeableness.
2) Formal properties of the responses might reflect personality styles. *Lambda*, the ratio of pure form responses to nonpure form responses, is thought to reflect "the tendency to simplify complex stimulus fields" (Meyer, Viglione, & Exner, 2001, p. 68) and might be a sign of low Openness to Experience.
3) Responses might have no direct relation to personality traits, but might represent a defensive distortion of trait levels. Tranquil scenes might, through reaction formation, indicate underlying anxiety.
4) Responses might be determined by unknown psychological mechanisms that do not bear any obvious relation to the traits they reflect, just as the subtle items of the MMPI bear no obvious relation to the constructs they are purported to measure (Wrobel & Lachar, 1982).

The distinction between (3) and (4) parallels that between classic psychoanalytic interpretations of the Rorschach and the views of Exner (1993), who has adopted a strictly empirical position in which scores and complex indices are justified solely on the basis of their predictive utility (Wiggins, 2003). If, say, attention to small details in color blots but not in achromatic blots were demonstrated to be a reliable sign of Conscientiousness, then no rationale would be necessary to infer Conscientiousness from such a response pattern.

Case (1) is clearly consistent with FFT, which states that behaviors (including Rorschach responses) are a function of Characteristic Adaptations that have been shaped by underlying traits. Individuals high in Neuroticism have many fears, and might well report threatening scenes in responding to an inkblot. Case (2) is also consistent with FFT, which holds that personality traits can influence dynamic processes like perception. It is known, for example, the people high in Openness score higher in measures of divergent thinking (McCrae, 1987); their cognitive styles might influence their perception of Rorschach cards.

Although, according to FFT, both manifest content and formal style could be associated with traits, there is little consistent evidence to date that they are. Megargee and Schwartz (1968) reported an association between Neuroticism and a manifest Anxiety score on the HIT, but Costa and McCrae (1986) failed to replicate it. Greenwald (1999) hypothesized that *Lambda* would be inversely related to Openness, but found no significant correlation. It is well known that behavior is only weakly related to personality traits unless it is aggregated over a large number of instances (Epstein, 1979). Perhaps the behavior sampled in the course of completing a Rorschach is simply not sufficient to make reliable inferences about traits. Or perhaps the wrong variables have been chosen. For example, although she hypothesized that *Zd*, "an index of response complexity and detail" (p. 521) would be related to Conscientiousness, Greenwald found that it was instead correlated with Openness. Given open individuals' cognitive complexity (Rouff, 1975), this is a reasonable correlate. There has been too little research relating Rorschach variables to the dimensions of the FFM to conclude that there are no reliable associations with any of the factors. Note that these reliable associations might, as case (2) supposes and the Zd/Openness correlation illustrates, have a straightforward interpretation, or they might, as case (4) supposes, be apparently meaningless.

Psychological Defenses and the Expression of Personality Traits

But the most interesting, if difficult, possibility is (c). In this case we would not expect that the Rorschach variable would be significantly correlated with self-reports of a trait, because we hypothesize that unconscious defences or other mechanisms disguise the relation of the response to the trait. Someone seething with inner rage might show unmistakable signs in the Rorschach protocol while consciously believing and reporting that he or she is calm and easy-going. This situation corresponds to the common belief that when self-report and projective data differ, they may both accurately reflect personality characteristics, but operate on different levels. FFT does not rule out such a possibility;

Basic Tendencies might in principle be expressed outside of conscious awareness.

What does it mean to say that projective measures reflect *the same trait at a different level* from self-reports? From the perspective of FFM, it means that the same trait is expressed in different ways in the person. These different manifestations may or may not be mutually consistent, but both must reflect the same underlying Basic Tendency, and thus we can make a number of predictions of how Rorschach variables ought to operate. Because Agreeableness is heritable (Riemann, Angleitner, & Strelau, 1997), valid Rorschach indicators of Agreeableness should also be heritable. Because Agreeableness increases with age (McCrae et al., 1999), its Rorschach signs should also increase with age. Because women are more agreeable than men (Costa, Terracciano, & McCrae, 2001), women's Rorschach protocols should show more signs of Agreeableness than men's. Ultimately, because Agreeableness affects interpersonal behaviors and relationships, it should be perceptible to outside observers, including clinicians and laypersons who know the individual well. Rorschach Agreeableness scores might not correlate with self-reports, but they ought to correlate with observer ratings of Agreeableness.

A quick check of PsycINFO shows that research testing these hypotheses has rarely been conducted. We found a single instance of a behavior genetic study of Rorschach variables (Lohrenz & Gardner, 1967), and one comparing peer ratings of a personality trait - dependency - to Rorschach data (Zuckerman, Levitt, & Lubin, 1963). There are, of course, studies relating Rorschach variables to age and gender (e.g., Greenwald, 1990), but they have not been organized and interpreted with respect to FFM traits. In principle, one might be able to use Meyer et al.'s (1999) correspondence scheme to classify Rorschach variables in terms of personality traits, and conduct a meta-analysis of age and gender differences.

Longitudinal and behavior genetic studies of Rorschach variables would be highly informative, but they are also difficult to conduct. However, it would be quite simple to conduct observer-rating studies. Spouses or friends of patients assessed by the Rorschach could complete the observer rating Form R of the NEO-PI-R to describe the patient. These data, themselves of value to the clinician in understanding the patient and how he or she is seen by significant others (Mutén, 1991), could be used as criteria in validating Rorschach variables.

More sophisticated research designs can easily be imagined. As a "gold standard" for evaluating assessments, two (or more) clinicians who were well acquainted with the patient but blind to test results could complete the RRS (Meyer et al., 1999) and Form R of the NEO-PI-R. These criteria could be used to assess the validity of patient self-reports on the NEO-PI-R, Rorschach responses, and their combination.

Statistical Considerations

The idea of equally valid but nonoverlapping information from self-reports and projective methods is appealing. It recognizes the strengths of both of these long-contesting camps, and it offers the prospect of dramatic improvement in the accuracy of personality assessment. If the correlation of both Rorschach and self-report measures with an external criterion were 0.50, and the correlation between the two predictors were 0.00, the multiple correlation with the criterion would be .71: Twice the variance would be explained.

So little research has been done along these lines that we cannot rule out that optimistic scenario, at least for the factors that seem to be represented in Rorschach variables, Neuroticism, Openness, and Agreeableness (Meyer et al., 1999). But it seems rather implausible to us. Statistically, two variables can be uncorrelated indicators of the same trait only if they show opposite correlations with another variable, which we might hypothesize to be defensiveness. We could model this by two equations, in which true trait scores and defensiveness are equally weighted:

1) Self-Report = Trait – Defensiveness + error
2) Rorschach = Trait + Defensiveness + error

These variables would both be related to the true score (Trait), but they would also be systematically distorted, in opposite directions. Highly defensive individuals would underestimate their level of Neuroticism in self-reports, whereas their Rorschach responses would overestimate it.

Although this model is statistically satisfactory, it is cumbersome. It is easy to see why people would be defensive about Neuroticism and perhaps low Agreeableness, but it is less clear why people would unconsciously distort their levels of Openness. Closed people value Closedness, as open people value Openness; Openness is ego syntonic at all levels. The model also requires that there be a different defensiveness mechanism for each different trait, because otherwise traits would not form orthogonal factors.* A given individual might be highly defensive with respect to Openness, moderately defensive with respect to Agreeableness, and not defensive at all with regard to Neuroticism. The number of variables needed to characterize a person will at the broadest level will have doubled, from five to ten.

These models are possible, but we do not think they are plausible. We suspect Rorschach variables in general do not agree with self-reports of personality traits because the Rorschach does not assess traits well. Zuckerman et al. (1963) found that self-reports of dependency were significantly correlated with peer ratings of dependency, but that Rorschach measures were not.

This does not mean that Rorschach variables are useless. They hold promise as measures of cognitive and perceptual aberrations that can differentiate psychotic from nonpsychotic patients (Jorgensen et al., 2000). They may be useful in describing the clinical state of the patient at the moment of the test administration. But until much more supportive evidence has been accumulated, it is probably unwise to make inferences about chronic anxiety, hostility, rigidity, or any other personality trait on the basis of Rorschach scores.

The Rorschach in Psychodynamic Assessment: A Case Study

Academic psychologists familiar only with the research literature are often puzzled by clinicians' faith in the Rorschach. Surely there must be something beyond sheer graduate school indoctrination that encourages the use of the test! We suspect that the perceived utility of the instrument comes from the fact that it is used in the context of a complete psychodynamic assessment that may include life history, clinical symptoms, other test data, and the patient's observable behavior in interaction with the clinician. An excellent example of that approach is given in Behrends and Blatt's (2003) assessment of Madeline G., the case study examined from multiple perspectives in Wiggins' (2003) volume. Behrends and Blatt administered the Wechsler Adult Intelligence Test, the

* Raw NEO-PI-R domain scores are intercorrelated, but orthogonal factor scores can be calculated, and it is these that we believe best operationalize the FFM (Costa & McCrae, 1995).

Thematic Apperception Test, and the Object Relations Inventory as well as the Rorschach and carefully observed her behavior and emotional reactions throughout the assessment procedure. From all this information, they concluded that she was "action-oriented and highly emotional, with a flair for the dramatic. She is a free spirit and a bohemian, who prides herself on her unconventionality ... Although her thinking is vulnerable to the intrusion of painfully disruptive associations, her openness to such experiences tends to enrich and enliven, rather than to disorganize, her overall functioning" (pp. 4–5).

With regard to Rorschach responses, "the predominant feature is the extensive affective and ideational elaborations" (p. 22) that might sometimes be considered confabulations. In isolation, these responses might be considered pathological, but in the context of other Rorschach indicators (e.g., *F*+% = 64%, suggesting good cognitive control) and other observations, they are viewed by Behrends and Blatt as indicators of a struggle between emotional vulnerability and creative integration.

A more prosaic interpretation would suggest a very active imagination. We know from self-report and partner ratings on the NEO-PI-R that Madeline is very high in Openness to Experience, especially Fantasy (T = 76; Costa & Piedmont, 2003). She is also very high in Openness to Feelings, which could account for her strong emotional reactions to many of the blots. Individual Rorschach variables are not necessarily good indicators of Openness – for example, Madeline's *Lambda* score is 1.17, suggesting a rather closed "tendency to simplify complex stimulus fields" (Meyer et al., 2001, p. 68)–but anyone who read the protocol and interacted with Madeline for a day would recognize that she is curious, sensitive, and open to a wide range of experiences.*

Although there appears to be concordance between the Rorschach, self-reports, and observer ratings with regard to Openness, that is not the case with regard to Neuroticism. Behrends and Blatt remarked that Madeline has strong defences against dysphoric affect, but "when these defences fail, Madeline can experience extreme feelings of depression, desolation, and hopelessness" (p. 25). She reports depressing or disturbing images in the Rorschach, but then jokes about them, or recalls happier content from earlier cards. In contrast, Costa and Piedmont (2003)

* Behrends and Blatt pointed out the presence of transparency responses that may indicate suicidal ideation. An alternative interpretation is to note that people high in Openness have thin boundaries (Hartmann, 1991; McCrae, 1994), which might be expressed in transparent imagery.

reported that Madeline sees herself as very low in Anxiety, Depression, Self-Consciousness, Vulnerability, and overall Neuroticism. Is she really so well-adjusted, or is she being defensive in her self-report responses? If we consult her partner, it appears that the Rorschach-based conclusion is right: He says she is average in Anxiety and Depression and high in Self-Consciousness and Vulnerability. (Both Madeline and her partner agree that she is very high in Angry Hostility and Impulsiveness, traits not singled-out in the Rorschach interpretation.) Most impressive is the fact that Behrends and Blatt essentially predicted the subsequent year-long depression that follows the break-up of Madeline G.'s common law marriage (Trobst & Wiggins, 2003).

This case study illustrates some of the clinical appeal of the Rorschach. In the hands of skilled clinicians who interpret it in conjunction with other observations and test results, the Rorschach can give a reasonably accurate picture of some personality traits – in some cases, perhaps, more accurate than self-reports. But does the Rorschach have incremental validity? Would Behrends and Blatt have drawn less accurate conclusions if the Rorschach had been omitted from their assessment battery? Lilienfeld et al. (2000) claim there is little evidence of incremental validity, although they admit that it "has not been studied for the vast majority of Rorschach scores" (p. 38).

Madeline G.'s Rorschach is particularly revealing because she is articulate, imaginative, and clearly engaged in the task, and her responses thus provide a relatively rich sample of behavior. A thoughtful individual who read her Rorschach protocol might make many of the same inferences that Behrends and Blatt did, without any training in the scoring and interpretation of the Rorschach, or any background in psychodynamic theory.

Clinicians and the Future of Rorschach Research

Considering the widespread use of the Rorschach and the number of published studies that have used it, it is surprising how little we know about it as a measure of personality traits. Mainstream personality researchers abandoned the Rorschach years ago – it last appeared in *JPSP* in 1987 – before modern findings on the Five-Factor Model and its stability, heritability, and consensual validity had been established. Even if they were interested, personality researchers would probably find it difficult to get funding for a study of Rorschach responses, because the instrument has lost scientific credibility in many quarters. And whatever its merits, the Rorschach will not regain credibility until a new body of research findings convinces the critics. Caught in this bind, Rorschach research is virtually lost to academic psychology.

The only practical solution is to turn clinicians into researchers. Everyone who now administers the Rorschach for clinical purposes should also collect self-report and informant ratings of personality using established measures of the FFM (De Raad & Perugini, 2002), as well as background and outcome data. Pooled across many clinicians, such a database would allow definitive conclusions about the validity and incremental validity of specific Rorschach scores. Clinicians should also summarize their overall psychodynamic assessment in terms of ratings on the five factors, to facilitate research on the contribution of the Rorschach to global assessment. Clinicians could publish their own results, or provide data to statisticians for a multi-center trial that might be sponsored by the International Rorschach Society. Clinical practice could only benefit from the inclusion of multiple measures of the FFM (Costa & McCrae, 1992a), and the end result could be either a vindication of the Rorschach or a compelling reason to abandon it as a measure of personality traits.

But there is much more to personality than traits, and the Rorschach may hold most promise as a measure of dynamic processes. As Figure 1 shows, Basic Tendencies, Characteristic Adaptations, and External Influences all interact through Dynamic Processes. Previous treatments of Five-Factor Theory (McCrae & Costa, 1996) have listed examples of these processes (such as perception, repression, and role-playing), but this aspect of the theory is not well developed. In particular, there are no techniques for assessing the operation of dynamic processes. Rorschach responses, and in particular the interaction of respondent and interpreter in the inquiry phase (Ritzler & Nalesnik, 1990) may provide telling examples of how individuals manifest their traits in characteristic adaptations and maladaptations, and how they express these adaptations in behavior across the life course. As Blatt (1990) expressed it, there are "exciting new possibilities for the use of the Rorschach ... if we have the imagination and creativity to develop methods for evaluating cognitive processes and the structures of mental representations from an individual's responses to relatively ambiguous stimuli" (p. 401).

Note that the study of dynamic processes cannot be carried out in isolation, any more than Figure 1 could represent the person if it were reduced to the connecting arrows. To understand how people operate, the clinician must also understand their Basic Tendencies, their Self-Concept, their Objective Biography. Self- and informant reports on measure of the Five-Factor Model provide valid information on some of the most important Basic Tendencies, and life history interviews can indicate how these traits have played out in real life. Responses to the Rorschach might be informative about the intervening mechanisms. Blatt (1990) observed that projective data were most useful "if one had a comprehensive theory of personality that provided a framework for interpreting the remarkable diversity of observation that became available through these procedures" (p. 396). Perhaps Five-Factor Theory can provide that framework.

References

Archer, R.P. (1996). MMPI-Rorschach interrelationships: Proposed criteria for evaluating explanatory models. *Journal of Personality Assessment, 67*, 504–515.

Archer, R.P., & Newsom, C.R. (2000). Psychological test usage with adolescent clients: Survey update. *Assessment, 73*, 227–235.

Bagby, R.M., Rector, N.A., Bindseil, K., Dickens, S.E., Levitan, R.D., & Kennedy, S.H. (1998). Self-report ratings and informant ratings of personalities of depressed outpatients. *American Journal of Psychiatry, 155*, 437–438.

Behrends, R.S., & Blatt, S.J. (2003). Psychodynamic assessment. In J.S. Wiggins, *Paradigms of personality assessment*. New York: Guilford.

Blatt, S.J. (1990). The Rorschach: A test of perception or an evaluation of representation. *Journal of Personality Assessment, 55*, 394–416.

Bouchard, T.J., & Loehlin, J.C. (2001). Genes, evolution, and personality. *Behavior Genetics, 31*, 243–273.

Conn, S.R., & Rieke, M.L. (Eds.). (1994). *16PF Fifth Edition technical manual*. Champaign, IL: Institute for Personality and Ability Testing.

Costa, P.T., Jr., Busch, C.M., Zonderman, A.B., & McCrae, R.R. (1986). Correlations of MMPI factor scales with measures of the Five-Factor Model of personality. *Journal of Personality Assessment, 50*, 640–650.

Costa, P.T., Jr., & McCrae, R.R. (1986). Age, personality, and the Holtzman Inkblot Technique. *International Journal of Aging and Human Development, 23*,115–112.

Costa, P.T., Jr., & McCrae, R.R. (1992a). Normal personality assessment in clinical practice: The NEO Personality Inventory. *Psychological Assessment, 4*, 5–13, 20–22.

Costa, P.T., Jr., & McCrae, R.R. (1992b). *Revised NEO Personality Inventory (NEO-PI-R) and NEO Five-Factor Inventory (NEO-FFI) professional manual*. Odessa, FL: Psychological Assessment Resources.

Costa, P.T., Jr., & McCrae, R.R. (1995). Solid ground in the wetlands of personality: A reply to Block. *Psychological Bulletin, 117*, 216–220.

Costa, P.T., Jr., McCrae, R.R., & Dye, D.A. (1991). Facet scales for agreeableness and conscientiousness: A revision of the NEO Personality Inventory. *Personality and Individual Differences, 12*, 887–898.

Costa, P.T., Jr., & Piedmont, R.L. (2003). Revised NEO Personality Inventory profiles of Madeline G. In J.S. Wiggins, *Paradigms of personality assessment*. New York: Guilford.

Costa, P.T., Jr., Terracciano, A., & McCrae, R.R. (2001). Gender differences in personality traits across cultures: Robust and surprising findings. *Journal of Personality and Social Psychology, 81*, 322–331.

De Raad, B., & Perugini, M. (Eds.). (2002). *Big Five assessment*. Göttingen, Germany: Hogrefe & Huber.

Epstein, S. (1979). The stability of behavior: I. On predicting most of the people much of the time. *Journal of Personality and Social Psychology, 37*, 1097–1126.

Exner, J.E. (1993). *The Rorschach: A comprehensive system* (vol. 1). New York: Wiley.

Funder, D.C. (1989). Accuracy in personality judgment and the dancing bear. In D.M. Buss & N. Cantor (Eds.), *Personality psychology: Recent trends and emerging directions* (pp. 210–223). New York: Springer.

Greenwald, D.R. (1990). An external construct validity study of Rorschach personality variables. *Journal of Personality Assessment, 55*, 768–780.

Greenwald, D.F. (1999). Relationships between the Rorschach and the NEO Five-Factor Inventory. *Psychological Reports, 85*, 519–527.

Hartmann, E. (1991). *Boundaries in the mind: A new psychology of personality differences*. New York: Basic Books.

Hathaway, S.R., & McKinley, J.C. (1983). *The Minnesota Multiphasic Personality Inventory manual*. New York: Psychological Corporation.

Holtzman, W.H. (1961). *Guide to administration and scoring: Holtzman Inkblot Technique*. New York: Psychological Corporation.

John, O.P., & Robins, R.W. (1994). Accuracy and bias in self-perception: Individual differences in self-enhancement and the role of narcissism. *Journal of Personality and Social Psychology, 66*, 206–219.

Jorgensen, K., Andersen, T.J., & Dam, H. (2000). The diagnostic efficiency of the Rorschach Depression Index and the Schizophrenia Index: A review. *Assessment, 7*, 259–280.

Kuhn, M.H., & McPartland, T.S. (1954). An empirical investigation of self-attitudes. *American Sociological Review, 19*, 68–76.

Lilienfeld, S.O., Wood, J.M., & Garb, H.N. (2000). The scientific status of projective techniques. *Psychological Science in the Public Interest, 1*, 27–66.

Lohrenz, L.J., & Gardner, R.W. (1967). The Mayman Form-Level scoring method: Scorer reliability and correlates of form level. *Journal of Projective Techniques and Personality Assessment, 31*, 39–43.

McAdams, D.P. (1993). *The stories we live by: Personal myths and the making of the self*. New York: William Morrow.

McAdams, D.P., Anyidoho, N.A., Brown, C., Huang, Y.T., Kaplan, B., & Machado,

M.A. (in press). Traits and stories: Links between dispositional and narrative features of personality. *Journal of Personality*.

McCrae, R.R. (1987). Creativity, divergent thinking, and openness to experience. *Journal of Personality and Social Psychology, 52*, 1258–1265.

McCrae, R.R. (1994). Openness to experience: Expanding the boundaries of Factor V. *European Journal of Personality, 8*, 251–272.

McCrae, R.R., & Costa, P.T., Jr. (1980). Openness to experience and ego level in Loevinger's sentence completion test: Dispositional contributions to developmental models of personality. *Journal of Personality and Social Psychology, 39*, 1179–1190.

McCrae, R.R., & Costa, P.T., Jr. (1996). Toward a new generation of personality theories: Theoretical contexts for the five-factor model. In J.S. Wiggins (Ed.), *The five-factor model of personality: Theoretical perspectives* (pp. 51–87). New York: Guilford.

McCrae, R.R., & Costa, P.T., Jr. (1999). A Five-Factor Theory of personality. In L.A. Pervin & O.P. John (Eds.), *Handbook of personality: Theory and research* (2nd ed., pp. 139–153). New York: Guilford.

McCrae, R.R., & Costa, P.T., Jr. (2003). *Personality in adulthood: A five-factor theory perspective* (2nd. ed.). New York: Guilford.

McCrae, R.R., & Costa, P.T., Jr. (1988). Age, personality, and the spontaneous self-concept. *Journal of Gerontology: Social Sciences, 43*, S177–S185.

McCrae, R.R., Costa, P.T., Jr., Lima, M.P., Simões, A., Ostendorf, F., Angleitner, A., Maruš ić, I., Bratko, D., Caprara, G.V., Barbaranelli, C., Chae, J.-H., & Piedmont, R.L. (1999). Age differences in personality across the adult life span: Parallels in five cultures. *Developmental Psychology, 35*, 466–477.

McCrae, R.R., Costa, P.T., Jr., Martin, T.A., Oryol, V.E., Rukavishnikov, A.A., Senin, I.G., Hřebíčková, M., & Urbánek, T. (in press). Consensual validation of personality traits across cultures. *Journal of Research in Personality*.

McCrae, R.R., Costa, P.T., Jr., & Piedmont, R.L. (1993). Folk concepts, natural language, and psychological constructs: The California Psychological Inventory and the five-factor model. *Journal of Personality, 61*, 1–26.

McCrae, R.R., & John, O.P. (1992). An introduction to the Five-Factor Model and its applications. *Journal of Personality, 60*, 175–215.

McCrae, R.R., Stone, S.V., Fagan, P.J., & Costa, P.T., Jr. (1998). Identifying causes of disagreement between self-reports and spouse ratings of personality. *Journal of Personality, 66*, 285–313.

Megargee, E.I., & Swartz, J.D. (1968). Extraversion, neuroticism, and scores on the Holtzman Inkblot Technique. *Journal of Projective Techniques and Personality Assessment, 32*, 262–265.

Meyer, G.J., Bates, M., & Gacono, C. (1999). The Rorschach rating scale: Item adequacy, scale development, and relations with the Big Five model of personality. *Journal of Personality Assessment, 73*, 199–244.

Meyer, G.J., & Handler, L. (1997). The ability of the Rorschach to predict subsequent outcome: Meta-analysis of the Rorschach prognostic rating scale. *Journal of Personality Assessment, 69*, 1–38.

Meyer, G.J., Viglione, D.J., & Exner, J.E. (2001). Superiority of *Form%* over *Lambda* for research on the Rorschach Comprehensive System. *Journal of Personality Assessment, 76*, 68–75.

Mutén, E. (1991). Self-reports, spouse ratings, and psychophysiological assessment in a behavioral medicine program: An application of the five-factor model. *Journal of Personality Assessment, 57*, 449–464.

Parker, K.C.H., Hanson, R.K., & Hunsley, J. (1988). MMPI, Rorschach, and WAIS: A meta-analytic comparison of reliability, stability, and validity. *Psychological Bulletin, 103*, 367–373.

Paulhus, D.L. (1984). Two-component models of socially desirable responding. *Journal of Personality and Social Psychology, 46*, 598–609.

Paulhus, D.L., Bruce, M.N., & Trapnell, P.D. (1995). Effects of self-presentation strategies on personality profiles and their structure. *Personality and Social Psychology Bulletin, 21*, 100–108.

Piedmont, R.L., McCrae, R.R., Riemann, R., & Angleitner, A. (2000). On the invalidity of validity scales in volunteer samples: Evidence from self-reports and observer ratings in volunteer samples. *Journal of Personality and Social Psychology, 78*, 582–593.

Rabin, A.I., & Limuaca, J. (1967). A comparison of the connotative meaning of Rorschach's inkblots for American and Filipino college students. *Journal of Social Psychology, 72*, 197–203.

Rapaport, D. (1942). Principles underlying projective techniques. *Character and Personality: A Quarterly for Psychodiagnostic and Allied Studies, 10*, 213–219.

Riemann, R., Angleitner, A., & Strelau, J. (1997). Genetic and environmental influences on personality: A study of twins reared together using the self- and peer-report NEO-FFI scales. *Journal of Personality, 65*, 449–475.

Ritzler, B., & Nalesnik, D. (1990). The effect of inquiry on the Exner comprehensive system. *Journal of Personality Assessment, 55*, 647–656.

Roberts, B.W., & DelVecchio, W.F. (2000). The rank-order consistency of personality traits from childhood to old age: A quantitative review of longitudinal studies. *Psychological Bulletin, 126*, 3–25.

Rolland, J.-P. (2002). Cross-cultural generalizability of the Five-Factor Model of personality. In R.R. McCrae & J. Allik. (Eds.), *The five-factor model of personality across cultures* (pp. 7–28). New York: Kluwer Academic/Plenum.

Rouff, L.L. (1975). Openness, creativity and complexity. *Psychological Reports, 37*, 1009–1010.

Trobst, K., & Wiggins, J.S. (2003). Constructive alternativism in personality assessment: Madeline G. from multiple perspectives. In J.S. Wiggins (Ed.), *Paradigms of personality assessment*. New York: Guilford.

Wiggins, J.S. (2003). *Paradigms of personality assessment*. New York: Guilford.

Wrobel, T.A., & Lachar, D. (1982). Validity of the Wiener subtle and obvious scales for the MMPI: Another example of the importance of inventory-item content. *Journal of Consulting and Clinical Psychology, 50*, 469–470.

Zuckerman, M., Levitt, E.E., & Lubin, B. (1963). Concurrent and construct validity of direct and indirect measures of dependency. *Journal of Consulting Psychology, 25*, 316–323.

Summary

Many of the constructs the Rorschach is used to assess are related to personality traits included in the Five-Factor Model, but studies to date have not shown convergence between Rorschach and self-report measures of these traits. This poses a problem for the Rorschach, because recent research on the universality, stability, heritability, and consensual validity of traits demonstrate that self-report measures cannot be dismissed. In an effort to understand these issues, we examine the Rorschach from the perspective of Five-Factor Theory (FFT), a systems model of the person. FFT is compatible with the projective hypothesis, but would generally lead to the expectation that Rorschach signs and self-reports should be correlated. Where they are not, the validity of Rorschach measures of personality traits would need to be confirmed by demonstrations of their heritability, stability, and convergence with observer ratings. The Rorschach may be more useful when interpreted in the context of a global psychodynamic assessment. Clinicians who use the Rorschach should gather the data necessary to test its validity as a measure of personality traits and related constructs, and clinicians and researchers should consider the possible use of Rorschach responses in assessing dynamic processes.

Résumé

Beaucoup de dimensions pour l'évaluation desquelles on utilise le Rorschach sont liées aux traits de personnalité retenus dans le modèle des cinq facteurs, mais les études n'ont montré à ce jour aucune convergence entre le Rorschach et la mesure de ces traits par l'auto-évaluation. Cela pose un problème pour le Rorschach, parce que les travaux récents sur l'universalité, la stabilité, l'héritabilité et la validité consensuelle de ces traits démontrent qu'on ne peut pas disqualifier les mesures fondées sur l'auto-évaluation. Dans un effort pour éclairer cette question, nous examinons le Rorschach du point de vue de la théorie des cinq facteurs. La théorie des cinq facteurs est compatible avec l'hypothèse projective, mais devrait conduire dans l'ensemble à attendre que les signes au Rorschach et l'auto-évaluation soient corrélés. Quand ils ne le sont pas, la validité des évaluations de traits de personnalité par le Rorschach devrait être confirmée par la démonstration de leur héritabilité, de leur stabilité et de leur convergence avec les évaluations faites par des observateurs. Le Rorschach est peut-être plus utile quand on l'interprète dans le contexte d'une évaluation psychodynamique globale. Les cliniciens qui utilisent le Rorschach devraient recueillir les données nécessaires pour tester sa validité en tant que mesure de traits de personnalité et de réalités du même ordre, et les cliniciens et les chercheurs devraient prendre en considération la possibilité d'utiliser les réponses au Rorschach dans l'évaluation des processus dynamiques.

Resumen

Muchos de los constructos teóricos que se usan en la evaluación con Rorschach se relacionan con rasgos de personalidad incluidos en el modelo de los Cinco Factores, pero hasta el momento no se ha podido demostrar una convergencia significativa entre Rorschach y medidas de autoinformes para valorar esos rasgos. Esto plantea un problema para el Rorschach, porque las más recientes investigaciones sobre la universalidad, estabilidad, herencia y validez consensual de dichos rasgos señalan que las medidas procedentes de los autoinformes no pueden ser ignoradas. Intentando comprender mejor estos aspectos, examinamos el Rorschach desde la perspectiva de la teoría de los Cinco Factores (Five-Factor Theory: FFT), un modelo sistémico de la persona. La FFT es compatible con la hipótesis proyectiva pero implica la expectativa de que los signos Rorschach y los datos de los autoinformes deberían correlacionar. Cuando no ocurre así, la validez de las medidas Rorschach sobre rasgos de personalidad debería ser confirmada mediante pruebas de heredabilidad, estabilidad y convergencia de las puntuaciones de observadores. El Rorschach podría ser más útil si se interpretara en el contexto de una evaluación psicodinámica global. Los clínicos que usan el Rorschach tendrían que recopilar los datos necesarios para probar su validez como medida de rasgos de personalidad y constructos relacionados. Tanto clínicos como investigadores deberían considerar la posible utilidad de las respuestas al Rorschach para evaluar procesos dinámicos.

Rorschachiana 27, 101–116

Discrepancies Between the Rorschach Inkblot Method and Self-Report Measures of Personality: Methodological and Theoretical Reflections

Jean-Michel Petot[1] and Dragana Djurić Jočić[2]

[1]*Laboratoire de Psychologie clinique des Faits culturels (EA 3460 – CLIPSY), Université de Paris X-Nanterre, France,* [2]*Institute of Psychiatry, Clinical Center of Serbia, Belgrade, Serbia & Montenegro*

Research results have repeatedly shown that the convergent validity between the Rorschach test and personality self-report questionnaires is low, especially when the sample is heterogeneous and certain variables of instruments are not controlled. The relationship between the Rorschach test and MMPI-2 is the best studied, and the relationship between the Rorschach test and the NEO PI-R questionnaire has been more recently dealt with. This article presents a brief review of the multiple theoretical and methodological factors that may have influence on the interrelation of the instruments, as good knowledge of these factors enhances our understanding of discrepant results obtained by instruments grounded on different epistemological and methodological basis. While for researchers low convergent validity may raise concern or doubt about the validity of individual instruments, it must be stressed that, in clinical practice, this fact justifies a multimethod approach to personality assessment, because the use of different instruments produces a larger number of different information of particular case, and such information are integrated by the process of clinical judgment.

The Lack of Convergence Between the Rorschach Inkblot Method and Self-Report Measures

It is expected that psychological tests measuring the same constructs correlate mutually and this characteristic is termed convergent validity. For example, indicators of depression (or anxiety and stress indicators, etc.) measured by questionnaire are expected to correlate with measures of depression determined by projective techniques. Divergent validity is present if the correlation between the same trait and constructs using different instruments is higher than the correlation between two different traits and construct using the same method. It would be the case when, for example, the correlation between the indicators of depression determined by Rorschach test and questionnaire would be lower than between indicators of depression and other constructs measured by the Rorschach Inkblot Method.

Another assumption is that instruments using similar methodology of assessment correlate more than instruments testing the same constructs, by using different methodology. Therefore, it is expected that the indicators of depression in different questionnaires correlate more than the indicators of depression determined by questionnaire and projective technique.

The relation of the Rorschach with intelligence tests (WAIS) and questionnaires, particularly the MMPI-2, was analyzed in an investigatory manner. It may be noted that studies dealing with other instruments were sporadic and insufficiently systematic, while the Rorschach – MMPI-2 relationship was examined in 37 studies during the last 50 years (Archer & Krishnamurthy, 1993). Unfortunately, the comparison of the results was not always possible on account of methodological incongruence, and it became easily feasible only during the last decade, when the Comprehensive System was used for scoring the Rorschach test (the reviewed research included six studies that used the Comprehensive system). General conclusion of these studies is that the correlations between the two instruments are low or absent.

Research literature on the Big Five Model or Five-Factor Theory (FFT) of Personality is vast, while the accumulation of data referring to the relation between the Rorschach test and NEO PI-R personality questionnaire has been initiated only recently (Greenwald, 1999; Petot, 2004). Therefore, the relation between the Rorschach and the MMPI-2, as it is supposed to raise the same kind of problems, will be used for definition of general research problems.

Possible Reasons for the Discrepancies Between the Rorschach and MMPI: Methodological Issues

The Rorschach test and self-report questionnaires such as the NEO PI-R and MMPI-2 are generally supposed to measure the same psychological constructs: characteristics of personality, defensive styles, current emotional state, and/or psychopathological symptoms. While the MMPI-2 questionnaire is primarily intended for detection of psychopathological states, the NEO PI-R is more focused on normal personality traits, and, therefore, more correlative conjunctions with the Rorschach constructs may be expected in these domains.

But in the last few years, the results of studies have raised serious problems. From a methodological point of view, the main topic to be discussed concerns the explanation of the low convergent validity, and the options to clarify such results by statistical procedures. In this context, instead of validity, the issue was power or limitation of particular methods, as well as understanding of how one method was sensitive for differentiation of the external reality.

The first issue to be questioned is the thesis that all instruments of evaluation should comprise the whole complexity of personality. A review of the available instruments would show that none of them meets this criterion, and, therefore, that different instruments are likely to cover different parts of the studied territory that is called "personality." For example, the difference between the conscious and unconscious or self-presentation and real traits of personality may account for heterogeneous results.

The obtained low correlations of instruments may also be the result of differences between their methodological options, validity and reliability. A series of independent studies has revealed satisfactory validity and reliability of both instruments, therefore it may be considered that they meet necessary psychometric criteria. Ganellen (1996) compared the diagnostic efficiency of the Rorschach and MMPI-2 for the detection of depression and psychotic disorder. He found that both instruments had satisfactory sensitivity for detection of depression, but higher percentage of false positive results and lower specificity was found with the

MMPI compared to the Rorschach. Concerning the diagnosis of psychotic disorders, MMPI questionnaire (scales 6, i.e., paranoia, and 8, i.e., schizophrenia) had higher proportion of false positive results than the Rorschach test (SCZI scale, an early version of what is now termed PTI).

Parker, Hanson, and Hunsley (1988) and Ganellen (1996) found that both instruments had satisfactory criterion-related validity, and, accordingly, they discriminate well different psychiatric categories of subjects. It is believed that criterion validity (relation between the psychological constructs and the instruments of evaluation intended for their measurement) is more significant for clinical evaluation than concurrent validity (relation between two instruments designed to measure the same psychological construct). The difference between these two kinds of validity may arise because of different degree of correlation of instrument and criterion variable or because two instruments are sensitive in a different way to specific aspects of the criterion variable. It especially occurs in cases when criterion variable and/or test variables are multidimensional. In that way, test variables may have significant correlation with criterion variable, while their interrelation may be very low. This thesis is partially overlapped with the observation that the same terms may be used within both instruments, whereas their operationalization reveals that it is a matter of different psychological constructs, as it will be explained below concerning the relationships between personality psychology extraversion and Rorschach extratensiveness.

Ganellen (1996) suggested that correlation analyses would yield better results if the relation between psychological constructs were tested, and not only the relation between individual indicators or discrete scales. Psychological constructs may be operationalized as a set of scores combined on the basis of theory or clinical judgment referring to individual domain; they also may be defined on the basis of study that verified the relation between specific configurations of test scores and constructs. The first case could be exemplified by the evaluation of anxiety, including the following indicators: MMPI-2 Scale 7 (psychasthenia), Welsh's anxiety scale and Rorschach indicators *Y* (Diffusion shading), *m* (inanimate movement) and *es* (experienced stimulation, i.e., the sum of shading, achromatic color, and nonhuman movement responses). Another example, individual MMPI scales 2 (depression), 4 (psychopathic deviation), and 7 (psychasthenia) do not express the dependence of subjects, but when combined in 2–4–7 profile, they may indicate strong, unsatisfied needs for attention and support, and dependence conflict. These data may be associated with Rorschach's indicators of the same meaning: Texture and Food responses or Oral Dependence Scale. Such experimental designs are more complex, but they are similar to the process of clinical data integration (Graham, 1993).

One should mention, as one of the issues, the heterogeneity of Rorschach variables, which may be expressed as raw scores, percentages or proportions. From the research point of view, especially important variables are: total number of responses (R), number of responses based on pure form (Lambda), and personal style (EB = experience balance or Erlebnistypus). It needs to be emphasized that these basic variables should be taken into account while comparing the results. As an example of the importance of the number of responses for the correlations, we refer again to the study by Meyer (1999), in which the sample was divided into short (R from 14 to 17 responses) and long protocols (R over 28). The correlations of Rorschach and MMPI-2 variables were negative in short protocols and positive in long protocols, while they were not significant in the whole sample. It was afterward demonstrated that R by itself does not moderate convergent validity, and Meyer later interpreted this finding not only as the impact of the number of responses, but as an instance of the more extensive concept of "style of answering." Notwithstanding, such finding advises us well how the ignorance of variable nature may result in misinterpretation of results.

Study designs should be devised in such a manner they can test specific hypotheses based on theory. A model accounting for the relation of questionnaire and projective instrument should be simple and testable. It means it is expected to be cost-effective considering the number of postulated constructs and the number of presented theoretical hypothesis. Moreover, a theoretical model may be supported or denied by means of empirical analysis of specific and testable hypotheses, which it explicates.

In the absence of such hypotheses, the studies of convergent validity meet the problem of variable selected number, that are included in research frames. The CS has more than hundred variables, and the questionnaires have tens of scales and subscales. Systematic correlation of all variables leads to a large number of analyzed relations, on a sample that is not commonly big enough for so large-scale designs. Too small samples used by various researchers (e.g., $N = 30$) may have significant fluctuations regarding the obtained correlation results (Meyer, 1999). Moreover, correlations computed on too small samples may be distorted because of the presence of "outliers." It is possible to recognize, by statistical procedures (number of aberrant observations identified by Mahalonobis' methods or Cook's D) the subjects who spoil the correlation of two instruments and their expelling from the sample would increase the convergent validity. However, the better solution would probably be to include only selected variables in the research design.

There are many other issues to be discussed concerning the selection of the variables to be included in the crossing.

First, whether to mutually cross each individual variable from the first test with every individual variable of the second one, or to cross one variable of the first test with a group of variables of the second one, or to cross only groups of variables.

Second, how to make selection of theoretically relevant variables that are the same not only by their names but also by their content. Some variables are multidimensional by their nature, and *per se* they are not appropriate for crossing. For example, the index of egocentrism, by its semantics, is also a measure of self-involvement and self-esteem. Therefore, when it is used in crossing, we can never be sure of the meaning of the observed relation.

Third, there is possibility to cross the groups of markers of some psychological function, e.g., emotionality, cognition or self-perception, or each of these markers individually. Their convergent validity may be individually lower, but it may be higher if united in the group.

In the forth place, individual markers may be in correlation with specific entities, although they are not in direct relation with this entity according to the interpretative principles of the Rorschach System utilized. For example, depressed persons are mostly inclined to passive fantasy (Mp > Ma), although this indicator is not included in the Comprehensive System index of depression, but it is disputable whether it should be included in the crossing of variables.

Finally, another problem is whether variables should be expressed as continuous (in values presented in methods) or categorical. A large number of Rorschach variables are interpretatively significant, if at all present in a protocol or if they exceed specified limits: Vista, Reflection, FD (dimensional form), MOR (morbid content), Color shading blends, Intell (intellectualization index), DEPI (depressive index), PTI (problems of thinking index), etc. It is more proper to address them as categorical variables, as exercised in individual evaluation. As a consequence of that, the examiner should be prudent when s/he opts for statistical tests that will be used for testing of interrelations of instruments. Exner's normative sample shows that even 48 out of 111 variables have no Gaussian distribution, and therefore nonparametric statistical procedures are more appropriate for their analysis (Exner, 1995).

Jean-Michel Petot and Dragana Djurić Jočić

Differences of Content and Structure Between Personality Psychology Dimensions and the Main Rorschach Variables

Conventional measures and Rorschach Inkblot Method opposes themselves concerning their relation to personality theory. The rationale of conventional personality measures (self-report or observer-report) presupposes a pre-established explicit model of personality, on which the definition of scores and scales are grounded, while the "Rorschach experiment" (Rorschach, 1921) does not: it produces data - scores and scales - which all stem out of clinical experience, are largely unrelated to a priori constructs, and remain open to a large gamut of interpretations. Historically, many Rorschach phenomena, (e.g., achromatic color, shading, animal movements, color-shading blends, etc.) were discovered before they received any interpretation. Moreover, conventional models of personality are dimensional, while the Rorschach generates personality characteristics whose structure is sometimes dimensional, often categorical, and often intermediate. The Rorschach is not intrinsically associated with any particular model, even though it has been for decades associated with psychodynamic or psycho-analytic models of the psychic structure. It assesses personality traits or psychological dimensions which are not directly related to personality psychology constructs - certain of them being specific to the Rorschach; and certain of them having only loose resemblance with some personality construct.

Rorschach constructs like restriction, dilatation, introversiveness, extratensiveness, constitute only the sketch of a possible model which could be *a posteriori* derived from the analysis of Rorschach responses, and this model remains partial, tentative, and open to further developments. The psychological variables comprised in this tentative model are neither fully categorical nor fully dimensional. It is hard to list the dimensions the Rorschach is supposed to assess, and it is difficult to align Rorschach constructs with Personality Psychology dimensions. On the one hand, some features assessed by the Rorschach like developmental quality, form quality, organizational factor Z or special scores, are without correspondence in personality psychology, and seem to correspond to cognitive dimensions, but it is also very hard to relate them with aptitudes recognized by cognitive psychology and assessed by aptitude tests. On the other hand, Rorschach constructs like egocentricity, self image or quality of self and other representations refer to constructs more or less neglected by empirical personality research, even though they are a central focus of clinicians and psychopathological theories. These constructs generally are categorical rather than dimensional.

Is this a serious argument against the validity of the Rorschach Inkblot Method? It is hard to relate the main Rorschach variables with conventional personality construct, but it is also very hard to find convergence between variables stemming from different and competing models of personality research. As each conventional instrument for the assessment of personality is closely associated with a precise theoretical model of personality, the concordance between the different questionnaires is sometimes very loose. The correlations between scales measuring similar constructs are generally fair, e.g., when subjects are administered both NEO PI-R and the Eysenck's personality Inventory (EPI), correlation between measures of extraversion is .69 and that between both scales of emotional stability/neuroticism is .75 (McCrae & Costa, 1985). *But as soon as there are some differences between the constructs to be correlated, correlations are generally low even if these differences are slight.* Thus agreeableness, that Eysenck (1992) held as "the obverse of P" (P = Psychoticism), has very low relationship (from $r = -.13$ to $r = -.38$) with this latter, whereas Conscientiousness, often considered as a good marker of low P, has only low correlation (from $r = -12$ to $r = -.28$) with it (McCrae & Costa, 1985; Avia et al., 1995). The findings are similar at the facet level (Costa & McCrae, 1995) and also when other questionnaires are compared (Barelds & Luteijn, 2002). It must be emphasized that the magnitudes of these correlations between measures based on self-description are not higher than the magnitudes of correlations between self-report measures and Rorschach variables that are in the same range (Petot, 2004). As the difference of the methods (self-report vs perceptual task) is an additional source of divergence, it is possible to assume that certain correlations between questionnaires and Rorschach measures (e.g., between FFM Openness and some Rorschach variables) are a little less disappointing than the correlations between Agreeableness, Conscientiousness, and Psychoticism across different self-report measures.

Even though some Rorschach variables seem to be very similar to the traditional personality psychology dimensions, and they are labeled with resembling names, they are strongly different. For example, if we compare the personality psychology construct Introversion/Extraversion with the Rorschach construct Introversiveness/Extratensiveness, there are striking differences concerning the content of each of them. The Five-Factor Theory (FFT) Extraversion is associated with warm sociability, gregariousness, assertiveness, high level of activity, excitement seeking, and positive emotions. With the exception of the strong link between Extratensiveness and orientation toward the others, these traits are not characteristic of Rorschach Extratensiveness, which is rather defined by strength and vividness of the affective contact with the outer world, especially the human beings. The contrast is even more striking as far as the pair introversion/introversiveness is concerned: while FFT introversion is no more than low extraversion, Rorschach introversiveness is rather defined as proneness to use one's inner life for the satisfaction of one's important needs. At a conceptual level, this definition is very similar to that of certain facets of Openness, even if, in fact, there are few correlations between Rorschach introversiveness and FFT Openness. Moreover, some aspects of Rorschach introversiveness resemble FFT Conscientiousness, like tendency to thinking prior to acting (deliberation), while some others resemble FFT Agreeableness, like tendency to mature identification.

There is no mirror symmetry between extratensiveness and introversiveness, because the structure of Rorschach dimensions is different from that of personality psychology dimensional models. Structure of personality as described by empirical personality research is relatively simple: according to these models, the components of personality are dimensions which are linear and bipolar, e.g., introversion is defined by a low level of extraversion and reciprocally. The structure of personality is no more than the addition of two, three or more of these unilinear dimensions. The main models are comprised of: two (Eysenck), three (Eysenck's 2nd model including psychoticism, Cloninger first model), four (Tellegen), five (Five-Factor Theory), seven (Cloninger second model), or eighteen (Cattel) dimensions. The most sophisticated personality models are hierarchical, i.e., the broad dimensions or "superfactors" are composed of facets or first order factors. The structure of the FFT of Personality, which is one of the main subjects of this special series, is very simple: five broad independent or orthogonal dimensions, each of them being composed of six interrelated facets, each facet expressing specific aspects of the broad dimension.

Whereas extraversion/introversion is a simple construct, extratensiveness/introversiveness is a very complex one. Extraversion opposes to introversion, but extratensiveness does not really oppose introversiveness. There is some ambiguity in the definition of Rorschach introversiveness/extratensiveness. Strictly speaking, introversiveness is defined by the excess of human movement over plain chromatic responses. But it is also possible to consider an ambitent subject is just as introversive as s/he is extratensive. What is the operational definition of extratensiveness/introversiveness? Is it defined only by the difference between sum M and Weighted Sum C or by the amount of each of them? The possibilities to be "pure extratensive" or "mixed extratensive" or "dilated extratensive" are without correspondence with FFT Extraversion, which is generally supposed to be the counterpart of extratensiveness in personality psychology. In case of true ambitendency (to be distinguished from restriction/coarctation), for example dilated ambitendency, a person can simultaneously present a high number of introversive M and a high quantity of extratensive FC, CF and C. Thus, paradoxically, an introversive person (e.g., with EB: 4 M/1.5 C) may have less "introversive" resources than certain ambitent persons (e.g., with EB: 6 M/6 C) or even than certain extratensive person (e.g., with EB: 5 M/7 C) – and vice versa.

According to personality psychology, introversion and extraversion are the two ends of the same dimension: the more a person is extravert, the less s/he is introvert. But Rorschach introversiveness and extratensiveness together opposes "coarctation," i.e., restriction, lack of inner resources as expressed by the absence or quasi-absence of M and C. Does this construct have some counterpart in personality psychology? I hypothesize coarctation is well described by "O^-" (low openness to experience). If so, both Rorschach extratensiveness and introversiveness would oppose Five-Factor Theory Closedness.

Test Taking Attitude and Response Style

Besides these problems stemming from the deep differences between the content and structure of the psychological realities assessed by self-report measures and the Rorschach inkblot method, other ones are raised by the deep differences in the task nature and presentation. The main question is: what is the meaning of the answer in a questionnaire or in a projective instrument? Although there are few theories on the kind of personality instances that are involved in the formation of responses to the Rorschach test, it may be stated that it measures psychological realities that are not under conscious control. On the opposite, in self-report questionnaires, the subjects give self-description of personality that may be more or less distorted, depending upon the following:

1) how aware s/he is of his/her characteristics
2) how s/he is willing to cooperate (careful or careless answers, simulation or dissimulation)
3) what image of him/herself s/he is willing to give
4) how exactly s/he is able of self-evaluation in relation to other people.

McClelland et al. (1989) believe that projective material evaluates the "implicit" aspects of personality (more unconscious and related to physiological characteristics, developed earlier in life, not requiring language and verbal communication, strongly associated with long-term trends of spontaneous behavior). The answers in questionnaires depend upon self-representation and "self-attributed" motivation, which has different developmental origin, and it is the predictor of conscious option and situation-related behavior.

The main concept that should reflect the influence of the personality factor on the test process expression is response style. A series of research by Meyer (1997, 1999) represents the most sophisticated attempt to elucidate the influence of the response style upon the Rorschach and self-report questionnaires (especially MMPI-2). If we define the variables that are the reflection of the response style, the supposition is that we can homogenize the samples and increase the convergent validity. But the results have shown that, not even skillful and complex research succeeded to clearly determine response style, the control of which would increase the convergent validity.

The main problem stems from the fact that, contrary to the MMPI, neither the NEO PI-R nor the Rorschach test was designed to measure the test-taking attitude. Therefore, when one wants to measure this attitude, s/he must select some items or variables which are supposed to express it. But these items – always in the case of self-report instruments, and often, in the case of the Rorschach – have some already recognized significance. What kind of evidence could allow us to assume that a score is understandable in some cases as a marker of negative emotionality, and in some other cases as a marker of honest and uninhibited test-taking attitude? For example, it may seem likely that a short Rorschach record, especially if the Lambda or F% is low, is a good marker of the subject's test-taking attitude, even though these characteristics may have other different meanings, like mental poverty, and even though it may happen that a very long record, with low Lambda, is rather a marker of lack of control. But when one hypothesizes the MMPI first factor is a marker of test-taking attitude, the problem arises because this factor is primarily a marker of negative emotionality and psychopathology. Therefore, it is impossible to disentangle the assessment of this factor and the assessment of the test-taking attitude, and this weakens the psychometric qualities of the assessment: is it not reasonable to assume a subject is all the more honest and expansive since s/he scores high on pathology – or conversely s/he is all the more reluctant to take the test since s/he answers negatively to items suggesting recognition of pathological thoughts, emotions, or behaviors. This would be imply that honest subjects are necessarily those with strong psychological problems, and conversely the subjects reporting low or no psychology are suspect of reticence of reluctance.

Besides these questions, there is another consideration which casts some doubt in the otherwise promising hypothesis of the influence of the test-taking attitude. As the assessment of the test attitude is linked with the assessment of another construct or psychological feature, e.g., the negative emotionality in the Meyer's attempts, the influence of the test-taking attitude on the content of the subjects' responses may be limited to this tautological assumption: correlation between Rorschach and self-report markers of negative emotionality is high when subjects scores high (or low) on both tests, and low when their scores are divergent. To sum up, the test-taking hypothesis may prove illuminating in the future, but this will need reliable identification of independent, specific, and therefore unambiguous markers.

Conclusions

From a theoretical point of view, all available evidence emphasize the sources of divergence between the Rorschach and self-report measures. It would not be reasonable to expect strong convergences between instruments which measure different constructs and use different ways of approach, and that says nothing against the validity of either method. Provided this point is well understood, and strong correlations are not expected, it may be useful to explore the many relationships which may prove enlightening between personality constructs and Rorschach variables.

From a practical point of view, most of the skilled clinicians, during the continuous integration of results, evaluate both instruments as useful for clinical judgment. When they get discrepant results, they are not worried, but, by procedure of clinical judgment and integration, they make an attempt to explain the discrepancy in the light of a particular case. Likewise, research studies have verified the validity of both instruments for the estimate of objective, external criteria (Acklin, 1993).

In the clinical context, the discrepancy of the variables of two instruments may be the result of differences of "the set of conscious answers" given by patients, depending upon the mechanisms of defence and the extent of impact of unconscious processes on the conscious functioning of the subjects. Recognition of such patients has therapeutic effects, since they are unable to recognize or attach importance to their symptoms and problems (denial or dissimulation). In this way, what appears to be a statistical weakness is, in clinical context, important diagnostic and therapeutic information.

References

Acklin, M.W. (1993). Integrating the Rorschach and MMPI in clinical assessment: Conceptual and methodological issues. *Journal of Personality Assessment, 60*, 125–31

Archer, R.P. (1996), MMPI-Rorschach Interrelationships: Proposed Criteria for Evaluating Explanatory Models. *Journal of Personality Assessment, 67*, 504–515.

Archer, R.P., & Krishnamurthy, R. (1993). A review of MMPI and Rorschach interrelationships in adult samples. *Journal of Personality Assessment, 61*, 277–293.

Avia, M.D., Sanz, J., Sanchez-Bernardos, M.L., Mártinez-Arias, M. R, Silva, F., & Graña, J.L. (1995). The five-factor model – II. The Relations of the NEO PI with other personality variables. *Personality and Individual Differences, 19,* 81–97.

Barelds, D.P.H., & Luteijn, F. (2002). Measuring personality: A comparison of three personality questionnaires in the Netherlands. *Personality and Individual Differences, 33,* 499–510.

Costa, P.T., & McCrae, R.R. (1995). Primary traits of Eysenck's P-E-N system: Three and five-factor solutions. *Journal of Personality and Social Psychology, 69,* 308–317.

Exner, J.E. (1995). *Issues and methods in Rorschach research.* Mahwah, NJ: Erlbaum.

Eysenck, H.J. (1992). Four ways five factors are *not* basic. *Personality and Individual Differences, 6,* 667–673.

Ganellen, R. (1996), *Integrating the Rorschach and MMPI-2 in personality assessment.* Mahwah, NJ: Erlbaum

Graham, J.R. (1993). *MMPI-2: Assessing personality and psychopathology* (2nd ed.). New York: Oxford.

Greenwald, D.F. (1999). Relationships between the Rorschach and the NEO Five-Factor Inventory. *Psychological Reports, 85,* 519–527.

McClelland,D.C., Koesatner, R., & Weinberger, J. (1989). How do self-attributed and implicit motives differ? *Psychological review, 96,* 690–702.

McCrae, R.R., & Costa, P.T. (1985). Comparison of EPI and psychoticism scales with measures of the five-factor model of personality. *Personality and Individual Differences, 6,* 587–597.

Meyer, G.J. (1997). On the integration of personality assessment methods: The Rorschach and MMPI. In J.A. Schinka & R.L. Greene (Eds.), *Emerging issues and methods in personality assessment.* Mahwah, NJ: Erlbaum.

Meyer, G.J. (1999). The convergent validity of MMPI and Rorschach scales: Extension using profile scores to define response and character styles on both methods and reexamination of simple Rorschach response frequency. *Journal of Personality Assessment, 72,* 1–35.

Parker, K.C.H., Hanson, R.K., & Hunsley, J. (1988). MMPI, Rorschach, and WAIS: A meta-analytic comparison of reliability, stability, and validity. *Psychological Bulletin, 103,* 367–373.

Petot, J.M. (2004). Le test de Rorschach et le modèle de personnalité en cinq facteurs [The Rorschach and the Big Five Model]. *Psychologie Française, 49,* 81–94.

Rorschach, H. (1921). *Psychodiagnostics.* Bern: Ernst Bircher.

Summary

Because the quasi-absence of correlation between Rorschach variables and the dimensions described in academic psychology of personality is now a well-established fact, this paper reviews the main reasons which could account for this puzzling discrepancies. Some of these reasons are methodological or statistical ones, and they are linked to formal properties of variables to be correlated: raw scores, ratios, or percentages, or broader constructs operationalized by specific pattern of scores and ratios. It is emphasized that some difficulties are related to the excessive number of variables addressed in studies lacking theoretical hypotheses, as to the categorical nature of many Rorschach variables, which opposes the dimensional nature of the constructs of academic personality psychology. More fundamentally, it is suggested that, as exemplified by introversion and introversiveness, psychological realities assessed by the Rorschach differ from those conceptualized by personality psychology not only by their content but also by their structure. Finally, the authors discuss the hypothesis suggested by Ganellen and Meyer: the correlation between the Rorschach and self-report measures would be moderated by the patients' response style or test-taking attitude; the absence of correlation in the studied samples would conceal strong positive correlations among subjects with the same attitude toward both tests, and strong negative correlations among subjects with test-taking attitude different toward each kind of instrument. It is suggested that this hypothesis is promising, but it will be illuminating only when a reliable and specific marker of attitude will be identified. To conclude, it is remembered that while these discrepancies between the two kinds of tests raise some problems at the theoretical level, at a clinical level they convey much valuable information about patient's self-representation and defence mechanisms.

Résumé

Partant du fait maintenant bien établi de la quasi-absence de corrélations entre les variables du Rorschach et les dimensions décrites en psychologie différentielle de la personnalité, les auteurs passent en revue les principales raisons susceptibles de rendre compte de ce décalage surprenant. Certaines de ces raisons sont d'ordre méthodologique, voire statistique et tiennent aux propriétés formelles des variables mises en relation: scores isolés, proportions ou pourcentages, ou dimensions plus vastes opérationnalisées par un ensemble de plusieurs scores ou proportions. On souligne également les difficultés liées au grand nombre des variables comparées dans certaines études dépourvues d'hypothèses théoriques, et à la nature catégorielle de nombreuses variables du Rorschach, qui s'oppose à la nature dimensionnelle des traits étudiés par la psychologie différentielle de la personnalité. Plus fondamentalement, on montre sur l'exemple de l'introversion et de l'introversivité que les réalités appréhendées par le test de Rorschach diffèrent par leur contenu et par leur structure de celles conceptualisées par la psychologie de la personnalité. Enfin, on discute l'hypothèse avancée par Ganellen et Meyer selon laquelle la corrélation entre le Rorschach et les questionnaires de personnalité serait influencée par le style de réponse ou attitude du patient par rapport au test: l'absence globale de corrélation dans les populations étudiées masquerait une corrélation positive élevée chez les sujets ayant la même attitude face aux deux types d'instrument, et une corrélation négative élevée chez les sujets ayant des attitudes différentes face à chaque instrument. On estime que cette hypothèse est prometteuse, mais qu'elle ne pourra tenir ses promesses que lorsqu'on aura identifié un marqueur fiable et spécifique de l'attitude de réponse. En conclusion, on rappelle que ces divergences entre les deux types de test, même si elles posent problème au plan théorique, sont porteuses au plan clinique d'informations précieuses sur la représentation de soi et les mécanismes de défense des patients.

Resumen

Dado que la casi ausencia de correlación entre ciertas variables Rorschach y las dimensiones descritas académicamente por la psicología de la personalidad es un hecho bastante aceptado, este artículo revisa las principales razones que podrían explicar estas enigmáticas discrepancias. Algunas de estas razones son metodológicas o estadísticas y están vinculadas a las propiedades formales de las variables cuando se intentan correlacionar: puntuaciones muy bajas, razones, porcentajes o constructos demasiado amplios que se tratan de operativizar mediante pautas específicas de códigos y relaciones. Otras dificultades tienen que ver con un excesivo número de variables que se estudian careciendo de hipótesis teóricas y con la naturaleza categórica de muchas variables Rorschach, que se opone a la naturaleza dimensional de los conceptos de la psicología académica de la personalidad. Fundamentalmente, se sugiere que, como ejemplifica el caso de la introversión y la introversividad, las realidades psicológicas evaluadas a través del Rorschach difieren de aquéllas que se conceptual izan en psicología de la personalidad, no solamente en su contenido sino también en su estructura. Por último, los autores discuten la hipótesis sugerida por Ganellen y Meyer: la correlación entre el Rorschach y las medidas de autoinforme estaría modulada por el estilo de respuesta del paciente o su actitud ante la administración de las pruebas. Así, la ausencia de correlación en las muestras estudiadas podría estar ocultando correlaciones positivas elevadas entre sujetos con la misma actitud ante Rorschach y autoinformes y correlaciones negativas elevadas entre sujetos con diferentes actitudes ante ambos tipos de prueba. Se sugiere que esta hipótesis es prometedora, pero que sólo podrá comprobarse cuando se consiga elaborar un marcador fiable y específico para identificar correctamente la actitud de los sujetos ante la situación de examen. Como conclusión, se recuerda que, si bien a nivel teórico estas discrepancias entre distintos tipos de tests plantean algunos problemas, también aportan a nivel clínico valiosas informaciones acerca de los mecanismos de defensa y de autorepresentación del sujeto.

Other Topics

Rorschachiana 27, 119–138

The Rorschach Ink-Blot Test as an Instrument for Evaluating Quality of Life in Breast-Cancer Victims

G. Marchioro, F. Barbato, G. Azzarello, and O. Vinante
Department of Oncology and OncoHematology, U.L.S.S. n° 13, Noale, Venice, Italy

Introduction

Breast cancer and treatment related factors are traumatic events for women. Besides representing life-threatening events, they strongly affect the patient's inner quality of life.

The breast, defined as a "somatic place" characterizing the female body image, is symbolically related to typical feminine functions such as motherhood and sexuality.

Therefore, surgery, inducing a distortion of body schema, causes important changes of self-image. In fact, radical or conservative surgery, associated with the side effects of adjuvant therapies, is an attack on a woman's identity. The psychological discomfort associated with the disease has been related either to premorbidity personality traits or to coping strategies with the stress of illness (Spiegel et al., 1996; Marchioro et al., 1996).

The need of psychological support during diagnosis and treatment for cancer diseases is universally recognized. However, homogeneous modalities of intervention are lacking, even if some areas of common interest have to be stressed:

1. Awareness of the disease and disclosure of cancer diagnosis,
2. Psychological defences as responses to the cancer diagnosis,
3. Assessment of quality of life according to the tumor stage and related treatments.

At present, in psycho-oncology research, the questionnaires are the most employed approach to study the personality traits and quality of life of cancer patients. However, to get qualitative data, it has to be considered that the reliability and validity of the questionnaires depend not only on the standardization of the tools, but on patient motivation, too. In fact, some omitted responses, or even refusal, generally underestimated, are recorded. Patient reluctance to use questionnaires to measure psychological variables is related to some factors such as the length of the protocols and a feeling of uselessness in a context where the problems are essentially somatic ones.

So, the questionnaires could not represent the best instrument to promote the empathic relationship, obviously related to motivation. On the other hand, counseling along with administered psychological tests allows listening and mutual relationship between the patients and the examiner.

In particular, the Rorschach test is applicable as a multidimensional method of collecting data on personality functioning, considering not only what patients say in their responses, but also why and how they say it. As reported by extensive published data, recently reviewed by Weiner, the specific characteristics of the Rorschach test demonstrate its strong research basis, the richness of the data it makes available and the wide applicability of its findings (Weiner, 1994).

The aim of this study is the evaluation of the impact of the Rorschach test as an instrument to assess possible mood disorders, object-relation, self-image and quality of life in breast-cancer patients.

Patients and Methods

135 consecutive patients, divided into three age groups (35–49, 50–59, and 60–67 years old) affected by operable breast cancer entered the study within 2–4 weeks after surgery.

The following exclusion criteria were adopted: previous psychopathological disorders and/or psychotherapeutic treatments or previous submission to the Rorschach test.

On admission patients were interviewed in a semi structured way (1 h for each patient) recording physical symptoms, stressful life events, family and social support, coping strategies. Patients finally underwent the Rorschach psychodiagnostic test.

The data were interpreted according to the structural approach, which focuses primarily on the structural features of the scores and their interrelations, taking into account also the experiential approach, a more subjective and phenomenological method, based on the examiner's empathy (Rausch & Boizou, 1977; Rausch & Sanglade, 1984).

Basically, we aim to evaluate:

1. spatial organization of the inkblot cards on the median line (referred to body schema);
2. limits of the inkblot shape (referred to self-image);
3. discrimination between compact and noncompact cards (referred to self- or non-self-integrity).

We compare our target group to both a sample of 736 healthy Italian women (18–65 years old, national sample) (Passi Tognazzo & Cristante, 1990) and a control group composed of 60 healthy age-matched women (20 females 35–49 years old, 20 females 50–59 years old and 20 females 60–67 years old) from the same Italian region (regional sample).

Results

The Rorschach test sequential mean scores for the 135 breast-cancer patients (experimental group) and for the national and regional control groups (Passi Tognazzo & Cristante, 1990) are reported in Table 1.

All observed results were comparable with respect to mean age and educational level, except for F+% (percentage of sharply seen forms), Anat% (percentage of anatomy) and Ban% (percentage of popular responses).

Low F+% along with high Anat% – Ban% values and low M (movement response), suggest that the patients' answers were qualitatively and quantitatively poor, with low abstract and symbolism attitude. No significant differences in terms of rejections were observed (25.1% for experimental vs 23.3% for regional control group).

On the basis of the Rorschach criteria for depression (Bohm, 1969), no patient fulfilled the parameters configuration corresponding to depressive disorders.

On the other hand, we observed a higher incidence of R < 15 (total responses and location) in the patients of the experimental group with

Table 1. Rorschach test sequential mean scores for 135 breast cancer patients, a regional control group (60 patients), and a national control group (736 nonpatients).

	Breast cancer		Regional sample		National sample	
Parameters	Mean	IQ range	Mean	IQ range	Mean	IQ range
R	19.3	13–24	15.0	11–17	20.2	14–23
W	7.3	5–9	6.8	5–9	9.3	7–11
W%	40.0	28–52	49.3	33–62	51.1	37–61
W(+)%	37.7	25–47	44.6	29–56	87.9	78–100
D%	57.1	44–68	45.1	33–61	43.6	33–56
Dd%	3.4	0–5	5.7	0.9	3.0	0–5
DO	0.0	0–0	0.0	0–0	0.1	0–0
DrS	0.6	0–1	0.35	0–1	0.7	0–1
F%	79.7	72–90	71.2	62–84	67.0	56–76
F(+)%	66.2	58–77	56.5	40–69	82.7	74–92
M	0.9	0–1	0.9	0–1	1.3	0–2
FM + m	0.5	0–1	0.9	0–1	na	na
FC	1.0	0–2	0.6	0–1	1.2	0–2
CF	0.3	0–0	1.3	0–2	1.4	0–2
C	0.2	0–0	0.4	0–1	0.2	0–0
F(C)	0.2	0–0	0.1	0–0	na	na
FCh	0.5	0–1	0.4	0–1	na	na
ChF	0.2	0–0	0.2	0–0	na	na
Ch	0.0	0–0	0.00–0	na	na	
A%	46.0	33–58	47.1	31–61	46.5	35–55
H%	14.0	6–20	16.0	6–25	15.6	9–21
Anat%	14.0	0–21	12.0	0–18	5.2	0–8
Sex	0.6	0–1	0.3	0–0	0.2	0–0
Ban%	57.1	44–68	14.3	7–20	27.7	20–36
Orig%	0.3	0–0	0.8	0–0	na	na
RC	0.2	0–0	0.2	0–0	na	na
F(+)%C	0.0	0–0	0.0	0–0	na	na

na = not available

lower educational levels vs regional control group (37.2% vs 22%; p = .08) (data not shown in the table).

On the contrary, a lower incidence of G < 5 (whole response) is recorded in the patients with higher levels vs lower educational (9.8% vs 25.5%; p = .0376); so, the patients' capacity for synthesizing seems to be related to the educational levels. The "introversive vs extratensive ratio" (Erlebnistypus or Experience Balance-EB parameter) resulted as mainly coarcted in the experimental vs Regional control group (60% vs 37%; p =

Table 2. Frequency of patients fulfilling the Rorschach criteria for depression: breast-cancer patients (135) vs regional controls (60).

	Breast cancer		Regional controls	
Parameters	%	LC 95%	%	LC 95%
R < 15	33	24–41	55	42–68
TMI > 1 min	30	22–37	42	29–55
G < 5	21	14–28	23	13–36
DO <>0	2	0–6	2	0–9
F(+)% > 80	0	–	0	–
A% > 60	0	–	0	–
U < 10	42	34–51	38	26–52
ΣM = 0	32	24–40	33	22–47
ΣC = 0	65	57–73	55	42–68
"coarcted" ET	60	52–68	37	25–50
Orig% = 0	93	88–97	92	82–97

95% LC = 95% Confidence Limits

Table 3. Affectivity control for breast-cancer patients (135), regional controls (60), and national controls (736).

	Breast cancer		Regional controls		National controls	
Parameters	Subjects	%	Subjects	%	Subjects	%
FC > (CF + C)	55	41	9	15	213	29
FC = (CF + C)	56	41	19	32	184	25
FC < (CF + C)	24	18	32	53	339	46
FC≥ (CF + C)	111	82	28	47	397	46

.0026), confirming the presence of a "state reaction" that can be interpreted as an "adjustment disorder with depressive mood" according to the DSM-IV (American Psychiatric Association, 1994).

Moreover, this trait was correlated with lower educational levels (73.4% vs 46.3%) and increasing age (55.3% vs 66.1% vs 79.3%; $p = .011$).

In particular, analyzing the color determining factors for Erlebnistypus, we observed the prevalence of the parameter FC (Form-Color Response) > (Color-Form Response) + C (Color Response) in the experimental group vs Regional and controls (41% vs 15% vs 29%; $p = .000$).

This difference is more relevant if the data are analyzed according to FC > CF + C (82% vs 47% vs 46%). Similarly, we recorded FC < CF + C in 18% of the experimental group vs 53% and 46% of the regional and control groups, respectively. These data confirm that breast-cancer patients express a higher affective control. On the contrary, no difference in terms of Chiaroscuro Response [F(C) parameter] was recorded.

Table 4. Chiaroscuro responses in breast-cancer patients (135), regional controls (60), and national controls (736).

	Breast cancer		Regional controls		National control	
Parameters	Subjects	%	Subjects	%	Subjects	%
FCho > ChoF + Cho	44	(33%)	16	(27%)	324	(44%)
Fcho = ChoF + Cho	7	(5%)	2	(3%)	162	(22%)
FCho < ChoF + Cho	14	(10%)	6	(10%)	147	(20%)
for Fcho = 0						
ChoF + Cho = 0	70	(52%)	36	(60%)	103	(14%)

Table 5. Kinesthetic determinant, figures and small movement in breast-cancer patients (135), regional controls (60), and national controls (736).

	Breast cancer		Regional controls		National controls	
Parameters	Subjects	%	Subjects	%	Subjects	%
M > FM + m	65	48	26	43	302	41
M = FM + m	52	39	18	30	280	38
M < FM + m	18	13	16	27	154	21

$p = .071$

Breast-cancer patients showed a Fch (Form-Chiaroscuro) response similar to the national control group (33% and 44% respectively); also in this case, high affective control is suggested.

Regarding M (Movement or Kinesthetic Determinant) response, no differences between the experimental and regional control groups (mean = 0.9; IQ range = 0–1) were recorded; on the contrary, M response production was inferior compared to the national control group (mean = 1.3, IQ range = 0–2). Moreover, when the determinants associated to the Contents Human-Animal (Figures) and m (Small Movement) of the experimental and regional control group were analyzed, we observed a limited difference ($p = .071$). This difference becomes statistically significant ($p = .029$) only for the condition M < FM + m (data not shown in the table).

Then, we compared the Experienced Stimulation and the Experience Actual indices, which make it possible to analyze the actual proportion between environmental demands and personal resources, according to the Exner system (Exner, 1977).

This analysis has great importance in psycho-oncology research to achieve predictive indices of the patients' coping and psychological responses to therapeutic approaches.

Table 6. Experience Actual (EA) versus Experienced Stimulation (es) in breast-cancer patients (135) and regional controls (60).

	Breast cancer		Regional controls	
	Subjects	%	Subjects	%
es > EA (D neg.)*	77	(57%)	44	(74%)
es ≤ EA (D pos.)**	58	(43%)	16	(26%)
	135	100%	60	100%

p = .030; *es < EA, ** es ≥ EA; EA = (FM + m) + [F(C) + FCh + ChF + Ch]; es = (M) + (C)

Table 6 shows that cancer patients have greater personal resources than control ones (43% vs 26%, p = .030), suggesting that anxiety and strain associated to illness promote adjustment.

The Exner Aspiration Index (ratio between W and M factors) has revealed a prevalence of the W factor, suggesting that cancer patients have higher aspirations than personal resources (Table 1).

Another important aspect of our research deals with the changes of the patients' identity during illness. We have analyzed the ten inkblot tables according to the method of discrimination between compact and noncompact tables (Arcostanzo et al., 1990), resulting in three parameters and relative scores: positive (+, score 1), ambivalent (+/– score 0.5) and negative (–, score 0). Assessing five positive parameters as a sufficient score of retained self-identity, we reported the significant prevalence of negative parameters in cancer patients compared to the control groups (43% vs 26%, p = .000).

Self-identity results are also affected by age and educational levels. In fact, elderly patients and women with lower educational levels show higher negative scores (50% for 60–69 years old vs 41% for 50–59 years old and 46% for primary education levels vs 36% for higher educational levels). The same trend was present in the control group. These results are further confirmed by the difference of positive responses to non-

Table 7. Self-image in breast-cancer patients (135) and regional controls (60).

	Breast cancer		Regionals controls	
	Items	%	Items	%
Negative	580	(43%)	156	(26%)
Negative/Positive	70	(5%)	49	(8%)
Positive	700	(52%)	392	(66%)

p < .000

Table 8. Self identity related to age in breast-cancer patients (135) and regional controls (60).

	35–49 years		50–59 years		60–69 years	
Breast cancer	Items	%	Items	%	Items	%
Negative	196	42%	240	41%	144	50%
Negative/positive	28	6%	28	5%	14	5%
Positive	246	42%	322	54%	132	45%
Regional controls	35–49 years		50–59 years		60–69 years	
Negative	36	18%	57	28%	63	32%
Negative/positive	12	6%	10	5%	24	12%
Positive	151	66%	133	67%	111	56%

Table 9. Self identity related to educational levels in 135 breast-cancer patients.

	Low		Middle + high	
Breast cancer	Items	%	Items	%
Negative	433	46%	147	36%
Negative/positive	52	6%	18	4%
Positive	455	48%	245	60%
Regional controls				
Negative	71	31%	85	23%
Negative/positive	22	10%	27	7%
Positive	135	59%	257	70%

compact tables between cancer patients and the control group (21% vs 45%, $p = .000$) (Table 12).

Moreover, only 31.6% of breast-cancer patients reported answers with H (Human) content and clear sexual valence, revealing a highly altered sexual identity.

It's generally reported that radical mastectomy plays a key role on altered self-identity compared to conservative surgery. Our results do not confirm this assumption, as revealed by the data reported in Table 10. On the contrary, we observed 46% of negative scores for quadrantectomy vs 41% for mastectomy.

Then we considered the following seven relation levels of the Mutuality of Autonomy (M.O.A.) scale according to Urist (Urist, 1977) and modified by Arcostanzo et al. (1990): Level 1°: Mutual Relation; Level 2°: Parallel Relation; Level 3°: Dependence Relation; Level 4°: Narcissistic Relation; Level 5°: Control Relation; Level 6°: Persecution Relation; Level 7°: Archaic Relation (Incorporation, Splitting, Fragmentation-Ex-

Table 10. Self identity by type of surgery in 135 breast-cancer patients.

Breast cancer	Quadrantectomy Subjects	%	Mastectomy Subjects	%
Negative	247	46%	306	41%
Negative/positive	32	5%	38	5%
Positive	294	49%	406	54%

Table 11. Grading of self image and object relations.

CARD	I	II	III	IV	V	VI	VII	VIII	IX	X
S.R.										
L 1										
L 2										
L 3										
L 0										
L 4										
L 5										
L 6										
L 7										

Table 12. Self identity in "compact tables" and "noncompact tables" in breast-cancer patients (135) and regional controls (60).

Compact tables		(+)		non (+)
Breast cancer		13		503
Regional controls		12		217
Noncompact tables	items		%	items
Breast cancer	165		21%	611
Regional controls	157		45%	189

plosion, Fusion-Symbiosis); Level 0: Lack of relation (Arcostanzo et al., 1990).

For every inkblot we look for the relational level of the subject, employing the grading reported in Table 11, allowing us to obtain other important information to apply in the clinical setting. In fact, the majority of the breast-cancer patients expressed levels 0 and 4 (81% of cancer patients vs 69% of the control ones, $p = .000$), that represent an isolation trend and narcissistic relation, respectively.

Table 13. Relations modalities in breast-cancer patients (135) and regional controls (60).

	Breast cancer		Regional controls	
	Items	%	Items	%
L_5 L_6 L_7	178	14%	169	29%
L_0 L_4	1048	81%	396	69%
L_1 L_2 L_3	66	5%	10	2%

$p < .000$
L_5 L_6 L_7 = archaic relation levels
L_0 L_4 = isolation trend/narcissistic relation
L_1 L_2 L_3 = adequate levels of object relation

Table 14. Relational modalities in breast-cancer patients (135) and regional controls (60) by age.

	35–49 years		50–59 years		60–69 years	
Breast cancer	Items	%	Items	%	Items	%
L_5 L_6 L_7	56	12%	89	16%	33	12%
L_0 L_4	371	82%	444	78%	237	86%
L_1 L_2 L_3	26	6%	33	6%	7	2%
Regional controls	35–49 years		50–59 years		60–69 years	
L_5 L_6 L_7	48	25%	65	33%	56	29%
L_0 L_4	133	70%	130	66%	133	70%
L_1 L_2 L_3	8	4%	1	1%	1	1%

Moreover, the fact that as much as 25.7% of breast-cancer patients report the figures as seen "from the back," indicates relational anxiety.

Archaic relation levels were more frequent in the control group compared to breast-cancer patients (29% vs 14%). This is an expected result that confirms mechanism of negation of regressive traits in cancer patients.

L1, L2 and L3 levels represent particular relational modalities, like reciprocity and collaboration, indicating adequate levels of object relation; they were present in 5% of the cancer patients compared to 2% of the control group. These data suggest the particular lifestyle of these patients, tending to "effort" and "sacrifice," and they have to be interpreted as a high psychological burden.

Tables 14 and 15 show that object relation levels are not affected by age or educational level. Similarly, they are not affected by type of surgery (mastectomy or quadrantectomy) as shown in Table 16.

Table 15. Relational modalities related with educational level in breast-cancer patients (135) and regional controls (60).

	Low		Middle + high	
Breast cancer	Items	%	Items	%
L_5 L_6 L_7	105	12%	73	18%
L_0 L_4	751	84%	297	74%
L_1 L_2 L_3	36	4%	30	8%
Regional controls	Subjects	%	Subjects	%
L_5 L_6 L_7	77	35%	92	26%
L_0 L_4	143	65%	235	71%
L_1 L_2 L_3	1	–	9	3%

Table 16. Relational modalities by type of surgery in 135 breast-cancer patients.

	Quadrantectomy		Mastectomy	
Breast cancer	Items	%	Items	%
L_5 L_6 L_7	78	14%	100	14%
L_0 L_4	464	81%	584	81%
L_1 L_2 L_3	29	5%	37	5%

$p <$ NS
L_5 L_6 L_7 = archaic relation levels
L_0 L_4 = isolation trend/narcissistic relation
L_1 L_2 L_3 = adequate levels of object relation

Within the frame of object relation, it is important to analyze the sexuality. While the majority of authors point out a reduced sexuality in breast-cancer patients (Ganz et al., 1989; Holmberg et al., 1989) our results do not show the presence of different sexual problems as expressed by the frequency of sex responses in cancer patients compared to the control group or national control group (0.6% vs 0.3% vs 0.2%) as reported in Table 1.

It is important to stress the parameter Anat% that showed a significant discrimination between the study groups (14% for breast-cancer patients vs 5.2% for control group). The anatomical responses, and in particular the visceral ones (65.8%), show evidence of the fracture between body, Ego and the lived death, as markers of personality disorders.

Finally, anatomical responses along with R, G, F+%, Ban% indices and Erlebnistypus type, resulted to be the most important parameters to identify the adjustment disorders of the study group.

Discussion

Breast-cancer patients represent the most frequently analyzed group in regard to psychosocial issues. Many authors report greater anxiety and depression in these patients than in other surgery patients or women with benign breast disease (Maguire, 1976; Morris et al., 1977).

Actually there is a plethora of studies with varying degrees of methodological rigor investigating psychosocial distress, quality of life of breast-cancer patients and their psychosocial adjustment to cancer diagnosis and treatment.

The most used approach is to formally assess psychological distress and quality of life with valid questionnaires, but, as reported in important Editorial "most measurements of quality of life in the medical literature seem to aim at the wrong target," as they lack valid indicators of the patients' overall quality of life (Lancet, 1995).

In fact, conflicting data concerning the supposed quantitative estimates of the questionnaires confirm that research about the best ways of assessing psychological discomfort and quality of life must continue. Trying to overcome the uncriticized acceptance of the questionnaires, the aim of our study was to evaluate of the impact of a multidimensional psychodiagnostic method, the Rorschach test, as an instrument to assess not only psychological traits but also the quality of life in breast-cancer patients.

Rorschach referred to his inkblot test as a "form interpretation test" (Rorschach, 1942): During the test the patient experiences particular perceptions arising by some processes, such as sensation, memory and association. Thus, it appears as a multivalent approach, inducing the patients to respond to the meaning they give to the stimuli and to the feelings they experience. In analyzing the relationship present among responses, one can deduce a wide range of personality traits and to formulate certain diagnostic patterns.

Our results clearly confirm the great impact of breast cancer on patients' emotional-social well-being and psychosocial adjustment, but also provide evidence of new important psychological traits.

Depression is usually reported in scientific literature as a frequent condition in breast-cancer patients (Fillon et al., 1996; Spiegel, 1997); in our series no patient fulfilled the Rorschach criteria for Major Depression. The evaluation revealed the sample study group as having a dysthymic trait, as revealed by the difficulties of cancer patients to project themselves into the task. To explain this phenomenon, it is important to emphasize the coarcted Erlebnistypus (EB) in breast-cancer patients. The EB represents the ratio between the sum of human movement (M) responses and the weighted sum of chromatic color (C) responses. M responses, defined by Rorschach as "Kinesthesia" (Rorschach, 1942), reflect introversion and the attitude to resonate to one's inner life. On the other hand, C responses reflect extraversion and represent a feeling-based adaptation to the external world.

So, EB reflects the coexistence of these traits in specific proportions demonstrating, as reported by Rorschach, "an equalization of introversive and extratensive features" (Rorschach, 1942).

Analyzing the C responses, there is a clear prevalence of the conditions FC > CF + C in breast-cancer patients compared to control groups, reflecting a high affectivity control and an altered psychological health and integration. These features have been reported as typical of cancer prone personality (Ganz et al., 1987; Irvine et al., 1991).

These results have been integrated by the data resulting from the comparative analysis of the Experienced Stimulation and the Experience Actual indices, which makes it possible to detect the actual proportion between environmental demands and personal resources, according to the Exner system (Exner, 1977).

We show that breast-cancer patients have higher personal resources to face environmental demands than the control group, suggesting that anxiety and strain associated to illness promote adjustment.

This analysis has great importance in psycho-oncology research to achieve predictive indices of patients' coping and psychological responses to therapeutic approaches. Moreover, the Exner Aspiration Index (ratio between W and M factors) has shown evidence of the prevalence of the W factor, suggesting that cancer patients have higher aspiration than personal resources.

All these data effectively confirm the unconscious conflict between Ideal Ego and Real Ego of the women affected by breast cancer.

Another altered psychological trait has been demonstrated in our research: the change of the patients' identity during illness. Analyzing the ten cards according to the method of discrimination between compact and noncompact cards, we reported the significant prevalence of negative parameters in cancer patients compared to control group. Moreover, only 31.6% of breast-cancer patients reported answers with H (Human) content and sexual valence. These data reveal that altered self-identity promote a disruption in life patterns, including sexual relationships;

otherwise, no difference between study and control groups in terms of sexual problems were recorded, suggesting that these findings could be previously present, as reported by other studies (Schain, 1985; Young & Caughan, 1996).

Interestingly, self-identity resulted as being also affected by age and educational levels. Elderly patients and women with lower educational levels show higher negative scores: these results do not confirm the common idea that breast surgery may cause more psychological discomfort in young patients (Rowland & Holland, 1991). Moreover, we cannot confirm that radical mastectomy plays a key role on altered self-identity compared to conservative surgery, as previously reported (Singer & Reznikoff, 1981; Wellish et al., 1989). On the contrary, we observed 46% of negative scores for quadrantectomy vs 41% for mastectomy, in accordance with published review of the literature that suggests that there is no solid proof of a better psychological adjustment after breast-conserving treatment (Kiebert et al., 1991).

In conclusion, breast-cancer patients presented depressive traits without clinical depressive mood disorders with high control of emotions and restricted affectivity, according to the diagnosis of Adaptation Disorder with Depressive Mood (DSM-IV), and alexithymic traits. As recently reported by others scientific and clinical results demonstrate the utility and the wide range of applications of this method. In fact it provides not only a description of personality structure and dynamics, but offers the possibility to evaluate differential diagnosis of psychological disorders and related interventions (Weiner, 1996; Weiner, 1997). In particular, as demonstrated by our research it may be useful to evaluate global aspects of quality of life, defined as a uniquely personal perception. May this work overcome the uncriticized acceptance of questionnaires, suggesting that the Rorschach method represents a valid tool of assessing quality of life with respect to the patient's point of view.

References

American Psychiatric Association. (1994). *Diagnostic and statistical manual of mental disorders* (4th ed.). Washington, DC: Author.

Arcostanzo, G., Beglia, G., & Lertorta, V. (1990). Rappresentazione di sè, relazioni oggettuali al Rorschach [Self-representation, object relations in the Rorschach]. In E. Cattonaro (1989), *I test proiettivi tra indagine clinica e ricerca psicometrica* [Projective tests in clinical samples and psychometric research] (pp. 151–163). Università di Padova: Dipartimento di Psicologia Generale.

Bohm, E. (1969). *Manuale di psicodiagnostica di Rorschach* [Manual for the Rorschach psychodiagnostic]. Firenze: Giunti Barbera.

Editorial (1995). Quality of life and clinical trials. *Lancet, 346,* 1–2.

Exner, J.E., Jr. (1977). *The Rorschach: A comprehensive system, Vol. 2: Interpretation* (2th ed.). New York: Wiley.

Fillion, L., Lemyre, L., Mandeville, R., & Piche, R. (1996). Cognitive appraisal, stress state and cellular immunity responses before and after diagnosis of breast tumor. *International Journal of Rehabilitation and Health, 2,* 169–187.

Ganz, P., A., Schag, C.C., Polinski, M.L., Heinrich, R.L., & Flack, V.F. (1987). Rehabilitation needs and breast cancer: The first month after primary therapy. *Breast Cancer Res Treat, 10,* 243.

Holmberg, L., Omne-Ponten, M., Burns, Adami, H.O., & Bergstroem, R. (1989). Psychosocial adjustment after mastectomy and breast-conserving treatment. *Cancer, 64,* 969–974.

Irvine, D., Brown, B., Crooks, D., Roberts, J., & Browne, G. (1991). Psychosocial adjustment in women with breast cancer. *Cancer, 67,* 1097–1117.

Kiebert, G.M., de Haes, J.C.J.M., & de Velde, C.J.H. (1991). The impact of breast-conserving treatment and mastectomy on the quality of life of early-stage breast-cancer patients: A review. *Journal Clinical Oncology, 9,* 1059–1070.

Maguire, G.P. (1976). The psychological and social sequelae of mastectomy. In J.G. Howells, *Modern perspectives in the psychiatric aspect of surgery* (pp. 390–421). New York: Brunner Mazel.

Marchioro, G., Azzarello, G., Checchin, F., Perale, M., Segati, R., Sampognaro, F., Rosetti, F., Franchin, A., Pappagallo, G.L., & Vinante, O. (1996). The impact of a psychological intervention on quality of life in nonmetastatic breast cancer. *European Journal of Cancer, 32,* 1612–1615.

Morris, T.A., Greer, H.S., & White, P. (1977). Psychological and social adjustment to mastectomy: A two-year follow-up study. *Cancer, 43,* 1613–1618.

Passi Tognazzo, D., & Cristante, F. (1990). Valori normativi attuali delle prestazioni al Rorschach nell'adulto italiano [New normative data on the Rorschach for Italian adults]. In E. Cattonaro, *I test proiettivi tra indagine clinica e ricerca psicometrica* [Projective tests in clinical samples and psychometric research] (pp. 37–49). Università di Padova: Dipartimento di Psicologia Generale.

Rausch de Traubenberg, N., & Boizou, M.F. (1977). *Le Rorschach en clinique infantile* [The Rorschach in child clinical practice]. Paris: Duonod.

Rausch de Traubenberg, N., & Sanglade, A. (1984). Representation de soi et relation d'objet au Rorschach-Grille de représentation de soi [Representation of self and object relation in the Rorschach: A self-representation grid]. *Revue de Psychologie Appliqué, 34,* 41–54.

Rorschach, H. (1942). *Psychodiagnostics: A diagnostic test based on perception.* (Lemkau, P., Kronenberg, B., Trans.). Bern, Switzerland: Hans Huber.

Rowland, J.H., & Holland, J.C. (1991). Psychological reactions to breast cancer and its treatment. In J.R. Harris, I.C. Henderson, & D.W. Kinne (Eds.), *Breast diseases* (pp. 152–64). Philadelphia: Lippincott.

Schain, W.S. (1985). Breast-cancer surgeries and psychosexual sequelae: Implications for remediation. *Seminars in Oncology Nursing, 1,* 200–205.

Singer, C.K., & Reznikoff, M.A. (1981). Comparison of the psychological effects of breast-saving procedures with the modified radical mastectomy. *Cancer, 48,* 2341–2346.

Spiegel, D. (1996). Psychological distress and disease course for women with breast cancer: One answer, many questions. *Journal of the National Cancer Institute, 88,* 629–631.

Spiegel, D. (1997). Psychosocial aspect of breast-cancer treatment. *Seminars in Oncology, 24*(Suppl. 1), 36–47.

Urist, J. (1977). The Rorschach test and the assessment of object relations. *Journal of Personality Assessment, 41,* 3–9.

Weiner, I.B. (1994). The Rorschach Inkblot Method (RIM) is not a test: Implications for theory and practice. *Journal of Personality Assessment, 62,* 498–504.

Weiner, I.B. (1996). Some observations on the validity of the Rorschach inkblot method. *Psychological Assessment, 8,* 206–213.

Weiner, I.B. (1997). Current status of the Rorschach Inkblot Method. *Journal of Personality Assessment, 65,* 5–19.

Wellish, D.K., Di Matteo, R., Silverstein, M., Landswerk, J., Hoffman, R., & Waisman, J. (1989). Psychosocial outcomes of breast-cancer therapies: Lumpectomy versus mastectomy. *Psychosomatics, 30,* 365–367.

Young, Mc., & Caughan, Y. (1996). Sexual functioning in women with breast cancer after treatment with adjuvant therapies. *Cancer Nursing, 19,* 308–319.

Summary

Background. The psychological discomfort associated to breast-cancer diagnosis and related treatments is universally recognized. However homogeneous modalities of intervention are lacking. The questionnaires are the most employed tools to analyze pre-morbidity personality traits and the quality of life of cancer patients, but they lack valid indicators of the patients' overall quality of life. On the other hand, counseling along with administered psychological tests allows listening and mutual relationship between patient and examiner. The aim of this study was to evaluate the impact of the Rorschach test, a multidimensional method of collecting data on personality functioning, as an instrument to assess mood disorders, object relation, self-image and quality of life in breast cancer patients. *Methods.* 135 consecutive women affected by operable breast cancer underwent psychological counseling and the Rorschach test within 2–4 weeks after surgery. Results of the test were interpreted according to the structural and experiential approaches. The discrimination between "compact" and "noncompact" tables makes it possible to study the changes of patients identity during the illness, while the Experienced Stimulation and Experience Actual indices, providing information about the patient's coping to therapeutic approach, were calculated according to the Exner system. The records from a sample of 60 healthy women, equally distributed in three age groups (< 50, 50–59, > 60) coming from the same Italian region (regional sample) and the results from 736 nonpatient Italian subjects (national sample) were used as controls. *Results.* Quantitative results were comparable within groups, except for parameters of cognitive characteristics regulating the approach to reality (G, G+, F+, Anat, Ban). No patient fulfilled the parameter configuration corresponding to depressive disorder, but alexithymia with a state reaction interpreted as an adjustment disorder with depressive mood was recorded. This trait was correlated with lower educational levels and increasing age.

Résumé

Contexte. L'inconfort psychologique associé au diagnostic du cancer du sein et à son traitement est universellement connu. On ne connaît toutefois pas de modalités d'intervention homogènes. Les questionnaires sont les outils les plus fréquemment utilisés pour analyser les traits de la personnalité prémorbide et la qualité de vie des patients cancéreux, mais ils n'ont pas d'indicateurs valides de la qualité de vie générale du patient. On sait par ailleurs que l'activité de conseil ainsi que l'administration de tests psychologiques permettent une relation d'écoute et une relation mutuelle entre le patient et l'examinateur. Le but de cette étude est d'évaluer l'impact du test de Rorschach, une méthode multi-dimensionnelle de recueillir des données sur le fonctionnement de la personnalité, pour évaluer les troubles de l'humeur, la relation d'objet, l'image de soi et la qualité de vie de patientes atteintes de cancer du sein. *Méthode.* 135 patientes consécutives souffrant d'un cancer du sein opérable ont reçu des conseils psychologiques et ont passé le Rorschach de 2 à 4 semaines après l'opération. Les résultats du test ont été interprétés selon l'approche structurale et phénoménologique. L'opposition des planches «compactes» et «non compactes» permet d'étudier les changements dans l'identité des patientes pendant leur maladie, tandis que les variables Stimulation ressentie (es) et Ressources actualisées (EA), qui procurent des informations sur l'ajustement (coping) des patientes à l'approche thérapeutique, sont empruntés au système d'Exner. Les groupes contrôles utilisés sont un échantillon de 60 femmes en bonne santé, réparties également en trois groupes d'âge (< 50, 50–59, > 60) et provenant de la même région d'Italie, ainsi que l'échantillon national de 736 adultes italiens non consultants. *Résultats.* Les résultats quantitatifs étaient comparables d'un groupe à l'autre, à l'exception des variables cognitives qui concernent l'approche de la réalité (G, G+, F+, Anat, Ban). Aucune patiente ne présentait une configuration dépressive, mais on a trouvé des indicateurs d'alexithymie réactionnelle que nous avons interprétée comme un trouble d'ajustement avec humeur dépressive. Cette caractéristique était corrélée avec les bas niveaux d'étude et l'augmentation de l'âge.

Resumen

Antecedentes. El malestar psicológico asociado al diagnóstico de cáncer de mama y a los tratamientos que lo acompañan es reconocido universalmente, sin embargo, aún no existen modalidades de intervención homogéneas. Los cuestionarios son las herramientas más utilizadas para analizar los rasgos de la personalidad premórbida y la calidad de vida de los pacientes con cáncer, pero faltan indicadores de la calidad de vida global del paciente. Por otro lado, la asesoría psicológica durante la administración de tests permite establecer una escucha y una relación mutua entre paciente y examinador. El objetivo de este estudio fue el de valorar el impacto del test de Rorschach, un método multidimensional de recopilación de datos sobre el funcionamiento de la personalidad y un instrumento para evaluar trastornos del estado de ánimo, relaciones objetales, autoimagen y calidad de vida en pacientes con cáncer de mama. *Método.* 135 mujeres afectadas por cáncer de mama operable se sometieron a un proceso de asesoramiento y se les administró el test de Rorschach 2–3 semanas después de la cirugía. Los datos del test se interpretaron según el enfoque estructural y experiencial. La discriminación entre tablas "compactas" y "no compactas" permitió estudiar los cambios de identidad de las pacientes durante la enfermedad y los índices de Experiencia Estimular y Experiencia Actual, calculados según los criterios del Sistema Comprehensivo de Exner, aportaron información sobre las estrategias de afrontamiento del paciente hacia el enfoque terapéutico. Se utilizaron como controles los protocolos de 60 mujeres no pacientes igualmente distribuidas en tres grupos de edad (< 50, 50–59, > 60) y procedentes de la misma región de Italia (muestra regional) y los resultados de 736 no pacientes italianos (muestra nacional). *Resultados.* Los resultados cuantitativos fueron semejantes entre los grupos, excepto en los parámetros de las características cognitivas que regulan la aproximación a la realidad (G, G+, F+, Anat, Ban). Ninguna paciente cumplía los criterios que configuran el trastorno depresivo, pero aparecía alexitimia como estado reactivo interpretada como un trastorno adaptativo con humor depresivo. Este rasgo correlacionaba con un nivel educativo más bajo y con una edad mayor.

Riassunto

E'universalmente riconosciuto come la diagnosi di tumore al seno e i trattamenti ad esso correlato siano fonte di disagio psicologico. Molte sono le modalità di intervento per evidenziare tale vissuto. I questionari sono stati e continuano ad essere gli strumenti più utilizzati per analizzare i tratti di personalità (premorbosa) e valutare la qualità di vita dei pazienti neoplastici, tuttavia risulta spesso che il paziente si senta inibito di fronte alla formulazione degli item. Il fattore "comprensione" è inoltre determinante nell'attendibilità dello strumento. D'altro lato il counseling promosso anche dall'utilizzo dei test psicologici è un "pretesto" per promuovere una valida relazione tra paziente ed esaminatore. Lo scopo dello studio è stato quello di valutare l'utilizzo del test di Rorschach come strumento atto a raccogliere dati sulle caratteristiche di personalità, valutare l'entità dei disturbi dell'umore, le relazioni oggettuali, l'immagine di sé e la qualità di vita nei pazienti affetti da cancro alla mammella. *Metodologia.* 135 donne prese consecutivamente, affette da cancro alla mammella operabile, sottoposte a counseling psicologico e test di Rorschach entro 2–4 settimane dopo l'operazione chirurgica. I dati del test sono stati analizzati secondo il metodo classico e secondo il criterio del Sistema Comprensivo di Exner, interpretati secondo l'approccio strutturale ed esprerienziale. La differenza tra tavole "compatte" e "noncompatte" hanno reso possibile lo studio dei cambiamenti dell'identità dei pazienti nel corso della malattia, mentre gli indici dell'Experienced Stimulation e Experience Actual, calcolati secondo il metodo di Exner, hanno consentito di avere informazioni sul coping all'eventuale approccio terapeutico. I risultati di un campione di 60 giovani donne sane, egualmente distribuite in 3 gruppi di età (< 50, 50–59, > 60) provenienti dalla stessa regione d'Italia (campione regionale) e i risultati di 736 soggetti Italiani nella norma (campione nazionale) sono stati usati come gruppo di controllo. *Risultati.* Quantitativamente i risultati sono equamente distribuiti tra i gruppi, eccezione fatta per gli indici cognitivi che regolando l'approccio alla realtà (G, G+, F+, Anat, Ban). Nessun paziente ha mostrato un disordine depressivo conclamato, tuttavia si è osservata prevalentemente una configurazione alexitimica con reattività interpretabile come un disturbo del tono dell'umore con aspetti emotivi misti. Tale risposta è parsa correlata ad un basso livello scolastico e al tempo stesso ad un aumento dell'età.

Rorschachiana 27, 139–163

The Rorschach and the TAT as Relational Instruments: Evaluating Young Couples with Consensus Rorschach and TAT*

Dorit Noy-Sharav

Senior Clinical Psychologist and Supervisor, now in private practice, Jerusalem, Israel

The sociologists Berger and Kellner (1964) write about marriage as "A dramatic act in which two strangers meet and redefine themselves." Each of them comes with his or her own autobiography, each brings both conscious and unconscious expectations to a relationship, and each has his or her own way of interpreting reality. One can say that creating an intimate marriage relationship entails realigning two individual definitions of reality. Maggie Scarf, in her book *Intimate Partners* (1987), calls this process "creating a couple script, in which the inner script of each partner about himself and about intimate relations undergoes scrutiny and rewriting." Sometimes this process is reasonably successful. However, often the process entails misunderstandings, disappointments, and power struggles, and sometimes it arouses bitter conflicts. The main struggle in the premarital or early marital stage evolves around the main themes in the new script that they create together. If the couple cannot agree about the main themes of their common reality, their couple dialog will stall, as they will feel misunderstood, of different worlds, will grow apart, and probably separate.

This formulation seemed to me very apt to convey the special features of my approach to the use of the Consensus Rorschach and Consensus TAT, as it requires couples to reach agreements about each card of the Rorschach and TAT. In the first phase, the individual phase of the method, each spouse's task is to construct for the examiner his

---

* Earlier versions of this article were presented at the IRS Congress in Amsterdam, July 1999, and as part of a panel led by Prof. Stephen Finn on *Innovative Uses of the Rorschach* at the IRS Congress in Rome, September 2002.

unique interpretation of reality. We are not talking here of simple perception of an objective piece of reality (if there is such a thing); as the Rorschach – and to a lesser degree the TAT – are loosely structured situations, i.e., projective tests, there is much leeway for personal interpretation. Through the Rorschach protocol, the enquiry, and the structural summary we gradually formulate a dynamic picture of each spouse's personality. The interaction phase that follows often comes as a surprise to spouses. Suddenly they are confronted with the fact that the other perceives things differently. Some of them, who are unaware that this is not a simple task of identifying correctly whether the card depicts a "bat" or a "spaceship," become perplexed and even seriously question their partner's or their own reality testing or commonsense. Said one client, after hearing his wife on Card VII, "How can you see here a woman's dress? This is more an elephant's dress!" Others, who are more sophisticated, and realize that an interpretation is involved, still become chagrined, or bewildered by the implication of these differences in the way they perceive reality. If they have widely divergent "scripts," does it not raise doubts about their compatibility? Let me quote from one protocol of a man who expresses himself with much feeling. When listening to his wife on Card I, he exclaimed: "God help us! No agreement! Married 20 years and we do not see the same thing!" Each disagreement increased this man's despair – "Again no agreement! Soon we will be exchanging blows!" When they reach a card where they can easily agree, his relief is tangible – "Hurray! Agreement! Thank heaven, there is hope for us yet!"

Of course, not every couple reacts with such distress. There are other reaction patterns, and several styles may be observed. One couple, for instance, found it necessary to emphasize on the first card that each of them has his unique perception of the situation, and they made no effort to search for agreement or compromise. However, once this foundation of *the legitimacy for each of them to maintain their own view* was laid and accepted, they could be quite flexible on the following cards, and discover various ways of reaching agreements. Another pattern was observed in a couple where the man was rigid and became defensive when his wife perceived the stimulus differently. His wife, however, adopted a different attitude – she enjoyed the differences, regarding his ideas as a welcome surprise. "Oh! Really? I did not think of turning the card upside down! Indeed we can see here two dancers; here are their feet and shoes." For this woman, her husband's different perceptions served as an opportunity for new and creative ideas, and she had no problem accepting his responses and adding them to her own. These different reactions point to important factors of personality. For example, we can predict that a person with a secure and cohesive sense of self will be less threatened by differences in perception, while an insecure person will feel endangered and, therefore, become defensive. However the differences also reflect the personal, partly unconscious "script" each partner carries in his or her mind about the ideal, or acceptable, couple relationship.

As we, the examiners, observe this process and record it, we have the opportunity to follow, on live show, how the spouses struggle to create their combined script, and this script is later depicted in the couple's structural summary, in their Interaction scores, and in the stories they create together on the TAT.

I will now recount how this evaluation procedure was constructed, then describe the procedure in detail, and finally present an example of a couple that had been referred for evaluation in the stage of vacillation about getting married.

Couple Evaluation

When evaluating a couple, we seek to grasp and conceptualize each spouse's personality as well as the dynamics of the relationship, in a way that will assist us in making decisions about the couple. The decision may be for selection purposes, such as screening couples who apply for special assignments, or for admission to a small community (in Israel – to a Kibbutz or Moshav), or couples wishing to adopt a child. Decisions may also be for clinical purposes – usually in the preliminary stages of couple therapy. There we need to diagnose the type and level of psychopathology of each partner, the areas of early wounding; to identify underlying conflict areas in the couple, where each partner's needs and defenses clash with or challenge the other's defensive armor and touch his early wounds. Depending upon the theory we adhere to about personal development and couple dynamics, we can also look for the degree of enmeshment, estrangement, collusion, or power struggles. A good evaluation also helps us in identifying positive resources – what keeps the spouses together, what is their potential for growth and for change, their ability of mutual support during crisis, etc.

Most traditional test instruments have been geared toward individual evaluation. In recent decades there have appeared numerous techniques and tools for assessing couples and families, following the growing interest in couple and family dynamics and in couple and family therapy. Each technique has its own advantages as well as its own shortcomings. There are several good surveys of the literature on this subject, and I refer interested readers to the following references: Wilkinson, 1987; Jacob and Tennenbaum, 1988; Cromwell, Olson, and Fournier, 1976.

When I tried to choose or construct my own battery, in the 1970s, I used my experience with couples as well as the suggestions of several good surveyors, such as Cromwell, Olson and Fournier (1976). Following the authors' suggestions I aimed for a procedure that would use both objective and subjective measures, combine outside observation with self-report, and respect the complexity of the individual as well as the relational dynamics. I was also interested in an instrument that would enable the examiner to observe the couple *in vivo* - that is - not just at one point in time, using one-time observation or a written declaration of attitudes about the spouse or the marriage, as is found in many marital questionnaires (for example: Olson's FACES, 1983). When I discovered the Consensus Rorschach, which originated in the work of Singer (1968), Blanchard (1968), Willi (1969) and several others in the late 1960s, I was fascinated by its possibilities, and started experimenting with couples in the psychiatric clinic where I had been working at the time. Another incentive had been the assignment to assess couples applying to the Israeli Adoption Services. I decided to add a Consensus TAT to the Consensus Rorschach, so as to get a different perspective on couple interaction.

To my mind, using well-known and long-established tests such as the Rorschach and TAT as a basis has additional assets, as it enables us to utilize the accumulated research literature and the accumulated experience of numerous clinicians. A recent comprehensive review of the literature can be found in Leonard Handler's chapter on the Consensus Rorschach (in Meloy, Acklin, Gacono, Murray et al., 1997).

Description of the Evaluation Procedure (cf. Table 1)

The procedure consists of two stages: The individual stage, and the couple stage.

The individual stage includes:

1. Clinical interview;
2. Two subtests of the WAIS R – Comprehension and Block Design (Wechsler, 1958);
3. A full Rorschach, administered and scored according to the Comprehensive System (Exner, 1993); and
4. 4–5 TAT pictures, usually numbers 1,2, 3BM, 4, and 13 MF.

The material from the individual stage is analyzed and used to construct a personality interpretation for each partner, using both formal scores and analysis of content, narrative, and defenses (Aronow, Reznikoff, & Moreland, 1995).

Table 1. Structure of the evaluation procedure.

Individual Stage. Aim: Assessment of each spouse's individual personality		
A.	Clinical interview	Biography, family relations in past and present, questions pertaining to the specific purpose of assessment
B.	Tests	**Comprehension subtest** (WAIS-R) – Assessing intellectual functioning, verbal expression, understanding of social situations, attitude toward social norms.
		Block design subtest (WAIS-R) – intellectual functioning, observation of problem solving style, of ability to work under pressure, persistence.
		Rorschach (10 cards) A dynamic personality assessment.
		T.A.T. (partial, 4–5 pictures) A dynamic personality assessment. Important themes
Couple Stage. Aim: Assessment of the couple relationship		
A.	Consensus Rorschach	Discussion between spouses of each card, attempt to reach agreement, *writing down* (notation of) agreed responses.
B.	Consensus T.A.T.	Discussion between spouses of several T.A.T. cards, writing agreed story for each card.
C.	Short Couple Interview	Patterns of everyday relations, main topics of fights and arguments, specific attitudes.

The couple stage includes:

1. Consensus Rorschach,
2. consensus TAT, and
3. short couple interview.

The procedure for the Consensus Rorschach I use is as follows: The couple is sitting with the examiner. Cards are presented consecutively. The couple are instructed to discuss each picture and to try and reach an agreement about one or more responses acceptable to both. If an agreement is reached, each writes down the response on a separate sheet. Then they delineate the response on a common location sheet. If no agreement is reached, they write down "no agreement" and move on to the next card. The examiner's inquiry at this stage is minimal, so as not to interfere with the couple interaction. (This has certain implications for analyzing the consensus responses, which at times have to rely upon the examiner's judgment.)

The procedure for the Consensus TAT I use is as follows: 3–4 of the pictures that were presented individually are now presented to the couple, consecutively, and they are asked to construct a story about the picture that they both agree upon. One or more new pictures, not presented before, may now be added. One spouse (decided upon by the couple) writes down the agreed upon story. The whole dialog is tape-recorded.

The examiner is present as an observer, he/she does not press for agreements. S/he merely notes the patterns of interaction such as – Who volunteers or is elected to write the story, who presses for agreement, are agreements reached easily or after long and bitter arguments. We assume that the motivation to reach agreement depends on the couple dynamics – is it important for them to cooperate and agree on everything, or can they endure conflict and difference of opinion? Are they flexible and open to receive new perceptions and ideas from the partner, or are they rigid, threatened by different perceptions, and unable to make a shift? Do they fight obstinately about autonomy, control, or power, or do they tend to give in or compromise? Is the giving in done with a sense of respect for self and other, or with a sense of being defeated in a power struggle, or of being engulfed and overwhelmed?

Scoring

There exist in the literature a few systems for scoring the consensus responses, the most exhaustive being Margaret Singer's (1968) that had mainly been used with families of schizophrenics. I developed a system that was inspired by Roman and Bowman's work with couples Intelligence tests (Bauman, Roman, Borello, Melzer, et al., 1967), and is more suited to evaluate the relational styles of ordinary couples.

The scoring system: Each agreed response is first scored according to the Comprehensive System (Exner, 1993). So in the end we have a "Couple Structural Summary" that can be compared to the individual structural summaries. Then each response gets an Interaction score (Table 2).

This score indicates whether it is a response that was originally common to both partners - scored Former Agreement (F.A.); or originally seen by the wife or husband - scored Dominance Wife, or Dominance Husband (D.W., or D.H.); or whether both contributed elements to the agreed response - scored Combination (COM.). For example - H. saw missile, W. saw campfire, and the agreed response was - "missile with fire coming out of it."

New responses created during the interaction are scored Creation Husband (Cr.H) or Creation Wife (Cr.W.), or if created by ideas from both - Creation Couple (Cr.Co).

Pseudo Agreement (Pse.Ag) is a kind of "as if" agreement in which the couple pretends or seems to agree, but covertly each keeps his own perception. This is often exposed when the couple delineates the responses on the location sheet. When no agreement is reached after discussion, No Agreement (N.Ag) is scored for the card.

Table 2. Interaction scores.

F.A.	Former agreement	Response originally present in both records
D.H.	Dominance husband	Response originally present in husband's record
D.W.	Dominance wife	Response originally present wife's record
COM.	Combination	Response combining elements of both original records
Cr.H.	Creation husband	New response suggested by husband
Cr.W.	Creation wife	New response suggested by wife
Cr.Co.	Creation couple	New response created by couple interaction
Ps.Ag.	Pseudo-agreement	Response verbally agreed, but the written record shows differences
No Ag.	No agreement	A card where no agreement has been reached

The consensus stories of the TAT are analyzed according to the same principles, but no formal scoring is given. The examiner notes the process, notes whether important themes given individually disappear from the couple stories, etc. (Cramer, 1996, Ch. 4).

In the end the examiner has available: the tape-recorded interactions and his notes, the three structural summaries, and the Interaction scores, which serve as a " snapshot" of the relational style.

An extensive description of this procedure with clinical examples was published in English in E. Hibbs (Ed.), *Adoption, International Perspectives* (Sharav, 1991) and in Hebrew (English summary) in the *Society and Welfare Journal* (Noy-Sharav, 1995).

After analyzing the material, the couple is invited for a feedback session in which the main findings (results) are shared with the couple – individually and/or with both together, as suits the purpose of the evaluation and the couple's wishes (Finn, 1996). Relevant hypotheses about the couple dynamics are discussed and modified according to additional material that emerges. A written report is then available to the therapist or to the referring agency to help in planning therapy or in reaching decisions about the couple.

To summarize: The procedure is characterized by:

1. A combination of individual and couple evaluation,
2. A combination of several dimensions and perspectives, and
3. A lucid representation of the process of interaction.

Case Presentation – to Marry or Not to Marry?*

Irit and Ami are an unmarried couple in a stage of courtship. They are 32 years old, single, coming from religious families, though not very orthodox ones. They were referred by a therapist with whom Irit has been in psychotherapy for the preceding 10 months.

I was informed that they have been in contact on and off for 2 years, but cannot make a decision about marriage. Ami was the more committed one, but since Irit had cut off relations two times already, he also has some reservations. Irit has entered therapy in an effort to better under-

* Names and identifying information have been changed to insure privacy.

stand her inner block to getting married. The testing was suggested in order to get a clearer picture of the sources of difficulty in each partner's personality and in the relationship, possibly helping them to remove obstacles on the road to the consolidation of their relationship. I would like to mention that this was an unusual referral for me. Usually couple evaluations I do are either for couples in conflict, who seek marriage therapy, or couples that need an assessment in order to become adoptive parents. So this evaluation offered a special challenge.

Irit, 32, has a Masters degree and holds an executive job in a publishing firm. Her appearance is well groomed; she is becomingly dressed in a religious-style outfit. She appears serious, but there is a liveliness and even a mischievous look in her eyes.

Background (from the interview): Irit is the youngest of three sisters. Her parents, now in their sixties, are of middle class, European origin, the mother a holocaust survivor. She describes a sad home, both parents very reserved and unexpressive emotionally. The mother is depicted as anxious and worrying, and both parents as very critical, with high expectations for Irit and her elder sisters. Irit has always been a good student, took part in many activities, but had no real close friends. She says: Everyone is my pal, but no one is really close. There was much rivalry and jealousy between the sisters, and the other two were not academically inclined and are by now married and mothers of children. She finds it hard to characterize the relationship between her parents. She does not remember acts of affection, and there were often arguments and fights, but they stayed together and to this date do everything jointly.

Since age 19 Irit dated often, but relationships did not lead to marriage. (The reader must realize that in religious families like hers, dating is usually arranged and purposeful. No lengthy, "boyfriend" relationships are expected, and no sexual contact before marriage.) Irit is aware that she fears marriage, and has difficulty in creating and maintaining an emotional relationship. She sometimes has made an effort to prolong a relationship, but sooner or later she was the one to cut off contact on one pretext or another. About Ami she says she feels attracted and more deeply attached to him, but is unsure whether she loves him. She worries about his being of a working class, North African background, which may influence his view of the woman's role, and is also fearful of engulfment by his large extended family, who usually embrace her warmly. She is also anxious about some of his character traits – says he is obstinate

Table 3. Rorschach data.

	Rorschach		
	Woman (Irit)	Man (Ami)	Couple
R	29	20	34
W	5	4 (DW 1)	6
D	21	14	24
Dd	3	1	2
S	1	1	0
EB	10:5	2:2	7:1
EA	15	4	8
Eb	9:3	9:3	4:2
es	12	12	6
X+%	59	50	61
Xu%	34	20	29
x-%	6.9	30	8.8
F%	31	10	56
Lambda	0.45	0.11	1.26
P	7	4 (barely)	5
D	+1	–3	
Adj.D	+3	–3	
FC: CF + C	2:4	4:0	2:0
H: (H)	6:3	0:2	3:3
Hd: (Hd)	0:0	0:0	2:0
An.	0	2	5
Sex	1	0	0
Fire	4	0	1
AG.	10	1	3
COP	3	0	1?
SUM6	2	2	0
CDI	0	4	1
PTI	0	1	0

Wechsler scaled scores Comprehension: Irit: 15 Ami: 10

and persuasive – apparently she fears being dominated and losing power. She also mentions he is highly emotional, and this for her is both attractive and repulsive. When asked how she visualizes her future marriage, she states she imagines a very calm home, with cooperation, love, and affection, where shows of emotion are permitted, and her need to follow her career is respected.

Irit's test showed high intellectual ability (Comprehension scaled score 15). But in spite of superior endowment and high academic achievements she is shy, insecure about her ability, and reticent about speaking or acting assertively. When asked how she would find her way out if lost in a forest she says: "I would not have found my way out. My navigation is bad. Perhaps by chance, intuitively." In other situations where assertiveness is called for her timidity holds her back although she is well aware what needs to be done. These inhibitions probably made her search for a confident, assertive man who can be counted upon. This choice, however, threatens to create dependence, a tendency that is in conflict with her need to be independent and in control.

Irit's projective tests are rich in ideas, emotional expression, and creative fantasy, though she keeps complaining she has no imagination. On the TAT there is much "press," pressure from outside, while inner needs are not fulfilled and have little legitimacy. The little boy in Card I has to give up his beloved violin. The young girl in Card II is not allowed to follow her inclinations, while a strong, controlling mother "keeps an open eye, so that everything that has to be done will be done. There is no joy. They will go on like this for the next 50 years." A certain need to rebel is expressed, with a hope of fulfilling her ambitions, but it is not prominent: "Maybe the girl will rebel and go work on the fields too, etc."

In contrast, on the less structured Rorschach test, the pressure of inner needs and drives is predominant (EB 10:5 eb 9:3). She seems to experience some loss of control, but a certain joy at being "unruly" is also conveyed, even at the expense of perceptual accuracy, with many responses scored "unusual" (Xu% 34, see Table 3). She does exert intellectual defenses, and has a sufficient ability to perceive the conventional (X+% 59, 7 P), but there are many unconventional responses.

There is a host of aggressive content (AG = 10) for example "Two fire creatures sending flames or fingernails toward each other," and "A missile launcher with smoke and fire" (Card IX). Threatening figures appear, the male or father figure "A threatening giant, he intends to trample someone," (Card IV, W) and male sexuality is also felt as frightening "A threatening creature with teeth." (D1 on Card IV). So it can be inferred that she is scared of the male's power and his sexuality. It is not always clear who it is that Irit identifies with; sometimes she is cowed by outside aggression, at other times she seems to identify with the aggressor, in a rebellious, playful manner: "War dances, kind of nice" (Card X); "girls fighting, with hate and envy, their hair sticking out" (Card VII). We must remember that she is in the process of dynamic psychotherapy so some defenses are probably relaxed, while formerly inhibited emotions and drives gain a certain amount of expression. Sexuality, however, still seems suppressed, and arouses anxiety, probably as a result of her religious upbringing and the lack of sensuality in the perceived relation between her parents.

As we know, Irit is struggling with the decision to commit herself to Ami. As a result of therapy she has become more aware of her inner inhibitions. Her response to Card II reflects both the yearning for contact and the inner barrier that is projected outward:

"Two are sitting opposite each other. They join hands, but there is a glass wall between them. They want very much to touch each other, but do not succeed." Later in the response and inquiry criminal associations surface – "A stocking on their face, perhaps they are prisoners, perhaps a glass wall between prisoner and visitor, and the red hats remind me of those condemned to death." It seems that on a semiconscious level she fears marriage will be a prison, with no exit; perhaps even a death sentence to parts of her self?

Taking into account the high level of aggression, it dawned upon me that although consciously Irit fears being dominated and overpowered by the man, on a deeper, less conscious level she is afraid of her own burning impulses, her destructive aggression, which may bring retaliation or destroy the man and the relationship. It seems that these anxieties are not specifically connected to Ami's person, and would probably reappear in every relationship with a man. In therapy these fears and inhibitions can loosen up, by learning to accept her inner impulses, and to differentiate between destructive fantasies and their realization in actuality.

Ami, 32, an informally dressed young man wearing a Kippa and small beard, looks uncomfortable.

Background, from the interview: Unlike Irit he grew up in a small village where educational opportunities were limited. His parents, Tunisian immigrants with little formal education, have worked all their life in menial jobs, and are now retired. He describes his father as very popular among his friends, but quiet and reserved at home, and Ami feels him to be remote. The mother he describes as warm and loving, and Ami has always been very attached to her. Even now he shares confidences with her and consults her. The relationship between the parents he perceives as one sided: the mother is giving and caring, while the father is not appreciative of her.

As a child Ami was obedient and studious, his parents counted on him, and he was "a key boy" (an expression used for children who own a key to the home and take care of themselves while the parents are at work.). The parents did not encourage higher education, but Ami was always interested in studies and spiritual development, and has found his way to a combination of military service and Yeshiva high education. There he encountered a stimulating environment that inspired his intellectual development. He is at present a graduate student and also a teacher. He is also artistically endowed and plays several instruments.

In the interview Ami is unaware of, and even uses denial about, why he has not yet married. He claims that he had dated several girls, but has not felt the closeness and depth of feelings he expected; there was no "click," and he was usually the one to sever contacts. Irit is the first woman he has felt deeply about, sensed that she was meant for him, and the first one he has talked about with his mother. When she let him know there was no option of a serious relationship he moved away. When they renewed contact upon mutual will, he was enthusiastic, as he admires her intelligence, and her chastity, which is rare among women nowadays. But her repeated wavering arouses his own misgivings. Ami is sure Irit will get along fine with his family, that she needs the warmth and generosity his mother will offer her.

Test Interpretation (cf. Table 3)

Ami was anxious and tense about the tests, and felt as if he was on probation. Although as examiner I tried to alleviate his fears, they still affected his functioning, both on intelligence and on projective tests.

It was difficult to assess his intellectual potential. We have to take into consideration his tension as well as his impoverished educational and cultural background. Because of his tension he misunderstood some Comprehension questions (scaled score 10) and offered tangential responses. There was also a tendency to lose distance and respond in a personal way. For example – "As an electrician I would first disconnect electricity." In other instances he tends to use idioms and quotations from the scriptures, in the style of a teacher, though not always in an adequate sense. In contrast to Irit, Ami is active, resourceful, willing to take initiative and responsibility. For example: On the question about fire in the movies he says: "I will take care to save people, help those who have been hurt by smoke and fire." On a deeper level, as shown on projective tests, there are also expressions of insecurity, and of feeling suspended, in waiting, unable to act.

His production on the Rorschach is restricted (R15). Perceptual accuracy and reality testing are low, below the normal range (X+% = 50), his ability to perceive the popular contents is also low (3–4 Populars that are not definitive) and there are few Human percepts. Again it is difficult to decide to what extent this pattern is the result of anxiety, initial test "shock" as well as other "shock" signs to color and dark blots, and to what extent they point to a character pattern with deeper personality disturbance. However, although there are too many minuses (X–% 30) there are no serious signs of psychotic thinking (Low sum special scores, low PTI). The combination of low ability to deal with stress (D = –3, Adj. D = –3) and a relatively high Coping Deficit Index (CDI = 4) point to a vulnerable personality structure, that might cave in under prolonged stress.

On the TAT, there is little expression of instinctual drives, and aggression is suppressed, sublimated, and even denied, with some use of reaction formation. He tends to identify with the role of "medic" – one who helps and saves others, or teaches and guides (TAT 8BM, see also Comprehension). In contrast to this identification, which he materializes in his social life and his occupation as teacher, there are many signs of immaturity in his fantasy life (A% = 55, FM = 9) and ungratified needs seem to interfere with attention and concentration.

His TAT stories show strong dependency needs, with craving for a supportive, formative father figure that will serve as subject for identification and idealization, and he still depends on an understanding, empathetic mother figure for advice, warmth, and support. For example, the boy on Card I remembers a deceased family member who used to play the violin, he misses him, and wishes he could play like him. He then shares his feelings with his mother.

It appears that Ami's self-image is at present insecure and dependent. While Irit's male image on Rorschach Card IV is huge, threatening, and destructive, Ami sees on this card "a creature standing on a strange object, wretched hands, feet in the air." On most stories, the protagonist – the boy on TAT 1, the young man on 6 BM and on 7 BM – is passive, tense, while help comes from outside. For example the grandmother (6BM) "will say the situation is not so bad, you can get out of it, she will encourage him." Ami also harbors an inner ideal self that is expressed for example on Card XVIIBM: "A strong, muscular man, very active person, who tries to climb the rope with all his might, and demonstrates his prowess"; but even here some misgivings peep through: "What will be the next step? I hope he will not fall down."

In several stories there is a recurring motive of loss and mourning over a close meaningful person (Upon inquiry he tells of the death of a dear friend and teacher in an accident not long ago). It seems that the present state of being uncertain of Irit's love and commitment affects his mood and his self-image. He feels in a waiting position, suspended in the air.

To summarize: He is a man who yearns for attachment and warm feelings from a motherly female figure, and is in need of guidance from a fatherly figure (his actual father has not served as a supportive role model for him in the past). Both Irit and Ami share a similar need for warmth, support, and reassurance against insecurity, though they have different ways of expressing these needs, and different ways of camouflaging them.

Irit and Ami as a Couple

On the interaction test the atmosphere is somewhat tense, but soon becomes more playful. Humorous remarks to and fro and meaningful coy glances coming from Irit, transmit a clear sense of a couple in passionate courtship, though of course as a religious couple there is no physical contact.

Irit and Ami are highly motivated for the task of creating the couple script. Each of them expresses confidence in the other, but also some apprehension. Ami says jokingly "two are better than one."

Their individual protocols were very different, so the task was not easy (there were only 2 Former Agreements), and they needed long discussions in order to clarify their ideas and to negotiate. We must remember that they are still in the initial stage of adjusting their individual "scripts." Yet they managed to reach 34 agreements(!) which is very high by any standard (see Table 4). It shows their high motivation as well as their ability to work together. Sometimes the agreement was only superficial, while each covertly held on to his initial view (3 Pseudo Agreements, mainly on Card IV, the male image).

The interaction also uncovered the gap in their cultural background. Irit's associations often refer to citations from poetry, and Ami has difficulty following her. He tries to counter with quotations from religious scripts. The final "product" was quite balanced as far as power and dominance are concerned (12 D.H. + Cr.H., versus 12 D.W. – see Table 4), and there were some Combinations and some Couple Creations that re-

Table 4. Irit and Ami interaction scores.

F.A.	Former agreement	2
D.H.	Dominance husband	9
D.W.	Dominance wife	12
Cr. H.	Creation husband	3
Cr.W.	Creation wife	0
COM.	Combination	3
Cr.Co.	Creation couple	2
Ps.Ag.	Pseudo-agreement	3
No Ag.	No agreement	0
Total number of agreements		34

flect an ability to cooperate and be creative together. However, the difficulty to bridge over differences, as well as Ami's restricted attitude led to consensus responses that were "anemic" – emptied of the emotional intensity of the original responses, mainly of Irit's responses (EB, eb). A similar tendency appears on the TAT "product." Irit lets Ami take the role of writing down the stories, the result being short, frugal stories, that fail to do justice to their lively verbal interaction.

Going Back to the Rorschach Structural Summary

Perceptual accuracy and popular content are higher (see Table 3, the couple column) especially when compared to Ami's protocol (X+% = 61, compared to Ami's 50, and Irit's 59; X–% = 8.8 compared to Ami's 30 and Irit's 6.9). So we can conclude that their interaction serves to correct some of the perceptual failures and idiosyncratic interpretations of reality of each spouse.

So far I have focused on *scores* – the Structural Summary and the Interaction Scores. However, many fruitful insights are reached through listening to the process of interaction and negotiation. So let us move on to some examples of the *process*.

Ami is repeatedly surprised by Irit's stormy responses, such as "Two creatures dancing a war dance together." The aggressive content arouses in him a mixture of resistance and fascination. He seems to be attracted and repelled simultaneously by her turbulent fire, while she seems to regard these as a challenge to his imagination, and often refuses to withdraw them or noticeably tone them down. For example on Card VIII Irit saw (among other responses) "An airplane flying skyward, spouting fire"(D + m.CFu). In the interaction stage she adds: "Like on Independence day, colorful smoke and fire." Ami: "Real wild, but interesting." During the discussion Ami says:

"The flames are exaggerated for such a small plane, don't you think?" Irit: "To me it also sounds exaggerated, but what do I care? It is all imaginary." Ami seems to agree, but in this case, the smoke and fire disappeared from the final consensus response.

Moving to TAT 3BM, Ami in his individual story disregarded the object in the left corner (the 'gun'). His story depicted a girl who perhaps had failed in exams, who is sad, crying, and maybe someone will come and try to cheer her up. Irit's individual story started immediately with "There is a gun here" and then she struggled to construct a story around the gun – "Perhaps he mourns someone who had died, or perhaps he tried to save him and failed."

In the relational process, Ami at first tends to accept her story, but when she mentions a gun, he flinches, and refuses to accept it. After long negotiations, they succeed in creating a combined story in which aggression is integrated in a heroic and altruistic plot – the hero had tried to save somebody in a violent incident, but has failed, and, therefore, he is now frustrated and sad. Another example (Rorschach Card II) deals with Irit's blocks to a close relationship:

Ami: "Two bears." Irit: "What? Bears?" Ami shows her some details.
Irit: "Why! You have such an imagination!"(on a popular response!)
Ami: "The bears are *so* connected to each other, there is some stuff that's hard to identify, that unites them. What did *you* see?"
Irit: "Mine is nicer, I think. Two people."
Ami: "Where is the head, the face, something?"
Irit: "With a stocking-like hat on their face."
Ami: "Well, maybe, you see things that are difficult to see."
Irit: "They hold out their hands to each other, but there is a glass wall separating them."
Ami: "Hm, two people I see. A glass wall I do not see."
Irit: "So there is no glass wall?"
Ami: "No, they want to come close to each other."
Irit: "So why don't they come together? That is why we are here"!.

They both laugh and it becomes clear that both understand the link or implication of this response to their problem. Finally they agree on both answers – The popular "two bears," and "2 people," not mentioning the glass wall.

The next example comes from TAT Card I, and deals with dependency needs. Irit's individual story was about a boy who is grieving because his beloved violin is to be taken away, or perhaps he is tired and sad after practicing without success. She associated to a childhood memory, when she used to practice on a borrowed violin, and it had been taken from her. Ami's individual story was about a boy who mourns the memory of a dear relative, a musician.

Interaction: Ami tells his version. Irit: "I wrote about myself, but I like your story better." Ami (flattered): "It is touching, no?" They joke around.

Ami: "So how do we continue? What will he do?"

Irit: "In your scenario? He will start playing the violin, trying to recall the one who has died."

Ami: "Very good! *You uncover how much more independent the boy is*. In my story he goes to tell his mother, tells her how much he misses the one who is gone, misses his music."

Irit: (Jokingly) – "Maybe you would have gone to tell your mother, and I would have gone to play the violin."

Ami: (laughs, embarrassed)

Irit: "Your story is more romantic."

Ami: "Violin tunes accompany the happiness. Yes, I accept your ending of the story. He is a smart boy, profound, he looks mature, don't you think?"

Irit: "You have to see maturity in his eyes and they are closed."

Ami: "My intuition says yes. Though, perhaps he wishes to share his feelings with his mother, will tell her how sad he is feeling."

Irit: "And she will tell him to play and so remember his friend."

So Ami is delegated to write down the approved story, and writes, consulting her with every step, though not always following her suggestions.

The final consensus story: A smart boy is looking intensively at a violin, and is reminded of a friend/acquaintance that had left, and he wishes to remember his music. He goes to his mother to share his feelings, and she advises that he play the violin, thus he will sense the presence of his friend/acquaintance.

The issue of dependence assists our comprehension about what these two young people need from each other. Ami impresses and attracts Irit with his strong, coping, and ambitious personae. But he needs her both as an accepting container of his insecurity and dependency needs, and as support and confirmation of his need to develop and become what he strives for.

Irit needs Ami to accept and even admire her hidden fiery, imaginative qualities. At the same time she could also help *him* loosen his own restraints. A hidden, probably unconscious yearning of hers is that he will help her restore parts of her repressed, lost self – the longed for violin.

The Feedback Session

The feedback session with Irit was geared to alleviate her conscious fears (of Ami's potential aggression), to hint at her deeper fears (of her own destructive impulses), and to arouse her empathy for his needs for support and security.

In Ami's feedback session, he was not open to much interpretation. However he was reassured by hearing that Irit really needs him, and that if he is patient about her hesitance and accepting of her impulsivity there is a good chance that she will work out her remaining fears in therapy, and will stay with the relationship.

From what I heard from the therapist, the couple felt reassured by the process. They took immediate steps such as meetings with both families, and later setting a date for the wedding ceremony. Will the relationship work? Will they live happily ever after? That remains to be seen.

Conclusion

The procedure presented enables the examiner to get a multifaceted, rich picture of each spouse's personality, highlighting inner needs and defenses that affect their ability to create a mutually satisfying "couple script."

Sharing this material with the couple and/or with their therapist serves as a valuable tool for reaching decisions about getting married, separating, or for delineating areas that need to be worked through in individual or couple therapy.

In all probability the article has demonstrated the benefits of using the whole Rorschach, including traditional scoring and structural summary, thereby taking advantage of the accumulated research and clinical experience. However, economical considerations of time and investment sometimes suggest shortening the procedure. The author has sometimes achieved good enough results with using a shortened version of the Rorschach with 4 or 5 cards. Though limited and partial, it does convey the flavor of the couple's unique relational style.

References

Aronow, E., Reznikoff, M., & Moreland, K.L. (1995). The Rorschach: Projective technique or psychometric test? *Journal of Personality Assessment, 64,* 213–228.

Berger, P., & Kellner, H. (1964). Marriage and the construction of reality: On exercise in the microsociology of knowledge. *Diogenes, 46*(Summer), 1–24.

Bauman, G., Roman, M., Borello, J., & Melzer, B. (1967). Interaction testing in the measurement of marital intelligence. *Journal of Abnormal Psychology, 72,* 489–495.

Cramer, P. (1996). *Storytelling, narrative, and the thematic apperception test.* New York, London: Guilford.

Cromwell, R.E., Olson, D.H.L., & Fournier, D.G. (1976). Tools and techniques for diagnosis and evaluation in marital and family therapy. *Family Process, 15,* 1–49.

Exner, J.E., Jr. (1993). *The Rorschach: A comprehensive system. Vol. 1: Basic foundations* (3d ed.). New York: Wiley.

Finn, S.E. (1996). Assessment feedback integrating MMPI-2 and Rorschach findings. *Journal of Personality Assessment, 67*, 543–557.

Jacob, T., & Tennenbaum, D. (1988). *Family assessment, rationale, methods, and future directions.* New York & London: Plenum.

Meloy, J.R., Acklin, M.W., Gacono, C.B., Murray, J.F., & Peterson, C.A. (Eds.). (1997). *Contemporary Rorschach interpretation.* Mahwah, NJ: Erlbaum.

Noy-Sharav, D. (1995). Assessment of couples wishing to adopt a child. *Society and Welfare, 15,* 65–88. (In Hebrew, English abstract).

Olson, D.H., Russel, C.S., & Sprenkle, D.H. (1983). Circumplex model VI: Theoretical updatc. *Family Process, 22,* 69–83.

Scarf, M. (1987). *Intimate partners. Patterns in love and marriage.* Ch. 1, pp. 41–53. New York: Random House.

Sharav, D. (1991). Assessing adoptive parents using a combined individual and interaction procedure. In E.D. Hibbs (Ed.), *Adoption, international perspectives* (ch. 7, pp. 73–90). Madison, CT: International Universities Press.

Singer, M.T. (1968). The consensus Rorschach and family transactions. *Projective Techniques, 32,* 348–353.

Wechsler, D. (1958). *The measurement and appraisal of adult intelligence.* (Fourth edition). Baltimore: Williams & Wilkins.

Wilkinson, Y. (1987). Family assessment: A review. *Journal of Family Therapy, 9,* 367–380.

Summary

The paper presents a procedure for evaluating couples for clinical as well as for screening purposes such as assessing couples for therapy or for adoptive parenting.

The procedure combines individual evaluation (a clinical interview, two subtests of the WAIS-R, the Rorschach, and TAT), with couple evaluation (Consensus Rorschach and Consensus TAT).

The author describes her method for administering and scoring the Consensus Rorschach and of administering and analyzing the Consensus TAT as follows:

Having completed an individual Rorschach and TAT, in the couple stage the partners discuss each card and try to reach agreements on one or more responses, and to create together stories about several TAT cards. The examiner tape-records the process, and notes patterns of interaction, such as who presses for agreements; who dominates the decisions; are they flexible or rigid and defensive; do they negotiate with a sense of respect for self and other or do they fight about autonomy, control, or power.

Each Rorschach response is scored according to the Exner system, and a structural summary for the couple's record is constructed. Then each response gets an Interaction score developed by the author (see Table 2). (Readers are referred to other publications by the author, describing this procedure and several relational styles of couples. See references.)

This method offers a representation of the couple dynamics and makes possible an appraisal of the process as well as the final product of the couple's interaction.

While in the individual tests each spouse creates for the examiner his unique interpretation of reality, in the relational part we watch the couple's effort to integrate each spouse's individual "script" – i.e., his/her interpretation of reality and of the relationship – and to create a "couple script." Spouses often experience surprise and even dismay at the dissimilarity of their perception, while others feel intrigued and excited at the opportunity of seeing things in a different, new way. In some cases relief or joy is experienced at seeing things the same way.

A number of vignettes illustrate how the unique style of the couple emerges in their test interaction, revealing their positive resources as well as their problematic areas.

An extended case is presented, of a couple in the stage of courtship, hesitating on the verge of getting married. Each spouse's background material and test material are presented and analyzed (see Tables 3 and 4), and some hypotheses are made as to their inner needs from a partner and their inhibitions about commitment to an intimate relationship. The interaction reveals their struggle in the first stages of creating a "couple script," as each of them presents his personae, but also reveals his hidden needs and fears, and his projected image of the other. Focusing on issues of dependence and of aggression, the reader can see what these two young people need from each other. The man, Ami, impresses and attracts the woman, Irit, with his strong, coping, and ambitious personae. But he needs her to contain his insecurity and dependency needs, as well as to support his needs to develop and become what he strives for. Irit needs Ami to accept and even admire her hidden fiery, imaginative qualities, but also to respect her individuality and not try to dominate her. She also unconsciously yearns for his help in restoring parts of her repressed, lost self.

On the basis of this material the author suggests ways of using the feedback session and the written report for counseling and for planning psychotherapy.

Résumé

Nous présentons ici une procédure pour l'évaluation de couples dans des contextes cliniques ou d'examen visant par exemple à faire des recommandations de traitement ou d'évaluer des candidats à l'adoption. La procédure combine une évaluation individuelle (entretien clinique, 2 subtests de la WAIS-R, le Rorschach et le TAT) avec une évaluation en couple (Consensus Rorschach et Consensus TAT).

L'auteur décrit la méthode qu'elle préconise pour administrer et coder le Consensus Rorschach et pour administrer et analyser le Consensus TAT: après que chacun a passé individuellement le Rorschach et le TAT, le couple réuni discute autour de chaque planche en essayant de se mettre d'accord sur une ou plusieurs réponses au Rorschach, et de créer en commun une histoire à plusieurs planches du TAT. L'examinateur enregistre le processus au magnétophone et note les patterns d'interaction, tels que qui insiste pour arriver à un accord, qui domine la prise de décision, sont-ils souples ou au contraire rigides et sur la défensive, négocient-ils en gardant un sens du respect de l'autre et de soi ou luttent-ils pour l'autonomie, le contrôle ou le pouvoir.

Chaque réponse au Rorschach est codée selon le Système Intégré (Exner) et un Résumé formel est établi pour le protocole de couple. On attribue ensuite à chaque réponse un score d'Interaction (voir Tableau 2), les lecteurs pouvant se référer aux autres publications de l'auteur qui décrivent cette procédure et présentent divers styles relationnels (voir bibliographie).

Cette méthode permet de se représenter la dynamique du couple et de se faire une idée du processus et du résultat final de l'interaction dans le couple. Tandis que dans les tests individuels, chaque protagoniste crée pour l'examinateur son interprétation personnelle de la réalité, nous observons dans l'étape relationnelle les efforts que fait le couple pour intégrer le "script" individuel de chacun - c'est-à-dire sa propre interprétation de la réalité et de la relation - pour créer un "script de couple." Les conjoints sont souvent surpris, voire interloqués, de découvrir leurs dissimilarités de perception, tandis que d'autres se montrent intrigués voire excités de pouvoir voir les choses d'une autre manière, sous un nouvel angle. Certaines fois, ils sont rassurés ou éprouvent de la joie à voir les choses de la même façon.

La méthode est illustrée par des vignettes qui illustrent comment le style original du couple émerge de l'interaction aux tests, et révèle leurs ressources positives ainsi que les zones problématiques. Nous présentons le protocole détaillé d'un couple de fiancés qui hésitent devant le mariage, qui comprend l'anamnèse de chacun d'eux ainsi que les résultats aux tests avec l'analyse que nous en faisons (voir Tableaux 3 & 4) et les hypothèses que nous en tirons concernant leur attentes l'un vis à vis de l'autre, et leurs inhibitions face à un engagement dans une relation intime. L'interaction révèle leur lutte dans les premiers temps de création d'un "script de couple," alors que chacun présente sa personnalité, mais aussi révèle ses besoins et craintes cachées, et l'image projetée de l'autre. L'homme, Ami, impressionne et attire la femme, Irit, par sa forte personnalité adaptable et ambitieuse. Mais il a besoin qu'elle contienne son sentiment d'insécurité et ses besoins de dépendance, et qu'elle conforte ses besoins de se développer et d'arriver à ses objectifs. Irit a besoin qu'Ami accepte et même admire ses qualités cachées de flamme et d'imagination, mais aussi qu'il respecte son individualité et n'essaie pas de la dominer. Elle désire aussi inconsciemment qu'il l'aide à restaurer des parties de son soi refoulées et perdues.

Sur la base de ce matériel, l'auteur indique la manière dont on peut utiliser la session de compte rendu et le rapport écrit dans une perspective de conseil et pour planifier la psychothérapie.

Resumen

Este artículo presenta un procedimiento de evaluación de parejas, tanto con objetivos clínicos como para la discriminación y asesoría a la hora de afrontar dificultades o adoptar niños. Este procedimiento combina la evaluación individual (una entrevista clínica, 2 subtests del WAIS-R, el Rorschach y el TAT) con la evaluación de la pareja (Rorschach de Consenso y TAT de Consenso).

La autora describe su método de administración y codificación tanto del Rorschach como del TAT de Consenso como sigue:

Una vez administrados Rorschach y TAT individualmente, se solicita a la pareja que discuta sus respuestas a cada lámina de Rorschach e intente llegar a acuerdos en una o más respuestas y, después, que elabore historias conjuntas a varias láminas del TAT. El examinador graba las respuestas en magnetófono y toma notas sobre la interacción que se produce durante el proceso, registrando aspectos tales como: quién presiona para llegar a acuerdos; quién adopta el papel dominante en las decisiones; si son flexibles o rígidos y defensivos; si negocian con respeto a su propio punto de vista y al del otro o pelean por su autonomía, control o poder.

Cada respuesta Rorschach se valora según el sistema de Exner y se construye un Sumario Estructural con las respuestas que constituyen el protocolo de la pareja. Además, cada respuesta incluye un código de Interacción desarrollado por la autora (ver Tabla 2). (Se remite al lector a otras publicaciones donde se describe el procedimiento y varios estilos relacionales de pareja. Ver Bibliografía).

Este método ofrece una representación de la dinámica de pareja y permite la valoración tanto del proceso como del producto final de las interacciones. Mientras en los tests individuales cada miembro ofrece al examinador su personal interpretación de la realidad, en la parte consensuada se puede observar el esfuerzo de la pareja para integrar conjuntamente ambas visiones, es decir, se valoran las interpretaciones individuales y la relación que permite crear una "interpretación de pareja." Unas parejas expresan su sorpresa e incluso su malestar al comprobar sus diferencias perceptivas, otras se muestran intrigadas y se animan ante la posibilidad de interpretar los estímulos de una manera nueva y diferente. En algunos casos la decepción o la alegría se experimenta cuando las interpretaciones son casi idénticas. Una serie de viñetas ilustra cómo el estilo único de cada pareja va emergiendo a través de las interacciones y revelando, tanto sus recursos positivos como sus áreas problemáticas.

Se presenta con mayor detalle el caso de una pareja de novios que se llena de dudas en las vísperas de contraer matrimonio. Se analiza el material de cada miembro de esta pareja (Ver Tablas 3 y 4) y se elaboran hipótesis acerca de sus necesidades internas de tener un compañero y sus inhibiciones ante el compromiso que supone una relación íntima. La interacción muestra su conflicto en las primeras fases para crear una "visión conjunta," ya que cada uno presenta la suya propia, pero también revela sus necesidades y temores ocultos y sus respectivas imágenes proyectadas del otro. Focalizando la atención en los temas de dependencia y agresión, el lector entenderá mejor lo que cada uno de estos dos jóvenes necesita del otro. El hombre, Ami, impresiona y atrae a la mujer, Irit, con su estilo personal fuerte y ambicioso, no obstante, él necesita que ella contenga su inseguridad y dependencia y que apoye sus deseos de desarrollo y de logro. Irit requiere que Ami acepte e incluso que admire su vehemencia oculta y sus cualidades imaginativas, pero también que respete su individualidad y no intente dominarla. Ella, inconscientemente, también anhela la ayuda de él para restaurar partes de su self reprimido y perdido.

Sobre la base de este material, la autora sugiere otras vías de utilización de la sesión interactiva y del registro escrito, como la asesoría y la planificación de la psicoterapia.

Rorschachiana 27, 164–190

The Rorschach Extended Aggression Scores

Carl B. Gacono[1], Lynne Bannatyne-Gacono[2],
J. Reid Meloy[3], and Matthew R. Baity[4]

[1]*Private Practice, Austin, TX,* [2]*Austin State Hospital, Austin, TX,*
[3]*University of California, San Diego, CA,* [4]*University of Arkansas, all USA*

The Extended Aggression Scores

The Extended Aggression Scores were developed to quantify the aggressive Rorschach imagery produced by violent Antisocial Personality Disordered (ASPD; American Psychiatric Association, 1980) offenders. Despite their histories of real world violence, these subjects produced few Aggressive Movement (AG; Exner, 1993) responses. Why didn't violent children, adolescents, and adults produce more AG responses? Considering their expression of uncensored pleasurable affect when relating their aggressive acts during their interviews, conscious censoring (Exner, 1993; Meloy, 1988) did not adequately explain the paucity of AG responses among *sentenced* adults. Why would they describe their violent acts with pride and bravado during an interview and subsequently censor AG on the Rorschach? Conscious censoring among the Conduct Disorder (CD) children and adolescents, who frequently produced sexual content, seemed an equally unlikely explanation (Gacono, 1997).

Earlier Rorschach research (Holt & Havel, 1960; Rapaport, Gill, & Schafer, 1946, 1968; Schafer, 1954) provided clues to understanding the discrepancies between Rorschach production and the interview/historical data. Direct or implicit aggressive content was thought to imply tensions of aggressive impulse (Rapaport et al., 1946/1968). Initial findings (Gacono, 1988, 1990; Heaven, 1988) suggested that the paucity of symbolized aggression, represented by AG movement, might be due, in part, to the ego-syntonic nature of aggression in ASPD and psychopathic subjects.* The clinical logic was that AG symbolized tensions of ego-dystonic aggression when produced by violent, antisocial patients. In the absence of binding the aggressive impulse, the violent individual would, instead, act it out, thus vitiating the need to symbolize it. Table 1 offers some support for this hypothesis: Exner's (1995) character disordered sample produced lower AG frequencies than his adult nonpatients; violent children and adolescents produce lower AG frequencies than child and adolescent nonpatients; and the majority of the forensic subjects with known histories of violence produce less AG than nonpatients and the Gacono and Meloy clinical samples without histories of violence (Gacono, 1997; Gacono & Meloy, 1994).**

Despite the paucity of AG responses in ASPD records, other aggression imagery was not absent. Rather, the presence of other potentially scoreable aggressive imagery (see Gacono, 1988, 1990, 1997) allowed for the development (Gacono, 1988) and refinement (Gacono & Meloy, 1994; Meloy & Gacono, 1992) of five additional scoring categories: Aggressive Content (AgC), Aggressive Past (AgPast), Aggressive Potential (AgPot), Aggressive Vulnerability (AgV), and Sado-Masochism (SM).

Since their introduction (Gacono, 1988), the Extended Aggression Scores have received considerable clinical interest and empirical study. As noted in the Rorschach Workshops' Alumni Newsletter (2000) concerning the work of the Rorschach Research Council, "Another project on which there has been good progress is the special score for Aggressive Content (AgC). Council has reviewed the criteria and guidelines for its applications and has evaluated the literature concerning it . . . A more precise interpretation of AgC responses will probably hinge on findings

* The psychopath's ego-syntonic relationship to aggression is exemplified by a psychopathic inmate who while intoxicated wandered through a section of town looking for an individual he planned to murder. Instead he killed a 15-year-old male stranger. His comment after killing the boy was, "I was going to kill someone anyway."

** The higher rates of AG among the sexual homicide perpetrators (compared to other forensic samples) might appear to be antithetical to this hypothesis; however, increased rates of AG (compared to other forensic samples) are theoretically consistent with their ambivalent relationship to aggression. Increased AG has been consistently predicted and found for this particularly disturbed group of individuals despite their histories of both affective and predatory real world violence (Gacono & Meloy, 1994; Gacono, Meloy, & Bridges, 2000; Huprich, Gacono, Schneider, & Bridges, 2002; Meloy, Gacono, & Kenney, 1994; Meloy, 2000).

Table 1. Frequency of Aggressive Movement Responses (AG).

Exner (1995) subjects			Gacono & Meloy subjects		
Group	*N*	Mean *(SD)* %[1]	Group	*N*	Mean *(SD)* %
Children			Conduct-Disordered		
Age 5	90	1.23 (.67) 91%	Ages 5–12*	72	.60 (1.04) 32%
Age 6	80	.30 (.56) 25%			
Age 7	120	1.20 (.40) 100%			
Age 8	120	.93 (.58) 80%			
Age 9	140	1.37 (.78) 91%			
Age 10	120	1.57 (.62) 100%			
Age 11	135	1.42 (.57) 100%			
Age 12	120	1.08 (.66) 82%			
Adolescents			Conduct-Disordered		
Age 13	110	1.18 (.91) 77%	Ages 13–17*	179	.53 (.84) 35%
Age 14	105	1.30 (.92) 85%	Males**	79	.65 (.96) 38%
Age 15	140	1.14 (.91) 74%	Females**	21	.33 (.66) 24%
Age 16	140	1.20 (.99) 76%			
Adults			Adult Antisocial (ASPD)		
Nonpatient			Males*	108	.50 (.85) 54%
Adults	700	1.18 (1.18) 67%	Females*	69	.62 (.84) 45%
Schizophrenic	320	1.26 (1.85) 50%	Schizophrenic*	100	.75 (1.17) 40%
Character Disordered	180	.41 (.67) 31%	Female Psychopaths*	28	.57 (.92) 39%
			Male Psychopaths*	30	.50 (.82) 43%
			Sexual Homicide*	38	.82 (.90) 58%
			Adult Outpatient		
			Forensic/Paranoid Schizophrenic***	90	.54 (.96) 36%
			Forensic/Bipolar***	40	.68 (1.09) 38%
			Forensic/Undiff Schizophrenic***	38	.74 (1.13) 37%
			Narcissistic[a]	18	.78 (1.21) 50%
			Borderline[a]	18	1.39 (1.33) 72%
			Borderline Female*	32	1.60 (2.2) 69%

Note. [1]% = is the percentage of subjects that produced at least one aggressive movement response. [a]Gacono, Meloy, & Berg (1992). *Gacono & Meloy samples. **Gacono & Meloy (1994). ***Bannatyne-Gacono & Gacono samples. * & *** are new unpublished data analyzed by Dr. Exner at Rorschach Workshops.

for other variables . . ." (p. 13). Additionally, the ROR-SCAN Version 6 Rorschach Interpretive Scoring System (Caracena, 2002) now includes AgC, AgPast, AgPot and SM. What began as an attempt to expand the scoring of Rorschach aggressive imagery in CD and ASPD subjects, has evolved into a larger study of aggression on the Rorschach. In this article we evaluate and summarize the reliability and validity of the Extended Aggression Scores and discuss their clinical meaning.

Interrater Reliability

A search of PsycINFO between 1989 and 2003 using the key words Rorschach and aggressive, aggression, AgC, AgPot, AgPast, sadomasochism, sado-masochism, Gacono, or Meloy, revealed that, since their introduc-

Table 2. Interrater Agreement for the Rorschach Extended Aggression Scores.

Study	*N*	AgC	AgPot	AgPast	SM	Sample studied
Baity & Hilsenroth (1999)	25	99% .95[a]	100% 1.0[a]	99% .79[a]	--	Cluster A, B, & C Personality Disorders
Baity & Hilsenroth (2002)	20	.88[a]	--	--	--	Psychiatric reference groups from Exner's (1993) normative sample
Cohan (1998)	20	86%	83%	88%	--	Forensic Outpatient sex offenders
Darcangelo (1997)	5	.97[b]	.92[b]	.95[b]	--	Male incarcerated rapists
Gacono et al. (1992)	30	95%	100%	96%	--	Cluster B/Personality Disorders
Huprich et al. (2002)	19	97% .90[a]	99% .83[a]	99% .89[a]	99% .91[a]	Psychopaths, Pedophiles, Sexual Homicide Perpetrators
Levy (1998)	14	93%	97%	98%	--	Physically abused children
Meloy & Gacono (1992)	30	95%	100%	96%	--	ASPD incarcerated males
Mihura & Nathan-Montano (2001)	50	.85[a]	.76[a]	.85[a]	--	Undergraduate college students
Mihura et al. (2003)	70	.89[a]	.88[a]	.94[a]	--	Undergraduate college students
Neubauer (2001)	20	95% .80[a]	99.6% .66[a]	97.7% .65[a]	--	Nonpatient adults
Riquelme et al. (1991)/Ephriam et al. (1993)	40	--	97%	97%	--	Nonpatient adults (Venezuela)
White (1999)	33	73%	50%	86%	--	Forensic outpatients

Note. N = Number of protocols scored for interrater agreement. [a]Kappa coefficients (κ). [b]Intraclass correlations (ICC). [c]Pearson *r*.

tion (Gacono, 1988), there have been eight published articles (Gacono, 1990; Gacono et al., 1992; Meloy & Gacono, 1992; Baity & Hilsenroth, 1999; Baity & Hilsenroth, 2002; Kamphuis, Kugeares, & Finn, 2000; Mihura & Nathan-Montano, 2001; Mihura, Nathan-Montano, & Alperin, 2003) and approximately 12 dissertations (several additional dissertations were discovered through additional searches) that have included the Extended Aggression Scores. When interrater agreement was reported, it has been excellent (i.e., > .75; Fleiss, 1981).

Table 2 summarizes the interrater reliability of the Extended Aggression Scores from six published studies (Meloy & Gacono, 1992; Baity & Hilsenroth, 1999; Baity & Hilsenroth, 2002; Kamphuis, Kugeares, & Finn, 2000; Mihura & Nathan-Montano, 2001; Mihura, Nathan-Montano, & Alperin, 2003; Huprich, Gacono, Schneider, & Bridges, 2004), six dissertations (Cohan, 1998; Darcangelo, 1997; Levy, 1998; Margolis, 1992; Neubauer, 2001; White, 1999), and one book chapter (Riquelme et al., 1991; Ephraim et al., 1993). Percent agreement means ranged from 86% (AgPot) to 99.5% (SM). One low percent agreement finding, 50% for AgPot (White, 1999), lowered the mean scores. The combined mean for kappa coefficients and intraclass correlation coefficients (ICCs) ranged from .84 (AgPast) to .96 (SM).

Validity Research

Not surprisingly, since these are the most frequently produced scores, AgC, AgPast, and/or AgPot have been studied in the majority of studies. Only three studies investigated SM and no studies investigated AgV. The following sections describe the validity research, primarily from published studies, for each of the Extended Aggression Scores. Dissertation studies will be used mostly to highlight methodological limitations. For readers unfamiliar with the Extended Aggression Scores, each section begins with a brief description of how the variable is coded along with sample responses.

Aggressive Content (AgC)

AgC is coded for content popularly perceived as predatory, dangerous, malevolent, injurious, or harmful (Gacono, 1988; Meloy & Gacono, 1992). Example: (Card VI) "It's a gun;" second example: (Card IX) "It's a demon with claws" (this second percept would only receive one AgC score; "A dragon attacking a demon" would receive two AgCs). Popular responses are not coded as AgC unless embellished with aggressive imagery (i.e., Card V "a bat" [not AgC]; "A vampire bat" [score AgC]).* Gacono's surveys of mental health workers and college students provided guidelines for scoring AgC (Meloy & Gacono, 1992; Gacono & Meloy, 1994). In order to ascertain the robustness of the Gacono and Meloy (1994) AgC guidelines, Baity, McDaniel and Hilsenroth (2000) surveyed an undergraduate student group utilizing the Gacono and Meloy aggressive objects, a sample of potentially aggressive objects not located in Gacono and Meloy's work (e.g., bear, bee, Bigfoot, etc.), and a list of neutral objects taken from practice scoring protocols in Exner's Comprehensive System Workbook (e.g., apple, butterfly, candle, etc.; 4th ed., Exner, 1995b). Most of Gacono and Meloy's aggressive objects fit the definition of AgC and could be further delineated by categories (weapons, animal/part animal, environmental danger, fictional creature) and aggressive adjectives (scary, frightening, evil, angry, or mean; Baity et al., 2000). This research reinforced using the original AgC tables as a scoring guide rather than an exhaustive list. The authors also demonstrated that AgC definitions remained consistent over time (a 1-month test-retest reliability check produced an $r = .99$).

AgC is the most frequently occurring Extended Aggression Score in all studies. This variable was thought to represent identification with aggressive objects, and in certain cases, highly cathected object representations of weapons or violent acts (Gacono & Meloy, 1994). The relationship between AgC and aggressive identification, ideation or preoccupation has been supported in several studies. In a sample of personality disordered outpatients, Baity and Hilsenroth (1999) found that AgC was the strongest predictor of both the total number of DSM-IV criteria for Antisocial Personality Disorder (ASPD) and scores on the MMPI-2 Antisocial Practices Scale (APS). The findings of Mihura and colleagues (Mihura & Nathan-Montano, 2001; Mihura et al., 2003) suggested that, in college samples, elevated AgC represented an ego-dystonic relationship to aggression that caused disorganization (feelings of less control)

* Some studies did not report excluding aggressive objects from AgC scoring that qualified as a Popular (e.g., a "tiger" to D1 on Card VIII). Many authors did not indicate that they had scored multiple occurrences of a single aggressive category within a response (i.e., if two different objects within a single response qualify for an AgC, score two AgCs; same for AgPast, AgPot, and so forth).

and defensive use of projection. Elevated AgC signals the need to explore the presence of aggressive figures and events in the client's past that may have contributed to an "identification with the aggressor."

Baity and Hilsenroth (2002) also linked AgC to histories of real world aggression. They found that more behavioral aggressiveness (based on an Aggression Chart Rating Scale) was significantly correlated with a greater number of AgC, AG, and Morbid responses (MOR; Exner, 1993). Among these three responses, AgC was the only nonredundant, significant predictor of aggressiveness; specifically, AG and MOR did not account for significant variance beyond that provided by AgC. An AG > 3 cutoff was also effective in ruling out nonaggressive chart summaries (Specificity = .88 and Negative Predictive Power = .84), but demonstrated only a limited ability to identify cases with aggression (Sensitivity = .28 and Positive Predictive Power = .36; Baity & Hilsenroth, 2002). The ability to identify aggressive cases was greatly improved when either the AgC > 3 or AgC > 4 cutoffs were used (Sensitivity = .72 and .61, respectively). In summary, the AG cutoff was more effective in excluding "nonaggressive" histories while the AgC cutoffs were more effective for identifying "aggressive" histories. Most important from the Baity and Hilsenroth (2002) research was the fact that increases in AgC scores were more strongly related to reports of highly aggressive behavior than current Comprehensive System variables (CS; Exner, 1993).

Darcangelo (1997) found that higher AgC and AG scores were associated with higher ratings of both general and sexual aggression for incarcerated male rapists. In female nonpatients without a criminal history, Neubauer (2001) found that AgC was related to self-reported contained anger, but not to self-reported physical aggression. He concluded that in his sample AgC "could be a means of sublimating aggressive energy" or indicate "one's current level of anger." In comparison, Mihura et al. (2003) investigated AgC in a college student sample and found that AgC correlated with the Personality Assessment Inventory (PAI; Morey, 1991) Physical Aggression subscale, Borderline Features scale and its Affective Instability and Identity Problems subscales. Methodological differences between the Neubauer and Mihura et al. studies could account for the contrast in finding a significant relationship between AgC and self-reported physical aggression.

Aggressive Past (AgPast)

AgPast is coded for any response in which an aggressive act has occurred or the object has been the target of aggression (Gacono, 1988). Example: (Card X) "It's a cat that had its head cut-off" (Gacono, 1988, p. 20). AgPast responses may represent masochistic tendencies (Meloy & Gacono, 1992) or internal representations related to victimization (Gacono & Meloy, 1994). By definition all AgPast responses would be scored as MOR; however, Morbid responses without aggressive connotations are not scored as AgPast (e.g., "It's a sad person"). Indeed, Baity and Hilsenroth (1999) found a strong relationship between MOR and AgPast scores in Axis II outpatient personality disorders. Of note, morbid responses have been associated with aggression turned against the self (Hilsenroth, Hibbard, Nash, & Handler, 1993; Westen, 1990).

Several studies have reported findings that are consistent with Gacono and Meloy's (1994) conceptualization of AgPast as indicating self-damage, masochism, or an early traumatic experience of having been aggressed against. Baity and Hilsenroth (1999) found that combined with Morbid responses and Holt's (1977) primary process variable, AgPast loaded (.90) onto a factor labeled, "Aggression at Objects." Stepwise regression analysis with the aggression variables and selected scales of the MMPI-2 indicated that AgPast was the only significant predictor of scores on the Anger scale. Consistent with previous theories (Gacono & Meloy, 1994), they noted, "This suggests that the identification of the self as damaged or spoiled might arise from a history of being in an unstable environment potentially resulting in victimization. More severe aggressive environments might be expected to foster greater feelings of resentment and inner turmoil that may manifest on certain indices of anger" (Baity & Hilsenroth, 1999; p. 106).

Kamphuis et al. (2000) included AgPast in their study of three nondissociative outpatient groups: those with a history of sexual abuse, those with suspected but unconfirmed sexual abuse, and a third group with no sexual abuse. Although there was no significant mean difference among these groups, the AgPast score was significantly correlated with the intensity of violent or sadistic sexual abuse in the group with confirmed sexual abuse. Based on these findings, Kamphuis and colleagues suggested that "... those sexually abused clients with significant numbers of AgPast scores in their Rorschachs will have the greatest difficulties overcoming the negative effects of their abuse" (p. 220).

Two studies discovered relative elevations of AgPast in the Rorschach records of a male offender group where an early history of victimization would be expected (White, 1999; Huprich et al., 2004). Pedophiles were 2 times more likely to have at least one AgPast than those without the diagnosis (White, 1999). Huprich et al. (2004) found even higher elevations of AgPast in the records of sexual homicide perpetrators compared to *nonviolent* pedophiles.

Similar to the Baity and Hilsenroth's (1999) findings, Neubauer (2001) found that AgPast was related to several self-report anger scales: contained anger, state anger, trait anger, and hostility in female college students. He concluded that the presence of AgPast suggested feelings of frustration, resentment, being mistreated and/or suspiciousness. The Mihura et al. (2003) findings shed further light on AgPast in a college sample as they found that AgPast was most strongly associated with interpersonal submissiveness, the PAI Borderline Self-Harm and Negative Relationships subscales, and, to a lesser degree, with the Physical Aggression subscale. In certain nonpatient samples, AgPast scores may signal a defensive strategy where internalization of one's anger and hostility results in passivity, and even impulsively self-destructive behavior.

Aggressive Potential (AgPot)

AgPot has been defined as any response in which an aggressive act is getting ready to occur. Usually the act is imminent (Gacono, 1988). Example: (Card X) "These two are going to give them a surprise. They are waiting to lop their heads off. They won't even know what hit them" (Gacono, 1988, pp. 20–21). AgPot was thought to relate to "sadism" (Meloy & Gacono, 1992) or an identification with predatory objects or a preoccupation with predation (Gacono & Meloy, 1994).

Early research suggested that AgPot may occur more frequently in Cluster B Personality Disorders (Gacono, Meloy, & Berg, 1992) than nonpatients (Margolis, 1992). Consistent with this observation, White (1999) found that female offenders with BPD were approximately 3½ times more likely to have at least one AgPot response than those not diagnosed with BPD. Other research has found AgPot related to problems modulating one's aggressive urges. For example, Huprich et al. (2004) found that AgPot scores were significantly higher for sexual homicide perpetrators than for both nonsexually offending psychopaths and nonviolent pedophiles. In a college sample, Mihura et al. (2003) found that AgPot was related to the PAI Aggression Scale and its Physical Aggression Subscale, the Borderline Self-Harm Scale, and their PAI measure of suicidal ideation with impulsivity.

AgC, AgPast, and AgPot Combinations

Two studies by Mihura and colleagues combined AgC (aggressive identity) with AgPot (aggressive urges) using *z*-scores to see if this variable was more highly related to their external criteria than either variable in isolation. Indeed, protocols that contained elevations of both AgPot and AgC, versus either of these scores alone, were more highly associated with a PAI measure of outwardly expressed aggression (Mihura et al., 2003). While elevated rates of AgC were associated with viewing a significant other as less controllable when the relationship felt threatened, elevated rates of both AgC and AgPot were associated with not only viewing the significant other as less controllable, but also as more *controlling*. Mihura et al. (2003) also combined AgPot (aggressive urges) and AgPast (victimization) using *z*-scores, and found that this combination was more highly associated with a PAI measure of inwardly expressed aggression than either of these scores in isolation.

Finally, Levy (1998) investigated gender differences for AgC, AgPot, and AgPast in children with severe and chronic physical abuse, hypothesizing that physically abused boys would show higher rates of externalized aggression on the Rorschach than physically abused girls. Consistent with expectations, the physically abused boys had higher levels of both AgC and AgPot than did physically abused girls, with no significant differences for AgPast.

Aggressive Vulnerability (AgV)

AgV is coded when the subject identifies a percept as vulnerable to attack, exploitation, or indicates that the object has taken steps to protect itself from predation. Example: “It’s a butterfly and here is where it needs to cover up so the predators can’t attack it” (Gacono & Meloy, 1994; p. 277). Like AgPast, it suggests a passive relationship to aggressive impulses. Unlike AgPast, rather than suggesting a masochistic identification, it implicates a sensitivity or preoccupation with vulnerability or being exploited, injured, or victimized. There has been no published research on this variable since its introduction in Gacono and Meloy (1994).

Sado-Masochism (SM)

SM is scored when a response contains devalued, aggressive, or morbid content accompanied by pleasurable affect expressed by the subject (Gacono, 1988). Example: (Card VII) "A lady dancing and she got her head blown off (laughs)." The pleasurable affect is usually expressed through smiling or laughing, but the examiner should be careful to not interpret anxious behavior as pleasurable affect. Since SM requires observation during test administration it can generally be accurately scored from archival protocols only when the examiner recorded the patient's affective expressions; consequently, it has been the second least researched of the aggression scores.

Studies that investigated SM, however, produced findings consistent with the interpretation of SM as reflecting a sadistic orientation. Gacono (1988, 1990) first reported frequencies for SM in groups of psychopathic and nonpsychopathic ASPD offenders. In an expanded sample ($N = 43$), Meloy and Gacono (1992) found that SM differentiated between Hare Psychopathy Checklist-Revised (PCL-R; Hare, 1991) identified psychopathic ASPD (PCL-R > 30) and nonpsychopathic ASPD offenders (P-ASPDs = 41%; NP-ASPDs = 14%). Huprich et al. (2004) found that sexual homicide perpetrators produced higher frequencies of SM than nonviolent pedophiles (none of the pedophiles met the criteria for ASPD or psychopathy; respective frequencies; 24% & 3%). In Darcangelo's (1997) adult rapist sample, SM was also significantly related to elevated PCL-R scores and ratings of sexual sadism. Neubauer (2001) also found no occurrences (0%) of SM in a female adult nonforensic sample.

Discussion

Since Gacono and Meloy wrote (1994), "The various indices of aggressive responses to the Rorschach appear to be a rich source for understanding the structure and dynamics of an individual's intrapsychic aggression . . ." (p. 278), additional research has supported and refined, rather than refuted, the original interpretations for these variables.

None of the extant research has discredited Gacono and Meloy's hypothesis that the paucity of the AG response in CD and ASPD populations may relate to the ego-syntonic nature of aggression in CD, ASPD, or psychopathic individuals.* This hypothesis does not exclude the possibility that any given patient may be consciously censoring AG. The impact of response style (Bannatyne, Gacono & Greene, 1999) and the assessment context (forensic, research) must always be considered when evaluating an individual protocol (Gacono, Evans & Viglione, 2002) for the presence or absence of aggressive imagery. However, the fact that a particular Rorschach response *can be censored* does not mean that it *was censored.* For the original Gacono (1988, 1990) ASPD samples and later Gacono and Meloy (1992, 1994) samples, consistent findings across age groups and discrepancies between interview and Rorschach administration suggest an ego-dystonic relationship to aggressive impulses that stimulates AG production.

The notion that AgC represents a preoccupation or an identification with aggressive objects has also been supported (Baity & Hilsenroth, 1999, 2002; Darcangelo, 1997; Mihura et al., 2003; White, 1999). AgC is produced frequently enough that when combined with AG, it has the potential to add incrementally to understanding both violent patients and nonpatients with no documented histories of violence. For example, with sexual homicide perpetrators (Gacono, Meloy, & Bridges, 2000; Meloy, Gacono, & Kenney, 1994) or rapists (Darcangelo, 1997) elevated AG (intensity of the ego-dystonic impulse) and increased AgC (aggressive identifications) in conjunction with other Rorschach identified sexual preoccupations, cognitive deficits, and personality vulnerabilities provide a window into the object relations, defences, and impulses that drive the perpetrator's real world sexual violence (Gacono et al., 2000). In these sexually violent subjects, Rorschach identified impulses (AG) and identifications (AgC) await only a situational spark to ignite them. While combined aggression coding more accurately captures the underlying psychodynamics of patients with histories of real world aggression, like many other Rorschach variables, interpretations should be made while also considering the degree to which poor reality testing, cognitive slippage, and other drive derivatives infuse the record.

Correlations with severe aggression in sexual trauma (Kamphuis et al.,

* While the Extended Aggression Scores first appeared in Gacono (1988), this hypothesis was developed subsequently and first appeared in Meloy and Gacono (1992).

2000), self-reported self-destructive behaviors (Mihura et al., 2003), interpersonal submissiveness (Mihura & Nathan-Montano, 2001), and anger (Baity & Hilsenroth, 1999; Neubauer, 2001), support links between AgPast and a history of having been aggressed against, a masochistic identification, a passive orientation toward aggressive impulses, and/or ambivalence concerning expressing aggression (aggression turned inward). AgPast appears to reflect internalized object relations related to victimization with accompanying resentment and anger (aggression directed toward self). However, while AgPast may signal a propensity for self-harm in some patients, for patients who are characterologically predisposed to commit violence toward others (ASPD, psychopaths) it may also be a marker for their feelings of entitlement to retaliate.

Research findings with AgPot are more limited, although the extant literature is consistent with the interpretation of AgPot as representing aggressive impulses. This is supported by AgPot's more frequent occurrence in protocols of sexual homicide perpetrators (compared to nonviolent pedophiles; Huprich et al., 2004), offenders with a BPD diagnosis (White, 1999), and in college students with higher PAI scores on inwardly and outwardly directed aggressive impulses (Mihura et al., 2003). Since many studies report rather low base rates of AgPot, interpretations of AgPot may be more useful when considered in conjunction with other aggression variables. For example, Mihura and her colleagues suggest that when a protocol contains both AgPot and AgC (vs either variable alone), aggressive urges are more likely (Mihura et al., 2003; Mihura & Nathan-Montano, 2001). Like its name, Aggressive Potential may represent a "potential" for acting on aggressive impulses; other variables in the protocol, such as AgC (toward others) or AgPast (toward self), may suggest the direction of the action. Given the low base rates for both SM (sadism) and AgPot (aggressive urges/potential) combining the two scores might be explored; however, the degree of conceptual overlap between these variables remains to be seen.

Although Gacono and Meloy (1994) have suggested that AgPot may represent sadism, SM is the Rorschach aggression score most obviously linked to sadism. Unfortunately, SM is one of the least studied of the aggression scores. This is likely due to the fact that it may be difficult to score using archival CS Rorschach data, since the pleasurable affect must be observed and recorded. Additionally, when it does occur, it does so infrequently. We don't want to, however, discount the extant research. The three studies that did include SM in investigating offender populations found that SM was related to psychopathy (Meloy & Gacono, 1992), higher PCL-R scores (Darcangelo, 1997), and/or sadism (Darcangelo, 1997; Huprich et al., 2004). Darcangelo (1997) found that SM was significantly related to ratings of sexual sadism expressed during rape as well as in other behaviors. These studies suggest that SM might be used as a type of behavioral coding that indicates a greater likelihood of psychopathic and sadistic behaviors in everyday life.

The senior author has also examined Rorschach responses for SM that can be coded in a manner that does not require examiner observation. Scoring verbalized projected sadism may be useful for identifying this worrisome trait. That is, when projecting sadism, rather than displaying pleasurable affect, the examinee attributes sadistic attitudes to the Rorschach percept or personalizes (often coded with a PER) the sadistic activity of the percept. An example of "sadistic attribution" includes a subject perceiving a human face and stating, "... he's smiling like he's going to hit you." The percept, rather than the examinee, contains the pleasurable affect. An example of "personalized sadism" includes (Card III), "It's a fly. It's far out. I've been going to mental health counseling since 13 or 16. (Inquiry?) A fly, got big eyes. When I was little, I used to pull flies' eyes off" (Gacono & Meloy, 1994, p. 277). Researchers must consider that while empirical links between real world behavior and the original SM coding have been demonstrated, there has been no research with this expanded coding. Also, this expanded coding may capture different aspects of a patient's relationship to sadism than the ego-syntonic relationship linked to the original coding. Quite likely, the manner in which the patient expresses their sadistic impulses (directly, projected, with anxiety, and so forth) on the Rorschach tells us something about their relationship to the impulse. The question that remains is not the importance of assessing the sadistic impulse, but the best empirical Rorschach measure with which to do it.

Trends in the research have also highlighted the need for interpreting these aggression scores within the context of the patient's personality organization and the presence or absence of real world aggression in their history. While still representing an identification, the presence of AgC aids in understanding the disruptive impact of aggressive impulses on certain college samples with little real world histories of aggression (Neubauer, 2001; Mihura & Nathan-Montana, 2001). These findings support an ego-dystonic relationship to aggressive impulse (AG) and identifications (elevated AgC scores). While AgC in these nonpatient samples coincides with feelings of less control and the need to modulate the impulse through projection, in forensic populations correlations with the number of ASPD criteria, scores on the Antisocial Practices Scale (MMPI-2), and institutional chart ratings of aggressive behavior, support an ego-syntonic relationship to the aggressive identification and aggressive preoccupations (Gacono & Meloy, 1994). The use of sequence analysis to study the presence of other variables in the record, such as diffuse shading (FY, YF & Y) and inanimate movement (m), may help further delineate the forensic patients' relationship to their aggressive impulses (Meloy & Gacono, 1992).

The unpublished dissertation studies help us to understand methodological problems when studying the Rorschach and aggression. Most frequently, studies have failed to incorporate a conceptually accurate basis for predicting group differences. A glaring example includes the use of chart reported offense histories, alone, as the independent measure for determining aggressive versus nonaggressive groups. This procedure is problematic for several reasons. First, it is not uncommon for violent offenders to have an absence of formal charges or convictions (arrestable offenses) in their records. Secondly, the impact of plea bargaining can result in convictions that are quite different from the actual charges. Finally, any particular offense category may capture a diverse array of motivations and behaviors. With the exception of an extreme behavior such as sexual homicide, with it's very low base rate of occurrence, researchers must carefully consider the limitations of using "rap sheets" or patient records to quantify levels of aggression. Whilc these studies may provide useful descriptive data (relative frequency of the extended aggression scores within the given population), they do little to aid in understanding the utility of the scores in differentiating among levels of aggression. A related conceptual error in the offender Rorschach research is predicting that a Rorschach variable(s) will differentiate among two heterogeneous, but similar groups (e.g., hypothesizing differences between a group of ASPD offenders and a group of control offenders; the appropriate comparison is comparing PCL-R identified psychopaths with low PCL-R scorers; see Gacono et al., 2001). When interpreting a lack of "significant between group differences," one must first consider if there was a carefully considered and valid theoretical rationale for predicting differences and evaluate whether the proposed or established clinical meaning of the variables was accurately reflected in the study's hypothesis (Gacono & Meloy, 1994; also see Gacono, Loving, & Bodholdt, 2001). An evaluation of this latter point requires a sophisticated understanding of violent offenders and, also, how the Rorschach actually works.

High Lambda forensic samples represent another concern when evaluating frequencies or proportions of any Rorschach content based item (see White, 1999; Cohan, 1998). Any comparison of content based items means and frequencies with more normally distributed Lambda samples must be done with caution. Constricted protocols (high Lambda) are consistent with certain forensic patients' inadequacy and limited psychological resources (Bannatyne et al., 1999), however, the corresponding reduction in content based items means and frequencies limit direct comparisons to nonconstricted samples. While findings from constricted populations may represent a true estimate of the relative proportion of the given variable within the population studied, comparing between study means or frequencies is not possible. In this regard, the vast majority of well designed studies in this area have produced findings consistent with the clinical meanings of the Extended Aggression Scores, however, issues related to Rorschach administration, scoring, and sample characteristics (Lambda, R) limit between study comparisons of descriptive data. While an important consideration whenever Rorschach content based items are studied, controlling for R may be especially important for AgC, since it occurs frequently enough that comparing AgC score proportions, means, or subjects who produce ≥ 3 may be more useful than comparing frequencies of individuals who produce at least one.* Regardless, Lambda and R must be considered when comparing mean scores or frequencies for the extended aggression scores across studies.

---

* Considering descriptive data within the context of Lambda and R is especially crucial when comparing AgC mean scores between criminal and noncriminal samples. For example, compared to the mean R for nonpatient adults (M = 22.32; SD = 4.40; CS, Exner, 2001), the mean R for most criminal samples is lower ($M \approx$ 17–19; e.g., Cohan, 1998; Darcangelo, 1997; Gacono et al., 1992; Gacono et al., 2000), while the mean R is *higher* for sex offender groups such as pedophiles, ephebophiles, and sexual homicide perpetrators ($M \approx$ 26–29; Bridges, Wilson, & Gacono, 1998; Gacono et al., 2000; Gacono & Meloy, 1994). It should also be noted that most studies finding AgC significantly related to ratings of aggressive behavior and self-reported aggressive urges have controlled AgC for R (Baity & Hilsenroth, 2002; Darcangelo, 1997; Mihura et al., 2003). However, Lambda and R maybe only two of several factors that account for descriptive differences between studies (mean scores). Administration errors, inherent qualities of the population studied (relationship to aggressive impulse), and so forth may also contribute to mean score differences. While a worthwhile endeavor, an in depth discussion of methodological errors in each of the unpublished studies represents a task beyond the scope of this article.

Research done by summing the raw Extended Aggression Scores assumes (1) that each score has the same meaning or assesses the same criteria and/or (2) that each type of variable contributes equally to measuring the criteria (e.g., one AgC is equal to one AgPot). While aggregated variables can be created by calculating *z*-scores per variable and summing the *z*-scores (see Mihura et al., 2003; Mihura & Nathan-Montano, 2001), the aggregation of variables should always be based on a theoretical rationale, rather than just convenience to increase variable frequencies. Two final problems were apparent in several of the dissertations. First, inappropriate statistical procedures were used for comparing categorical data. Secondly, researchers failed to report interrater agreements for the Extended Aggression Scores, level of aggression measure, diagnosis, and so forth.

Conclusion

Research findings have been consistent with Gacono and Meloy's (1994) interpretations for the Extended Aggression Scores. While the integration of other assessment data, including Rorschach scores, provides the best picture of personality, these single Rorschach Extended Aggression Scores each appear to capture unique aspects of aggressive drive derivatives: AG representing aggressive drive intensity (ego-dystonic or ego-syntonic dependent on the population studied), AgC symbolizing an aggressive identification (forensic samples) or preoccupation (forensic and college samples), AgPot indicating aggressive urges or a potential to translate aggression into action, AgPast suggesting a victimized object representation, and SM indicating sadism and a link to psychopathy.*

In addition to capturing unique aspects of the aggressive impulse, these variables expand the examiner's ability to code a variety of aggressive imagery not included in the Comprehensive System. The importance of increased scoring potential needs to be underscored. This was the senior author's sole intent when he observed the paucity of AG

* Huprich et al. (2004) found significant correlations in the proportionally predicted directions (which would not have occurred with AG alone) between aggression and oral dependency among nonsexually offending psychopaths, nonviolent pedophiles, and sexual homicide offenders when including the extended aggression scores.

movement coupled with the presence of these scores; that was to be able to code the diverse Rorschach aggressive imagery produced in the forensic samples (see Table 1; Gacono, 1988, 1997). The forensic examiner always integrates data from multiple sources in formulating hypothesis and offering opinions. In this regard, the Extended Aggression Scores are very useful idiographically; however, the sophisticated researcher always couches interpretation within a throughout understanding of the difference between aggressive preoccupations and identifications and violent action. Quite likely, no combination of Rorschach variables in isolation, and certainly not a single variable, will ever be successful in predicting violent behavior. Violence does not occur in a vacuum, but is best understood within a psycho-biological-situational context (Espinosa, 2001). To expect otherwise is naive and asks too much of the Rorschach. Like any Rorschach variable, the usefulness of the Extended Aggression Scores occurs when they are viewed in conjunction with a patient's psychology, history, and situation.

Recent research with nonforensic populations also supports the need to examine Extended Aggression responses, particularly AgC, AgPast, and AgPot. The extant research suggests that there are individual differences for the production of Rorschach aggressive imagery, and that it can be qualitatively and quantitatively different depending on the person's legal and psychological history. As exemplified in Exner's *Rorschach Primer* (2000) and Rorschach computer software (e.g., Caracena, 2002), Rorschach technology is becoming more sophisticated. The days of generic interpretations of variables applied to everyone are over, and advanced algorithms individualizing interpretations of Rorschach findings are becoming the standard of practice. While AgV, AgPot and SM hold promise and should not be forgotten (due to their low frequencies of occurrence), this current research supports consideration of including the more frequently appearing AgC and AgPast in the Comprehensive System.

Acknowledgments

The authors wish to thank Chris Piotrowski and Amy Mashberg for conducting literature searches and Drs. Joni Mihura and Donald Viglione for their comments and suggestions related to the article's contents. The views expressed in this article are solely the authors' and may not reflect the views of any of the authors' past, present, or future affiliations.

References

American Psychiatric Association. (1980). *Diagnostic and statistical manual of mental disorders* (3rd ed.). Washington, DC: Author.

Baity, M.R., & Hilsenroth, M.J. (1999). Rorschach aggression variables: A study of reliability and validity. *Journal of Personality Assessment, 72,* 93–110.

Baity, M.R., & Hilsenroth, M.J. (2002). Rorschach Aggressive Content (AgC) variable: A study of criterion validity. *Journal of Personality Assessment, 78,* 275–287.

Baity, M.R., McDaniel, P.S., & Hilsenroth, M.J. (2000). Further exploration of the Rorschach Aggressive Content (AgC) variable. *Journal of Personality Assessment, 74,* 231–241.

Bannatyne, L.A., Gacono, C.B., & Greene, R. (1999). Differential patterns of responding among three groups of chronic psychotic forensic outpatients. *Journal of Clinical Psychology, 55,* 1553–1565.

Bridges, M.R., Wilson, J.S., & Gacono, C.B. (1998). A Rorschach investigation of defensiveness, self-perception, interpersonal relations, and affective states in incarcerated pedophiles. *Journal of Personality Assessment, 70,* 365–385.

Caracena, P.F. (2002). *ROR-SCAN version 6 Rorschach interpretive system.* Laredo, TX: ROR-SCAN.

Cohan, R.D. (1998). A comparison of sex offenders against minors and rapists of adults on selected Rorschach variables. *Dissertation Abstracts International, 59,* 2471B. (UMI No. 9834544).

Darcangelo, S.M. (1997). Psychological and personality correlates of the Massachusetts Treatment Center classification system for rapists (Doctoral dissertation, Simon Fraser University, Canada, 1997). *Dissertation Abstracts International, 58,* 2115B.

Ephraim, D., Occupati, R., Riquelme, J., & Gonzales, E. (1993). Gender, age and socioeconomic differences in Rorschach thematic content scales. *Rorschachiana, 18*, 68–81.

Espinosa, S. (2001). The difference between aggressive and nonaggressive hospitalized adolescents in their projected aggression and developmental levels of object relations functioning (Doctoral dissertation, Seton Hall Univ., College of Education and Human Services). *Dissertation Abstracts International, 61(12-B), 6703.*

Exner, J.E. (1993). *The Rorschach: A comprehensive system: Vol. 1: Basic foundations* (2nd ed.). New York: Wiley.

Exner, J.E. (1995). *A Rorschach workbook for the comprehensive system* (4th ed.). Asheville, NC: Rorschach Workshops.

Exner, J.E. (2000). *A primer for Rorschach interpretation.* Asheville, NC: Rorschach Workshops.

Exner, J.E. (2001). *A Rorschach workbook for the comprehensive system (5th ed.).* Asheville, NC: Rorschach Workshops.

Fleiss, J. (1981). *Statistical methods for rates and proportions.* New York: Wiley.

Gacono, C.B. (1988). *A Rorschach analysis of object relations and defensive structure and their relationship to narcissism and psychopathy in a group of antisocial offenders.* Unpublished doctoral dissertation, United States International University, San Diego.

Gacono, C.B. (1990). An empirical study of object relations and defensive operations in antisocial personality. *Journal of Personality Assessment, 54,* 589–600.

Gacono, C.B. (1997). Is the Rorschach aggression movement response enough? *British Journal of Projective Psychology, 42,* 5–10.

Gacono, C.B., Evans, B., & Viglione, D. (2002). The Rorschach in forensic practice. *Journal of Forensic Psychology Practice, 2*(3), 33–53.

Gacono, C., Loving, J., & Bodholdt, R. (2001). The Rorschach and psychopathy: Toward a more accurate understanding of the research findings. *Journal of Personality Assessment, 77,* 16–38.

Gacono, C.G., & Meloy, J.R. (1992). The Rorschach and the DSM-III-R antisocial personality: A tribute to Robert Lindner. *Journal of Clinical Psychology, 48,* 393–405.

Gacono, C.B., & Meloy, J.R. (1994). *The Rorschach assessment of aggressive and psychopathic personality.* Hillsdale, NJ: Erlbaum.

Gacono, C.B., Meloy, J.R., & Berg, J.L. (1992). Object relations, defensive operations, and affective states in narcissistic, borderline, and antisocial personality. *Journal of Personality Assessment, 59,* 32–49.

Gacono, C.B., Meloy, J.R., & Bridges, M.R. (2000). A Rorschach comparison of psychopaths, sexual homicide perpetrators, and nonviolent pedophiles: Where angels fear to tread. *Journal of Clinical Psychology, 56,* 757–777.

Hare, R. (1991). *Manual for the revised psychopathy checklist.* Toronto: Multihealth Systems.

Heaven, T.R. (1988). *Relationship between Hare's psychopathy checklist and selected Exner Rorschach variables in an inmate population.* Unpublished doctoral dissertation, United States International University, San Diego.

Hilsenroth, M.J., Hibbard, S.R., Nash, M.R., & Handler, L. (1993). A Rorschach study of narcissism, defence, and aggression in borderline, narcissistic, and Cluster C personality disorders. *Journal of Personality Assessment, 60,* 346–361.

Holt, R.R. (1977). A method for assessing primary process manifestations and their controls in Rorschach responses. In M.A. Rickers-Ovsiankina (Ed.), *Rorschach psychology* (2nd ed., pp. 375–420). Huntington, NY: Krieger.

Holt, R.R., & Havel, J. (1960). A method for assessing primary and secondary process in the Rorschach. In M.A. Rickers-Ovsiankina (Ed.), *Rorschach psychology* (pp. 263–315). New York: Wiley.

Huprich, S.K., Gacono, C.B., Schneider, R.B ., & Bridges, M.R. (2004). Rorschach oral dependency in psychopaths, sexual homicide perpetrators, and nonviolent pedophiles. *Behavioral Science and the Law, 22,* 345–356.

Kamphuis, J.H., Kugeares, S.L., & Finn, S.E. (2000). Rorschach correlates of sexual abuse: Trauma content and aggression indices. *Journal of Personality Assessment, 75,* 212–224.

Levy, A.E. (1998). Gender differences among physically abused children on Rorschach indices of adaptive patterns. (Doctoral dissertation, California School of

Professional Psychology at Alameda, 1997). *Dissertation Abstracts International, 58,* 5127B.

Margolis, J.D. (1992). Aggressive and borderline-level content on the Rorschach: An exploratory study of some proposed scoring criteria. (Doctoral dissertation, California School of Professional Psychology at Alameda, 1992). *Dissertation Abstracts International, 54,* 2805.

Meloy, J.R. (1988). *The psychopathic mind: Origins, dynamics, and treatment.* Northvale, NJ: Aronson.

Meloy, J.R. (2000). The nature and dynamics of sexual homicide: An integrative review. *Aggression and Violent Behavior, 5,* 1–22.

Meloy, J.R., & Gacono, C.B. (1992). The aggression response and the Rorschach. *Journal of Clinical Psychology, 48,* 104–114.

Meloy, J.R., Gacono, C., & Kenney, L. (1994). A Rorschach investigation of sexual homicide. *Journal of Personality Assessment, 62,* 58–67.

Mihura, J.L., & Nathan-Montano, E. (2001). An interpersonal analysis of Rorschach aggression variables in a normal sample. *Psychological Reports, 89,* 617–623.

Mihura, J.L., Nathan-Montano, E, & Alperin, R.J. (2003). Rorschach measures of aggressive drive derivatives: A college student sample. *Journal of Personality Assessment, 80*(1), 41–49.

Morey, L.C. (1991). *Personality assessment inventory: Professional manual.* Odessa, FL: Psychological Assessment Resources.

Neubauer, L.M. (2001). The relationship between behavior ratings of aggression and an aggression coding system of the Rorschach in a nonpatient female sample. (Doctoral dissertation, California School of Professional Psychology at Fresno, 2001). *Dissertation Abstracts International, 61,* 6143B.

Rapaport, D., Gill, M.M., & Schafer, R. (1946). *Diagnostic psychological testing (Vol. 1).* Chicago: Yearbook Publishers.

Rapaport, D., Gill, M.M., & Schafer, R. (1968). *Diagnostic psychological testing.* New York: International Universities Press.

Riquelme, J., Occupati, R., & Gonzales, E. (1991). *Rorschach: Estudio de contenidos. Datos normativos para de sujetos no pacientes di Caracas y su area metropolitana. Aportes al sistema comprensivo de Exner* [Rorschach: Study of the content. Normative data for nonpatient subjects from the greater Caracas area. According to Exner's Comprehensive System]. Unpublished raw data.

Rorschach Workshops. (2000). *2000 alumni newsletter.* Asheville, NC: Author.

Rosenthal, R. (1991). *Meta-analytic procedures for social research* (revised). Newbury Park, CA: Sage.

Schafer, R. (1954). *Psychoanalytic interpretation in Rorschach testing.* New York: Grune & Stratton.

Shaffer, T.W., Erdberg, P., & Haroian, J. (1999). Current nonpatient data for the Rorschach, WAIS-R, and MMPI-2. *Journal of Personality Assessment, 73,* 305–316.

Westen, D. (1990). Toward a revised theory of borderline object relations: Contributions of empirical research. *International Journal of Psycho-Analysis, 71,* 661–693.

White, D.O. (1999). A concurrent validity study of the Rorschach extended aggression scoring categories. *Dissertation Abstracts International, 59,* 5152B. (UMI No. 9907543).

Summary

The Extended Aggression Scores were developed to quantify the aggressive Rorschach imagery produced by violent Antisocial Personality Disordered (ASPD; American Psychiatric Association, 1980) offenders. Despite their histories of real world violence, these subjects produced few Aggressive Movement (AG; Exner, 1993) responses. Why didn't violent children, adolescents, and adults produce more AG responses? Considering their expression of uncensored pleasurable affect when relating their aggressive acts during their interviews, conscious censoring (Exner, 1993; Meloy, 1988) did not adequately explain the paucity of AG responses among *sentenced* adults. Why would they describe their violent acts with pride and bravado during an interview and subsequently censor AG on the Rorschach? Conscious censoring among the Conduct Disorder (CD) children and adolescents, who frequently produced sexual content, seemed an equally unlikely explanation (Gacono, 1997).

Earlier Rorschach research (Holt & Havel, 1960; Rapaport, Gill, & Schafer, 1946, 1968; Schafer, 1954) provided clues to understanding the discrepancies between Rorschach production and the interview/historical data. Direct or implicit aggressive content was thought to imply tensions of aggressive impulse (Rapaport et al., 1946\1968). Initial findings (Gacono, 1988, 1990; Heaven, 1988) suggested that the paucity of symbolized aggression, represented by AG movement, might be due, in part, to the ego-syntonic nature of aggression in ASPD and psychopathic subjects. The clinical logic was that AG symbolized tensions of ego-dystonic aggression when produced by violent, antisocial patients. In the absence of binding the aggressive impulse, the violent individual would, instead, act it out, thus vitiating the need to symbolize it. Existing data supported this hypothesis: Exner's (1995) character disordered sample produced lower AG frequencies than his adult nonpatients; violent children and adolescents produce lower AG frequencies than child and adolescent nonpatients; and the majority of the forensic subjects with known histories of violence produce less AG than nonpatients and the Gacono and Meloy clinical samples without histories of violence (Gacono, 1997; Gacono & Meloy, 1994).

Despite the paucity of AG responses in ASPD records, other aggression imagery was not absent. Rather, the presence of other potentially scoreable aggressive imagery (see Gacono, 1988, 1990, 1997) allowed for the development (Gacono, 1988) and refinement (Gacono & Meloy, 1994; Meloy & Gacono, 1992) of five additional scoring categories: Aggressive Content (AgC), Aggressive Past (AgPast), Aggressive Potential (AgPot), Aggressive Vulnerability (AgV), and Sado-Masochism (SM).

Since their introduction (Gacono, 1988), the Extended Aggression Scores have received considerable clinical interest and empirical study. As noted in the Rorschach Workshops' Alumni Newsletter (2000) concerning the work of the Rorschach Research Council, "Another project on which there has been good progress is the special score for Aggressive Content (AgC). Council has reviewed the criteria and guidelines for its applications and has evaluated the literature concerning it . . . A more precise interpretation of AgC responses will probably hinge on findings for other variables . . ." (p. 13). Additionally, the ROR-SCAN Version 6 Rorschach Interpretive Scoring System (Caracena, 2002) now includes AgC, AgPast, AgPot and SM.. What began as an attempt to expand the scoring of Rorschach aggressive imagery in CD and ASPD subjects, has evolved into a larger study of aggression on the Rorschach. In this article we present information concerning the reliability, psychometric properties, and construct validity of the scores and discuss their clinical meanings. We conclude that while AgPotential, AgVulnerability and Sadomasochism need additional research, the current research supports inclusion of the more frequently appearing AgContent and AgPast scores in the Comprehensive System.

Résumé

Le codage d'agressivité a été élaboré pour quantifier les connotations agressives dans les Rorschach de criminels violents présentant un Trouble de la Personnalité Antisociale (ASPD; American Psychiatric Association, 1980). Malgré leur passé de violence avéré, ces sujets ne produisaient que peu de réponses de Mouvements agressifs (AG; Exner, 1993). Pourquoi les enfants, les adolescents et les adultes violents ne produisaient-ils pas plus de réponses AG ? Étant donné l'expression non censurée de plaisir dans le récit de leurs actes d'agression au cours des entretiens, l'explication par la censure consciente des contenus agressifs (Exner, 1993; Meloy,

1988) n'était pas satisfaisante chez des criminels déjà condamnés. Pourquoi décriraient-ils leurs actes avec fierté et panache pendant un entretien, pour ensuite censurer les réponses AG au Rorschach ? L'explication ne tient pas plus pour les enfants et adolescents présentant des Troubles de la conduite (CD), qui donnent fréquemment des contenus sexuels dans leurs Rorschach (Gacono, 1997).

Des études Rorschach antérieures (Holt & Havel, 1960; Rapaport, Gill, & Schafer, 1946, 1968; Schafer, 1954) apportaient des indices pour comprendre ces différences entre la production au Rorschach et celle des entretiens. On pouvait faire l'hypothèse qu'un contenu agressif direct ou implicite provoquait des tensions de la pulsion agressive (Rapaport et al., 1946\1968). Nos premières recherches (Gacono, 1988, 1990; Heaven, 1988) suggéraient que la pauvreté de symbolisation de l'agressivité, représentée par le mouvement AG, seraient en partie due à la nature ego-syntonique de l'agressivité chez les sujets ASPD et psychopathes. Le concept sous-jacent était que les réponses AG des sujets violents et antisociaux symbolisaient une agressivité ego-dystonique. Par défaut de liaison de la pulsion agressive, l'individu violent l'agirait, faisant ainsi l'économie de la symbolisation. Cette hypothèse était étayée par certaines données: Exner (1995) a trouvé moins de réponses AG dans son groupe de trouble de caractère que dans l'échantillon normatif, les enfants et adolescents violents produisent moins de réponses AG que dans l'échantillon des nonconsultants, et la majorité des sujets judiciarisés au passé violent avéré produisent moins de réponses AG que les nonconsultants et que les groupes cliniques sans passé de violence de Gacono et Meloy (Gacono, 1997; Gacono & Meloy, 1994).

Malgré la pauvreté des réponses AG dans les protocoles ASPD, on trouve d'autres formes d'expression agressive. La présence d'autres formes d'expression agressive qui paraissaient codables (voir Gacono, 1988, 1990, 1997) ont permis d'élaborer (Gacono, 1988) puis d'affiner (Gacono & Meloy, 1994; Meloy & Gacono, 1992) de cinq catégories de cotation: Contenu agressif (AgC), Agressivité passée (AgPast), Agressivité potentielle (AgPot), Vulnérabilité agressive (AgV) et Sado-masochisme (SM).

Depuis leur introduction (Gacono, 1988), le codage de l'agressivité a suscité un grand intérêt clinique et a été l'objet d'études empiriques. Dans la lettre annuelle des Rorschach Workshops (Alumni Newsletter, 2000) il est écrit, concernant les travaux du Rorschach Research Council " Un autre projet à l'étude est le score Contenu agressif (AgC). Le Conseil scientifique a passé en revue les critères et directives pour son application ainsi que la littérature qui s'y rapporte. (. . .) Une interprétation plus précise des réponses AgC va probablement dépendre de la prise en compte d'autres variables (. . .)," p. 13. en outre, le logiciel ROR-SCAN Version 6 Rorschach Interpretive Scoring System (Caracena, 2002) inclut maintenant les scores AgC, AgPast, AgPot et SM. Ce qui était au départ une tentative pour expliquer l'expression de l'agressivité chez les sujets ASPD et CD s'est transformé en une étude plus générale de l'agressivité au Rorschach. Dans cet article, nous présentons des informations concernant la validité, les qualités psychométriques et la validité de construit de ces cotations et nous discutons de leur signification clinique. Nous en concluons que les scores AgPotentiel, AgVulnérabilité et Sado-masochisme demandent de plus amples recherches, tandis que ceux de AgContenu et AgPassée méritent d'être inclus dans le Système Intégré.

Resumen

Los Códigos Ampliados de Agresión se desarrollaron para poder cuantificar las imágenes agresivas que producía en Rorschach los delincuentes violentos con Trastorno de Personalidad Antisocial (TPA, Asociación Americana de Psiquiatría, 1980). A pesar de que en sus historias biográficas suele haber violencia real muy evidente, estos sujetos producen pocas respuestas de Movimiento Agresivo (AG, Exner, 1993). ¿Por qué los niños, adolescentes y adultos abiertamente violentos no generan más respuestas AG? Si se tienen en cuenta sus claras expresiones de placer cuando narran sus actos agresivos durante las entrevistas, los procesos de censura consciente (Exner, 1993; Meloy, 1988) no explican adecuadamente la escasez de respuestas AG en adultos que han sido condenados. ¿Por qué van a describir sus conductas violentas con orgullo y bravuconería en una entrevista y luego van a censurar las respuestas AG en Rorschach? La censura consciente en niños y adolescentes con trastornos de conducta (TC), que producen frecuentes respuestas de contenido sexual, resulta asimismo una explicación poco satisfactoria (Gacono, 1997).

Las investigaciones con Rorschach más antiguas (Holt y Havel,1960; Rapaport, Gill y Schafer, 1946, 1968; Schafer, 1954) ya aportaron ciertas claves para comprender la discrepancia entre la producción en Rorschach y en una entrevista de recopilación de datos histórico-biográficos. Se indicaba que el contenido agresivo directo o implícito implicaba tensiones en el impulso agresivo (Rapaport et al., 1946/1968). Los hallazgos iniciales (Gacono, 1988, 1990; Heaven, 1988) sugerían que la pobreza de agresión simbolizada representada por el movimiento agresivo (AG) podría ser debida, en parte, a la naturaleza egosintónica de la agresividad en sujetos con TPA y en psicópatas. La lógica de esta hipótesis clínica consistía en que las AG simbolizarían tensiones de la agresión egodistónica cuando eran aportadas por personas violentas o antisociales. En ausencia de controles adecuados para los impulsos agresivos, el individuo violento tiene que actuarlos, evitando así la necesidad de simbolizarlos. Existen datos en apoyo de esta idea: la muestra de Exner (1995) de sujetos con trastornos caracteriales produce menos AG que su muestra de adultos no pacientes; muestras de niños y adolescentes violentos producen menores frecuencias de AG que niños y adolescentes no pacientes; la mayoría de sujetos del ámbito forense con historia conocida de conductas violentas producen menos AG que los no pacientes y que las muestras clínicas de Gacono y Meloy de sujetos sin historia de comportamiento violento (Gacono, 1997; Gacono y Meloy, 1994).

No obstante, a pesar de la escasez de AG, fue muy importante registrar que aparecían muchas otras imágenes agresivas en los protocolos de TPA. Así, la presencia de estos otros elementos agresivos potencialmente codificables (ver Gacono, 1988, 1990, 1997) permitió el desarrollo (Gacono, 1988) y posterior refinamiento (Gacono y Meloy, 1994; Meloy y Gacono, 1992) de cinco categorías de codificación adicionales: Contenido Agresivo (AgC), Agresión Pasada (AgPast), Agresión Potencial (AgPot), Vulnerabilidad Agresiva (AgV) y Sado-Masoquismo (SM).

Desde su introducción (Gacono, 1988) estos Códigos Ampliados de Agresión han sido objeto de considerable interés y de numerosos estudios empíricos. Como se señalaba en la Alumni Newsletter de Rorschach Workshops (2000) en referencia al trabajo del Consejo de Investigación de Rorschach: "Otro proyecto en el que ha habido considerables progresos ha sido en el código especial para Contenido Agresivo (AgC). El Consejo ha revisado los criterios para su valoración y la literatura sobre el mismo ... Probablemente, una interpretación más precisa de las respuestas AgC dependerá de los hallazgos sobre otras variables ..."(p. 13). Por otro lado, el ROR-SCAN Versión 6 (Rorschach Interpretive Scoring System, Caracena, 2002) ya incluye AgC, AgPast, AgPot y SM. Lo que comenzó como un intento de ampliar la codificación de las imágenes agresivas en Rorschach de sujetos TC y TPA se ha convertido en un estudio muy amplio sobre la agresividad en Rorschach. En este artículo se presenta información sobre fiabilidad, propiedades psicométricas y validez de constructo de estos códigos y se discute sobre su significado clínico. Se concluye que AgPot, AgV y SM necesitan seguir siendo estudiados, mientras que los datos de investigación actuales permiten incluir AgC y AgPast en el Sistema Comprehensivo.

Rorschachiana 27, 191–210

Cognitive Functioning and Other Discriminatory Variables in Anorexic Patients

Carmen García-Alba

Psychiatric Institute José Germain of Leganés, Madrid, Spain

Introduction

The existence of Eating Disorders (ED) can be traced back to a remote past; they cannot be considered a new problem. However, the truth is that in recent years they have become an important health problem in industrialized and postindustrialized societies, not only because of the increase in these pathologies, but also because they are considered as serious illnesses with a lasting clinical course, which require specialized treatment and frequent hospitalization, and very often become chronic and produce high rates of mortality. The emergence of this pathology usually takes place during adolescence when an identity and value crisis occurs, typical of this developmental period, along with the bodily changes and the importance adolescents attach to physical looks. Consequently, during this period the adolescent is especially vulnerable, allowing for the creation of behavioral stereotypes (Morandé, Casas, Calvo, Marcos, Hidalgo, Lareo, García-Alba, & Eisman, 1995). At this moment, the existing stereotype in the occidental culture, in which anorexia nervosa (AN) appears most frequently, is slimness that comprises the ideal of beauty, intelligence, and success, which image is widely promoted by the media. It is a fact that the number of new cases in specialized clinics is increasing, and an appropriate treatment providing high rates of long-term efficacy has not yet been developed. The variety of problems present in this disorder makes a multi-factorial insight into the subject necessary, leading to an etiopathogenic understanding of the disorder from all possible angles. In fact, a strictly biological perspective must be taken into account if we consider that AN has medical implications that may lead to death. Similarly, the existence of a psychological dimension becomes obvious if we take into account its connection with other illnesses such as depression, anxiety or obsessive disorders. Finally, the family and social factors of this pathology are relevant since, once established, the clinical symptoms of AN can be devastating.

A review of the available literature reveals some flaws in the reported studies: The sample size is usually small and, most important, the subtypes of AN (restrictive and binge-eating/purging) are mixed together. Also, age ranges are excessively broad, mixing subjects who have very different psychological traits; not taking into account or not specifying the evolutive stage of the illness can be another common confusion. On other occasions, the normative data of the tests, which should normally be used as guidelines or references, is used as a control group of nonpatients, which can lead to erroneous conclusions when comparing heterogeneous groups (normative data) to homogeneous groups (participants in the research). It is also noted that the tests used in the psychological evaluation of these patients are usually personality questionnaires or inventories, or more specific anxiety/depression/ED questionnaires. For reasons of obvious difficulty and cost (economic, time consumption, and degree of training required), more exhaustive psychodiagnostic studies are scarce.

All of these factors determined not only the interest in, but also the possible usefulness of this study. It is meant to provide material to contribute, if possible, to a major insight into this pathology by means of a series of psychological tests, which have sufficiently proved the study's validity and reliability.

The *main objective* is to study the existing relationship between AN and Depression (D) which, even if undeniable from some perspectives (neurobiological, psychiatric/psychological, family, therapeutic), is not yet completely clear. These results have been previously published (García-Alba, 2000, 2004).

The *second objective*, consequent and complementary to the one mentioned above, is to complete a description of the *personality traits* of the female anorexic patients from the Rorschach protocols and, if possible, to detect the significant differences of this pathology with regard to the other evaluated groups. To achieve this, Exner's proposed schema of analyzing the variables by clusters was followed (Exner, 2003); Sendín also, summarizes the schema well (Exner & Sendín, 1995). The analyzed clusters were: *Affective Features, Capacity for Control and Stress Tolerance, Self-Perception, Interpersonal Relationships, and Cognitive Functioning*. In each one of these clusters the starting point of the hypothesis is that significant differences between the evaluated samples will be found.

In this article only the findings related to the cognitive functioning of these adolescents will be presented. The aim of this study is to analyze the cognitive difficulties of the restricting-type anorexic subjects and to specify in which part of the process these dysfunctions appear, what is their nature and how they facilitate and/or maintain the illness. The hypothesis to be verified in this part of the research assumes that there will be differences detected in the cognitive functioning of the groups composing this sample: restricting-type anorexic patients, depressed patients, and nonpatients as control group.

Method

To test this hypothesis a *comparative study of cases vs controls* has been designed.

Participants

The *common characteristics* are:

1. Age: between 13 to 16 years old, which is intended to: (1) eliminate childhood AN, which is significantly different being, in general, a measure of protest against the environment; (2) position oneself at the start of the illness to avoid the influx of other variables such as chronic development; (3) embrace a developmental period marking significant changes in physical, psychical, and educational functioning, without being so broad as to eliminate differences relative to age.
2. Gender: the sample is composed of girls, as the anorexic pathology has a greater incidence in the female gender. (The male group, evaluated in parallel, is still a very small sample, and will be examined in future studies and comparisons.)
3. Collected from public institutions: educational or health care. The socioeconomic level is, therefore, around middle and middle-low.
4. Sample size: 50 individuals in each group, determined by the considerations of the expected effect.

The *specific criteria* for each group are listed below:

1. Anorexic patients (ANP): (1) diagnosed following the criteria of the DSM III-R (APA, 1987) in force at the start of this research. Furthermore, when the DSM IV (APA, 1994) appeared, all DSM III-R criteria were revised with hardly any significant changes in these criteria. Only the subtypes of restricting AN and binge-eating/purging AN were added, modalities that had already been taken into consideration at the start of this research. (2) Restricting-type anorexic subjects, where the influence of the binge-eating/purging variable has been eliminated. This decision has slowed down the fieldwork considerably as 50% of anorectic patients develop bulimic symptoms, causing a symptomatic alternation in one or the other direction. The interview conducted at the beginning of the evaluation of these patients has been effective for eliminating all these cases. (3) First hospitalization was because of the anorexic problem so as to avoid doubtful diagnosis, as well as already chronic cases.
   Constitution of the sample has been possible through contact with public hospitals in Madrid, which had a special dedication to this pathology and also pediatric beds available. The University Hospital of Getafe, the Hospital of Móstoles, and the University Hospital «Niño Jesús», pioneers in the treatment of infant-juvenile AN, have collaborated in this study. The AN group has a mean age of 14.84 years, with a standard deviation of 1.13.
2. Patients diagnosed with depression (DP), following the clinical criteria of the DSM III-R (APA, 1987), later revised according to the DSM IV (APA, 1994). This criterion is the most widely accepted, even though the nosological problem of this pathology in infancy and adolescence has not yet been solved. The structured interview of Research Diagnostics Criteria has been used (Revised RDC: Endicott, Andreasen, & Spitzer, 1978) to attain greater objectivity in the data collection process. No differences have been established between a major depression and a dysthymic disorder because of the difficulties imposed by this differentiation, especially within the child and juvenile population (DSM IV, APA, 1994) and also the lack of utility for the purposes of this research.
   The sample was obtained in two mental health centers in Madrid (Leganés and Fuenlabrada), specialized in infant and juvenile care. The mean age of these adolescents was 15.02 years, with a standard deviation of 1.13.

3. Control group (NP) includes (1) individuals who have never required any psychiatric or psychological aid at any time, (2) adequate academic performance to eliminate possible intellectual limitations.

The sample was obtained in a Secondary Education School in Madrid (Leganés), with prior application of parental informed consent, and the availability of adequate resources and coverage to deal with the possible detected pathology, as these types of studies are inadvisable without the support of adequate health care resources. This group had a mean age of 14.90 years and an *SD* of .95.

Measuring Instruments

Rorschach, which is basically used as a perceptual-cognitive test, follows the guidelines of Exner's Comprehensive System (2003). Only the structural information of the protocol is used, basically quantitative, to facilitate statistical/computerized processing of the data.

Variables

Cognitive Functioning is identified by three Rorschach clusters:

1. *Information Processing*, which indicates how the subject incorporates information coming from his/her environment (motivation and efficiency). Variables: Lambda *(L)*; Obsessive style index *(OBS)*; Hypervigilance index *(HVI)*; Z frequency *(Zf)*, complemented by the location of responses: whole *(W)*, common detail *(D)*, and unusual detail *(Dd)*; Processing efficiency *(Zd)*; Developmental quality *(DQ)*; Perseveration *(PSV)*.
2. *Cognitive Mediation*, which indicates how the subject identifies and translates the previously processed information into responses (conventionality degree and distortion levels).
   Variables: *L; OBS; Populars;* Form quality: Conventional form use *(X+%; F+%; FQo)*; Distorted form *(X–%)*; Unusual form use *(Xu%);* Space minus *(S–)* frequency; Confabulation *(CFB)*.
3. Finally, *Ideation* indicates how the information is conceptualized and used as ideas (ideative efficiency, flexibility, and clarity of judgments). Variables: Erlebnistypus *(EB)* and *EB* pervasive *(EB Per);* Left side of

experience base *(eb: FM + m);* Ratios *active: passive* and ratios human movement *(M) Ma: Mp;* Intellectualization index *(Intellect);* Morbid contents *(MOR);* Special scores *(Sum6 Sp Sc; WSum6; Lvl 2 Sp Sc)*; Human movement: Form quality *(M; MQo; MQnone; MQ–).*

These three clusters are essential in the psychological functioning of the subject and the errors found in any of them will have important repercussions in his/her behavior.

In some cases (because of group accessibility) other examiners were used to obtain Rorschach protocols of the nonpatient sample. In this case, the possible influence of this fact as well as the interscorer reliability has been analyzed. We also studied the Rorschach variables related to validity criteria: Total number of responses (R) and Lambda (L).

Statistical Procedures

The statistical program SPSS/PC+ was used for data analysis. The problems raised by the data analysis of the Rorschach test are known in advance, because many of its variables are nonparametric and, even so, they can present asymmetric distributions, which invalidate the use of parametric analyses. That is why the following statistical calculations have been included after the exploratory analysis of the variables.

1. Univariant statistics providing a more solid base to the type of analysis selected, as well as giving information about these samples. Those Rorschach variables with $z \geq 1.96$ are considered nonparametric, both in the skewness and kurtosis.
2. Variance analysis of a three-factor independent variable. In all cases, the samples were independent and had equal variances (Bartlett's test). The assumption of normality was judged as less important because of the samples' characteristics. The F and the Tukey contrasts were used, and a significance level of $\alpha = .05$. The statistical power was calculated with the Bavry statistical program. The effect size (η) is also calculated.

When the basic assumption of equal variances is not met, a double solution is adopted: (1) the logarithmic transformation proposed by Tukey that, if unable to provide equal variance distributions, is not subjected to further possible transformations; and (2) use of the nonparametric

Kruskal-Wallis contrast. We used this procedure because of the the inconveniences of both options, as the transformations produce scales with a doubtful and questionable interpretation of the quantitative meaning (Exner, 1995) and the Kruskal-Wallis test is less powerful.

3. χ^2, under two assumptions: (1) In some nonparametric variables, with many values around zero, the ranges are very limited and the relations nonlinear. In these cases, Exner proposes nonparametric statistical and interpretative cut-off points. (2) In parametric variables it is useful to determine a cut-off point to distinguish between the expected values and those which denote some type of psychological alteration. A residual analysis was done to provide an in-depth study of the contingency tables.
4. Finally, a discriminant analysis was done with the Rorschach variables that were regarded as significant during the research.

Procedure

The procedure was basically as follows: (1) initial interview with the adolescent, (2) application of Rorschach individually, and (c) feedback on the results.

Results

Table 1 presents the variables that reached statistical significance between groups. In this table, the degrees of freedom are not shown, as they are the same in all cases ($df = 2$). In order to better interpret the data, a summary of some univariant statistics corresponding to each variable is included in all of them.

Our comments on the results will focus on two aspects: first, the characteristics that the ANP patients share with other adolescents and, second, those which are specific to this group.

Table 1. Variables that resulted as significant when analyzing the clustering of the Cognitive Triad: Processing, Mediation and Ideation.

	Anorexic patients (ANP) ($N = 50$)	Depressed-Patients (DP) ($N = 50$)	Nonpatients (NP) ($N = 50$)	Sign.	η	Pow.
Information processing						
DQv	$M = .98$; $SD = 1.10$	$M = 1.20$; $SD = 1.28$	$M = 1.94$; $SD = 2.05$	NP > ANP *	.26	.65
Zd	$M = -.16$; $SD = 5.31$	$M = .34$; $SD = 5.03$	$M = -2.53$; $SD = 4.57$	ANP, DP > NP *	.24	.79
Ideation						
M	$M = 4.46$; $SD = 3.88$	$M = 2.98$; $SD = 2.47$	$M = 2.82$; $SD = 1.97$	ANP > DP *	.24	.68
MQo	$M = 2.10$; $SD = 1.62$	$M = 1.42$; $SD = 1.40$	$M = 1.38$; $SD = 1.01$	ANP > DP *	.24	.74
MQsin	$M = .14$; $SD = .35$	$M = .02$; $SD = .14$	$M = .04$; $SD = .20$	ANP > DP, NP *	.20	.64
Mp	$M = 2.90$; $SD = 2.96$	$M = 1.84$; $SD = 1.72$	$M = 1.58$; $SD = 1.36$	ANP > NP *	.26	.78
Passive	$M = 5.08$; $SD = 3.47$	$M = 3.40$; $SD = 2.47$	$M = 3.72$; $SD = 2.81$	ANP > DP, NP *	.24	.77

Note. η = Expected effect; Pow. = Power; *M* = Mean; *SD* = Standard Deviation; $^*p < .05$.

Information Processing

As can be observed, this cluster is not very differentiating. With regard to the ANP, one can conclude, in a very synthetic way, that:

1. The style in which these patients register information coming from their environment is similar enough to that of the other evaluated adolescents. *All of them:*
   - Get involved in the task to be done, making an effort to organize the stimuli and create significant relationships among them *(Zf)*.
   - Have low practical skills (*D%*, ↓) (↓ = low) in facing different situations, as they become involved in perceptions that are too general (*W%*, ↑) (↑ = high) and/or in aspects that are much too partial, too biased (*Dd%* ↑).
   - Do not fall into repetitions (*PSV*, absent) nor into an excessive amount of detailed and/or an overwhelming perfectionism (neg-

ative *OBS*). They do not hold a state of continued alert (negative HVI).
- Their hostile and negative attitude (*S* ↑) could make them less efficient.

2. However, it is the ANP who better understand the information, with all its complexity, coming from their environment (*Lambda* ≤ *.99* = 70%; *DQv*).
3. They register well the key points of the information, being able to distinguish the essential from the additional *(Zd)*.
4. Consequently, the processing work of the stimulus field is adequate enough. These patients will have sufficient data available, which will allow them, at the start, to behave adequately.

Cognitive Mediation

The way these adolescents interpret the information they have gathered from their environment is similar across the three groups. Now we can complete the description of the cognitive functioning we have been performing by concluding that:

5. The lack of perceptive adjustment we find in the ANP, the biases when they codify the processed information, are similar enough in the *three groups*, so that we can highlight the following shared characteristics:
   - They can understand the most obvious and evident information, and even provide adequate responses that comply with the norms and expectations of their reference group *(Populars)*.
   - With the exception of these more obvious aspects, their perceptive adjustment is quite precarious, not only when they understand a situation in its entire complexity *(X+%)*, but also when they simplify the stimulus field *(F+%)* and reduce it to the strictly formal.
   - This perceptive disturbance is not caused by any hostile-type emotional interferences *(S–%)*, but is from an excessive degree of auto-centricity *(Xu%)* and a very arbitrary way of interpreting the information *(X–%)*.
   - The lack of perceptive precision, common to all three groups, could be partly linked to the inherent biases if the type of sampling conducted. These are, however, less serious and more understandable during the developmental period in which they appear, name-

ly during adolescence, a stage of great questioning, biases, confrontations and disagreements with the environment.

Ideation

This cluster appears as pathognomonic, as a clear differentiator of these ANP. These results allow us to add that:

6. In the final process of cognitive functioning, that is, at the conceptualization of the information that the adolescents have previously compiled from their environment and have codified, the three groups share only the following *traits*:
   - There is not any type of peripheral ideational overload *(FM + m)* that hampers and hinders the adolescent's thinking process and deliberate thinking.
   - Their thinking is sometimes slightly distorted (*MQ–; M– > 1*), but as there are not any significant cognitive slippages that can be observed *(Sum6 Sp Sc)*, these alterations could have minor psychopathologic importance.
   - Their way of thinking is occasionally tainted with some degree of pessimism and pessimistic ideas or attributions *(MOR)*.
   - They do not use any intellectualization mechanisms to neutralize the impact of emotions *(Intellect)*.
7. Despite the similarities mentioned above, this ideation cluster is the one that differentiates the anorexic patients from the rest of the adolescents, in a much more clear and firm way, and it is one of the constellations that provides more information on this pathology.
8. Even though there is a slight predominance of the *ambitent* response style (38%), the most curious thing about this group (ANP) as compared to the other adolescents is the fact of having a much more defined response style, in the sense of *introversive* (34%) or *extratensive* (28%), as can be observed from Figure 1.

As a result, only in 38% of the cases *(ambitents)* will the behavior of the ANP be unpredictable, as their way of thinking will occasionally be influenced by their emotions, while on other, maybe even similar, occasions, the emotions will play a secondary role. However, responses of the rest of the anorexic patients (62%) will be much more defined, more consistent. This determination, firmness, and consistency in the ide-

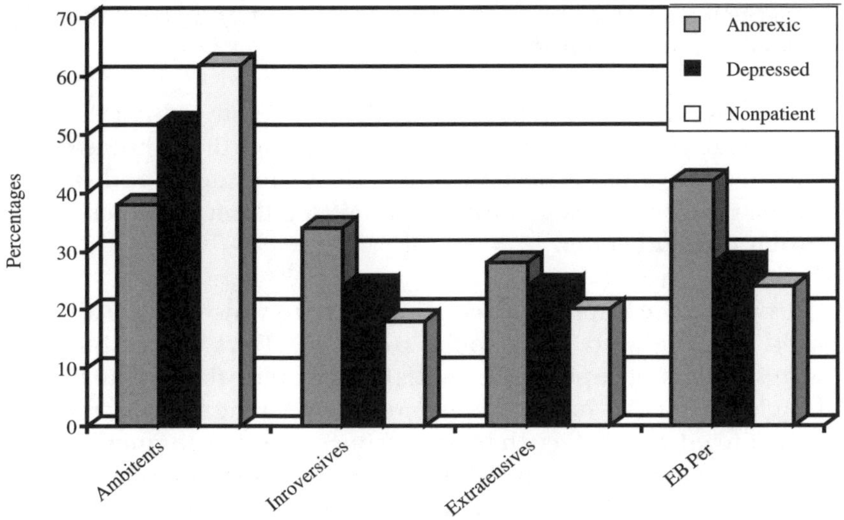

Figure 1. Erlebnistypus *(EB)* in adolescent samples (*N* = 150).

ational patterns shown in these patients would, at first, seem a positive finding, which will have to be compared with the information obtained from the analysis of other variables.

9. If this consistency (defined EB) goes with a lack of flexibility (EB Per = 42%), there will be adaptation difficulties and greater inefficacy among ANP. This problem also results in a major resistance to change and, in summary, to its psychotherapeutic approach.
10. The ANP make great use of thinking *(M)*.Their usually well-adjusted thinking *(MQo)* has occasional alterations, as also happens to the other evaluated adolescents *(MQ–),* but it occasionally presents some characteristics that are similar to the delusional-type ideation *(MQnone).*
11. Also, this thinking is very passive *(passive),* above all when deliberate thinking is used *(Mp).* It is a kind of thinking that repeatedly turns ideas and worries - sometimes distorted and passively accepted– over and over, causing trouble and wasting energy. This kind of thinking does not help ANPs to find solutions to their problems.

The responsibility and decision-making process is then delegated to others, with the expectation that the decisions of others will match their needs. Such a thought process is very inefficient and keeps the subject occupied in a very unproductive way.

12. This passivity does not at all imply that they easily submit themselves to the decisions of their environment, it makes them, however, more vulnerable with respect to other ideas, messages, and opinions, which they can accept without submitting them to the criticism of their own judgment.

At this point, the important social pressure to which we are all subject should be reiterated. This social pressure offers successful models where slimness occupies an essential place, and which, widely spread through the media, have a great impact on young people, especially. This is linked to the fact that adolescence is a developmental period of great disorientation in which the changing, corporal image is highly questioned, subject to very critical attitudes, and probably results in many conflicts. That is why the rejection of one's own body results in a relatively easy and irrational search for ideas such as slimness to solve all problems. These adolescents, who are more vulnerable because of their passivity, could be attracted by these arbitrary and distorted ideas. They do not even manage to reason about these ideas adequately, although they do seem to do reason without difficulty on other topics *(MQo)*.

13. In this ideation, used in such a rigid way even if the situation requires another type of response *(EB Per)*, we can find one of the many causes contributing to difficulty of treatment, and resistance to change.
14. The discriminant analysis performed with the variables that were significant throughout the research (García-Alba, 2000) reinforces this ideative disorder through one function, in which these ANP emphasize the following: Human movement none *(MQnone ↑)*; Human movement passive *(Mp ↑)*; Form dimension *(FD ↓)*; Human movement *(M ↑)*; Human movement ordinary *(MQo ↑)*; Adjusted D score *(AdjD ↑)*; All human contents *(SumH ↑)*; Whole human, fictional or mythological [*(H)* ↑]. The interpretation of this constellation makes full sense when taken together with the variables of the diverse Rorschach clusters that resulted as significant; we can thus broaden our knowledge on the personality traits of these ANP. On top of the thinking problems *(MQnone ↑; Mp ↑; M ↑; MQo ↑)* we can detect:

- Worrying and conflict surrounding the human element *(Sum H ↑)*. ANPs have quite a distorted vision, not only of themselves, but also of others *[(H) ↑]*. This alteration of the image is not caused by perceptive misadjustments, which they share with the other evaluated groups; the distortion is from a highly fantasized image, as a result of the imaginary experiences, which is not supported by real data coming from ordinary situations. That may be why it is so hard to modify.
- Lack of inclination to introspection and self-questioning *(FD ↓)*.
- Presence of good resources (*EA* > NP, $p < .05$, power .72, $\eta = .22$) to decide on behaviors and end them deliberately, without impulsiveness (*AdjD* > DP, $p < .05$, power .65, η .22). These data indicate that distorted thinking *(MQnone)* and fantasy *(Mp)* have great influence on the decision to not eat.

Measuring Errors

Even though valid protocols were initially used ($R \geq 14$ and $L \leq .99$), it is important to state that there are no significant differences between the groups with reference to *R*, nor in the *Lambda* score, as observed in the variance analysis that was performed ($p = .15$ and $p = .11$, respectively). Nevertheless, it is the ANP who, qualitatively, present a lower L, inferior to .99 in 70% of the protocols, as compared to the DP (64%) and the NP (52%). This finding is important, as it implies that the obtained data in this group is not shadowed by any avoidant and simplifying style, characteristic of a high L (L > .99).

We can also conclude that the possible examiners' bias (1 examiner in ANP, 2 in DP, and 3 in NP), has not significantly altered the length of the protocols obtained.

The percentage of interscorer reliability exceeds the recommended levels by Exner and Sendín (1997) and they are above 80% in all areas.

Discussion

The findings in cognitive functioning of these restricting-type ANPs have a series of implications and allow the clarification of some aspects of personality of these adolescents.

1. Currently, many authors discuss *thinking problems as most serious* in AN (Radomsky, de Silva, Tood, Treasure, & Murphy, 2002; Shafran, Teachman, Kerry, & Rachman, 1999), highlighting that these can participate in predisposition to the illness or in its maintenance. These problems persist even after clinical recovery and are important in possible relapses. The relevance to this research of the obtained data lies in the fact that:
   - They provide a solid empirical base to these theories and explanatory hypotheses. This empirical support, performed from the perspective of the psychological evaluation of the personality, has not found any equivalent study in the literature with which the results could be compared, considering the number of subjects and instruments used.
   - Within the cognitive functioning of the subject they emphasize the processes in which the problem lies: the ANP can grasp information in their environment in a very adequate way, even if they somehow bias it when interpreting it. Where one can really appreciate their problems is in the elaboration of this information, when they conceptualize and build up new concepts with the data they have grasped and partly interpreted in a quite correct way.
2. Maybe it is now easier to understand the frequent relationships that are established between the AN and *obsessive pathology*. Many authors, as Toro (2001), for example, consider that AN progresses with obsessive symptoms constituted by intrusive cognitions related with the figure, the weight, and the food, and these authors tend to assign these symptoms to the neurotransmitter dysfunction provoked by the starvation. But on top of these specific symptoms, one can find a frequent association of the AN with all obsessive-compulsive disorders (García-Camba, 2001). According to these authors, the rates of comorbidity among both pathologies vary enormously (5–25%).

However, the data of this research does not confirm the presence of an obsessive disturbance in the anorexic patients. The way in which the information is processed and codified does not correspond with obsessive cognitive functioning, however, passive deliberate ideation, which keeps the subject unproductively and inefficiently busy, could symptomatically be taken as an obsessive trait. On the other hand, the thoughts described by the Rorschach test are free of the intrusive or irrational properties common to obsessive pathology. There is an increase of deliberate passive ideation *(Mp)* in ANPs; this means that these ideas have been deliberately initiated by the subject, even if they are acritically and passively accepted. Thus, from our Rorschach data we can conclude that cognitive anorexic functioning differs from cognitive obsessive functioning in its three clusters. Nevertheless, to be able to make a rigorous statement it would be necessary to create a design in which the Rorschach results could be compared to the ones provided by other more specific obsession tests.

3. Another important consequence of the results of this research refers to the *treatment* of the AN. When designing a global plan of therapeutic intervention for these patients, a part should be included to modify this ideation, this altered way of thinking, for which cognitive restructuring is an ideal therapy. Similarly, it will be necessary to take into account the modification of this quite distorted and fantasized self-image. An adequate approach of such a complex pathology would require the coordinated effort of various professionals and the integration of diverse theoretical models.
4. Through some of the Rorschach variables we can also understand the difficulties posed by the treatment of the AN and that the prognosis for this illness is generally not good. Confirming unfavorable *prognosis* rates for a psychotherapeutic treatment are: (1) strict response style *(EB Per)*, (2) passive and inefficient ideation *(Mp)*, (3) scarce tendency toward introspection and self-questioning *(FD)*, (4) good resources to decide on behaviors *(EA)* and the possibility of carrying them out without impulsivity *(AdjD)*, and (5) highly fantasized self-image *[(H)]*, which is hard to compare to reality.
5. Finally, it should be mentioned that the data obtained throughout the research seem to indicate that the underlying pathology in this anorexic illness matches the diagnostic criteria of the DSM IV for *Personality Disorder* (1994). Various authors agree with this criterion (García-Camba, 2001). It would be necessary to verify this hypothesis with a design customized for this purpose, in which older subjects are used, as such a diagnosis is not reasonable until the age of 18.

Acknowledgments

To Dr. John Exner and the Dr. Concepción Sendín, for their continuous help and support during the elaboration of this dissertation. Their confidence in this project has been a constant stimulus. Subsequently, their opinions on the results obtained have substantially contributed to my interest in disseminating them.

This article is part of a larger investigation (doctoral dissertation).

References

American Psychiatric Association. (1987). *Diagnostic and statistical manual of mental disorders* (3th ed., Rev.) *(DSM III-R)*. Washington, DC: Author.

American Psychiatric Association. (1994). *Diagnostic and statistical manual of mental disorders* (4th ed.) *(DSM IV)*. Washington, DC: Author.

Endicott, J., Andreasen, N., & Spittzer, R. (1989). Criterios Diagnósticos de Investigación-Historia Familiar: FH-RDC [Research Diagnostic Criteria: FH-RDC]. In R.L. Spitzer, J. Endicott, & E. Robins (Eds.), *Criterios diagnósticos de investigación: RDC Revisado* (J. Bueno, M. Humbert, F. Sabanés, & L. Salvador, Trans.) (pp. 137–169). Madrid: Editores Médicos. (Original work published 1978).

Exner, J.E. (1995). Introduction. In J.E. Exner (Ed.), *Issues and methods in Rorschach research* (pp. 1–24). Mahwah, NJ: Erlbaum.

Exner, J.E. (2003). *The Rorschach. A comprehensive system. Basic foundations and principles of interpretation* (Vol. 1, 4th ed.). Hoboken, NJ: Wiley.

Exner, J.E., & Sendín, C. (1995). *Manual de interpretación del Rorschach para el sistema comprehensivo* [Handbook of Rorschach interpretation for the comprehensive system]. Madrid: Psimática.

Exner, J.E., & Sendín, C. (1997). Some issues in Rorschach research. *European Journal of Psychological Assessment, 13,* 155–163.

García-Alba, C. (2000). *Anorexia y depresion. Evaluación de personalidad en muestras adolescentes* [Anorexia and depression. Personality assessment in adolescent samples]. Madrid: Universidad Complutense de Madrid.

García-Alba, C. (2004). Anorexia and depression. Depressive co-morbidity in anorexic adolescents. *The Spanish Journal, 7,* 40–52.

García-Camba, E. (2001). *Avances en trastornos de la conducta alimentaria. Anorexia nerviosa, bulimia nerviosa y obesidad* [Advances in eating behavior disorders. Anorexia nervosa, bulimia nervosa, and obesity]. Barcelona: Masson.

Morandé, G., Casas, J., Calvo, R., Marcos, A., Hidalgo, I., Lareo, J., García-Alba, C., & Eisman, G. (1995). *Protocolo de trastornos del comportamiento alimentario* [Protocol for eating disorders]. Madrid: Instituto Nacional de la Salud.

Radomsky, A.S., de Silva, P., Tood, G., Treasure, J., & Murphy, T. (2002). Thought-shape fusion in anorexia nervosa: An experimental investigation. *Behavior Research and Therapy, 40,* 1169–1177.

Shafran, R., Teachman, B., Kerry, S., & Rachman, S. (1999). A cognitive distortion associated with eating disorders: Thought-shape fusion. *British Journal of Clinical Psychology, 38,* 167–179.

Toro, J. (2001). Anorexia nerviosa [Anorexia nervosa]. *Medicina Clínica, 117*, 334–335.

Summary

This study is part of a larger research study (doctoral dissertation), in which a comparative study with adolescent samples is done: 50 anorexic restricting patients (ANP), 50 patients diagnosed with depression (DP) and 50 non patients (NP). The proposed objective is two-fold: 1) To try to clarify the existing relationship between Anorexia (AN) and Depression (D), investigated from diverse disciplines but without conclusive results. 2) To detect in the ANP personality different traits from those of other groups, which should, if possible, allow to detect them at an early stage for an adequate prognosis.

The current article presents the Rorschach findings in relation to the cognitive functioning of the ANP. In them, the following has been detected: (1) An information processing similar to that of the other groups, even with a more complete *(L ≤ .99*), more complex *(DQ+*↑*)* and better discriminated *(Zd*↑*)* grasp of the stimulus; (2) Mediating processes very similar to those of the other groups, sharing with them the perceptive maladjustments *(X–%*↑*)* and an excessive individualism *(Xu%*↑*)*; (3) A clearly differentiating ideation disorder.

Definitely, the ANP use predominantly ideation *(M*↑*)*, but their thought, usually well-adjusted *(MQo*↑*)*, presents eventual operations of delusional type *(MQnone*↑*)*. Above that, their thinking is marked by a great passivity *(Mp*↑*)*, which makes them more vulnerable to accept ideas without criticizing them and it results in a very inefficient thinking, which spins around these concepts without finding solutions, entering into a sort of ruminating which is completely unproductive. The differences toward the obsessive pathology are established.

The discriminant analysis conducted with all the Rorschach variables that resulted as significant throughout the research, provides quite a consistent function which discriminates the ANP: *MQnone*↑, *Mp*↑, *FD*↓, *Ma*↑, *MQo*↑, *AdjD*↑, *Sum H*↑, *(H)*↑. Based on this we can understand that these adolescents, being in a developmental period of big changes and disorientations in relation with their own image, confronted with life events, and possibly starting off with some biologic vulnerability: (1) Due to the alterations of their ideation, accept without criticism *(Mp)* irrational ideas dominating in our culture, in which slimness appears as the only model, synthesis of intelligence, beauty and success; remaining captured in this type of mental activity *(MQnone)*, which they cannot escape nor criticize *(Mp)*, despite they reason adequately on other topics *(MQo)*; (2) Their alterations of self-perception *[(H)]* make them hide themselves in a fantasized image, which is the axis of their interests and the only thing that really matters to them; (3) The resources they have to decide on behaviors and to finish these deliberately *(AdjD)*, and their scarce tendency to the introspection *(FD)* lead to their decision of not eating, based on distorted and passively accepted thinking, which has great power and thus, so difficult to modify. Finally, based on the Rorschach data obtained, the hypothesis of a *personality disorder* as underlying pathology is pointed out.

Résumé

L'étude présentée ici fait partie d'une recherche plus large (thèse de doctorat) qui a comparé trois groupes d'adolescents: 50 patientes présentant une anorexie restrictive (ANP), 50 patientes présentant un Trouble dépressif (DP) et 50 nonconsultantes (NP). L'objectif de cette recherche est double: 1/tenter de clarifier les relations entre Anorexie (A) et Dépression (D), qui ont été investiguées par différentes disciplines mais sans résultat concluant; 2/détecter dans la personnalité ANP des caractéristiques qui seraient différentes des autres groupes, ce qui permettrait éventuellement de les dépister plus tôt.

Cet article présente les résultats Rorschach portant sur le fonctionnement cognitif des ANP. Les éléments suivants ont été mis en évidence: (1) le traitement de l'information est similaire à ceux des autres groupes, avec même une façon de saisir le stimulus plus complète (L ≤ 0,99), plus complexe (DQ+ ↑) et plus précise (Zd↑); (2) des processus de médiation très similaires à ceux des autres groupes et partageant avec eux une mauvaise adaptation perceptive (X–% ↑) et un individualisme excessif (Xu% ↑); (3) une perturbation de l'idéation qui les différencie nettement des autres groupes.

Il apparaît nettement que les ANP utilisent de façon prédominante l'idéation (M↑), mais leur pensée, généralement bien adaptée (MQo↑) présente des moments de déconnexion (MQnone↑). En outre, leur pensée est marquée par une plus grande passivité (Mp↑), ce qui les rend plus vulnérables à accepter des idées sans les critiquer, leur pensée devient très inefficiente, elle tourne autour de ces concepts sans trouver de solution, produisant une sorte de rumination totalement stérile. La différence avec les pathologies obsessionnelles est montrée.

L'analyse discriminante réalisée avec toutes les variables constamment significatives dans l'étude a produit une fonction très cohérente qui décrit les ANP: MQnone↑, Mp↑, FD↓, M ↑, MQo↑, AdjD↑, Sum H↑, (H)↑. À partir de ces résultats, nous pouvons comprendre que ces adolescentes, se trouvant à une période du développement de grand changement et de perte des repères dans l'image de soi, et confrontées aux événements de la vie, et peut-être en lien avec quelque vulnérabilité biologique: (1) en raison de l'altération de leur idéation, acceptent sans critique des idées irrationnelles qui dominent leur culture (Mp), qui présentent la minceur comme modèle unique, synthèse de l'intelligence, de la beauté et du succès; sont prisonnières de cette activité mentale (MQnone) qu'elles ne peuvent pas critiquer (Mp) bien qu'elles raisonnent de manière adaptée dans d'autres domaines (MQo); (2) l'altération de la perception de soi [(H)] les pousse à se réfugier dans une représentation imaginaire d'elles-mêmes, qui est leur intérêt principal et la seule chose qui compte à leurs yeux; (3) les ressources dont elles disposent pour prendre leurs décisions et diriger leur comportement (AdjD), et le peu d'activité d'introspection (FD) les amènent à décider de ne pas manger, ce qui devient, en raison des distorsions et de la passivité de leur pensée, si difficile à modifier. Les données obtenues au Rorschach nous amènent à faire l'hypothèse de l'existence d'une pathologie de la personnalité sous-jacente.

Resumen

Este trabajo forma parte de una investigación más amplia (Tesis Doctoral), en la que se realiza un estudio comparativo con muestras adolescentes: 50 pacientes anoréxicas restrictivas (ANP), 50 pacientes diagnosticadas de depresión (DP) y 50 no pacientes (NP). El objetivo propuesto es doble: 1) Intentar esclarecer la relación existente entre Anorexia (AN) y Depresión (D), investigada desde distintas disciplinas, sin que se hayan aportado aún resultados concluyentes. 2) Detectar en ANP características de personalidad distintas de los otros grupos evaluados que permitan, si es posible, su detección precoz, primordial para un buen pronóstico.

El presente artículo desarrolla los hallazgos Rorschach relativos al funcionamiento cognitivo de las ANP. En ellas se detecta: (1) Un procesamiento de la información similar al de los otros grupos evaluados, incluso con una captación del campo estimular más completa (*L* ≤ *.99*), más compleja *(DQ+↑)* y mejor discriminada *(Zd↑)*; (2) Procesos mediadores muy similares a los de los otros grupos, compartiendo con ellos los desajustes perceptivos *(X–% ↑)* y un individualismo excesivo *(Xu% ↑)*; (3) Se señala una alteración de la ideación como claramente diferenciadora.

En efecto, las ANP utilizan la ideación en mayor medida *(M↑)*, pero su pensamiento, habitualmente bien ajustado *(MQo↑)*, presenta eventuales operaciones de tipo delirante *(MQnone↑)*. Además, su reflexión está marcada por una gran pasividad (*Mp*↑), que las hace más vulnerables a la aceptación de ideas sin someterlas a crítica y supone un pensamiento muy poco eficaz, que da vueltas a estos razonamientos sin buscar soluciones, entrando en una especie de rumiación totalmente improductiva. Se establecen diferencias con la patología obsesiva.

El análisis discriminante realizado con todas las variables Rorschach que resultaron significativas en el conjunto de la investigación, aporta una función bastante consistente, que discrimina a las ANP: MQnone↑, Mp↑, FD↓, M ↑, MQo↑, AdjD↑, SumH↑, (H)↑. Según estos resultados podemos entender que estas adolescentes, estando en un periodo evolutivo de grandes cambios y desorientaciones en relación con la propia imagen, ante algún acontecimiento vital, y posiblemente partiendo de cierta vulnerabilidad biológica: (1) Debido a las alteraciones de su ideación aceptan sin crítica (Mp) ideas irracionales dominantes en nuestra cultura, en la que la delgadez aparece como modelo único, compendio de inteligencia, belleza y éxito; quedando atrapadas en este tipo de juicios (MQnone), de los que no pueden salir ni hacer crítica (Mp), aunque razonen adecuadamente en otros temas (MQo); (2) Sus alteraciones de autopercepción [(H)] hacen que se refugien en una imagen fantaseada, que es el eje de sus intereses y lo único que realmente les importa; (3) Los recursos que poseen para decidir conductas y llevarlas a término deliberadamente (AdjD), y su escasa tendencia a la introspección (FD) conducen a que su decisión de no comer, basada en reflexiones distorsionadas y aceptadas pasivamente, tenga una gran fuerza y, por ello, sea tan difícil de modificar. Finalmente, según los datos Rorschach obtenidos, se señala la hipótesis de un trastorno de la personalidad como patología subyacente.

Rorschachiana 27, 211–217

Rorschachiana
Contents of Previous Volumes

Volume 19, 1994

Speaking Rorschach: Building Bridges of Understanding
Irving B. Weiner (United States)
The Rorschach and the Study of the Individual
John E. Exner, Jr. (United States)
The Rorschach and Other Projective Methods in Portugal
Danilo R. Silva and Maria Emilia Marques (Portugal)
Family Changing Process: Integration of Two Modalities of Rorschach Test Administration
Concepcion Sendin and Carmen Garcia Alba (Spain)
Object Relations Theory and the Integration of Empirical and Psychoanalytic Approaches to Rorschach Interpretation
Bruce L. Smith (United States)
Projective Approach to Personality Study in Soviet Psychology: A Summary of Research
Leonid F. Burlatchuk and Elena Yu. Korzhova (Ukraine)
Expression of Narcissistic Fantasy in the TAT
Francoise Brelet-Foulard (France)
The Battery as "Perceptual Hold" in Structural Diagnosis
Helena Lunazzi de Jubany (Argentina)
Some Contributions of Cognitive Science to the Rorschach Test
Marvin W. Acklin (United States)
Rorschach's Psychodiagnosis in Peru
Matilde Raez de Ramirez (Peru)
Recurring Objects in Rorschach Records Over a Period of About 30 Years: How Often Do People Report the Same Thing Again?
Harald Janson and Kakan Stattin (Sweden)

Volume 20, 1995

Speaking Rorschach: Let Not Theory Come Between Us
Irving B. Weiner (United States)
Words of Remembrance: In Memory of K. W. Bash
Walter Jäger (Switzerland)

Psychosomatic Diseases and the Rorschach Test
K. W. Bash (Switzerland)
Rorschach Variables As Possible Prognostic Indicators in Cases of Serious Psychic Trauma
Montserrat Ros Plana (Spain)
Interpretation and the Response Process
Anne Andronikof-Sanglade (France)
A Comparative Study of the Comprehensive System and a Psychoanalytic Sequence Analysis
Reiko Baba (Japan)
Anxiety, Productiveness, Performance, and Culture in the Rorschachs of a Multiethnic Group of Adolescents
Cicero Emidio Vaz (Brazil)
Healing the Past: An Incest Victim's Journey Back to Health
Mary S. Cerney (United States)
Is the Rorschach of Psychopaths the Same on Both Sides of the Atlantic?
Odile Husain (Canada)
The History of the Rorschach: Overcoming Bias in Multicultural Projective Assessment
Giuseppe Costantino, Rosemary Flanagan, and Robert Malgady (United States)
Transsexualism and Connection with Reality: Rorschach Data
Christian Mormont, Aude Michel, and Jacques Wauthy (Belgium)
On the Use of the Rorschach in the Assessment of Psychological Functioning Following Sexual Abuse in Adolescent Girls
Ana Lorena Rojas Breedy (Costa Rica)

Volume 21, 1996

Speaking Rorschach: A Test For All Seasons
Irving B. Weiner (United States)
Hermann Rorschach, M.D.: His Life and Work
Wolfgang Schwarz (United States)
The Rorschach in the Study of Coronary Heart Disease: A Review
Ana María Tuset Bertran (Spain)
The Stockholm Comparative Psychotherapy Study (COMPASS): Project Presentation and Preliminary Rorschach Findings
Anna Maria Carlsson, Marianne Nygren, David Clinton, and Berit Bihlár (Sweden)
Adolescence and Borderline Functioning: A Case Study
Catherine Chabert (France)
Beyond Subjects' Response: Detecting Suicidal Inclinations in the Rorschach Inkblot Technique
Alicia M. Passalacqua, Sylvia Echenique, María Teresa Herrara, and Dolores Orcoyen (Argentina)
Internalized Achievement or External Authority: Some Cultural Comparisons of Responses to TAT Card 1
George A. De Vos (United States)

The Rorschach: From Formal Factors to Forms of Organization: A Study of the Spatial Axis
Etel S. de Kacero (Argentina)
Alexithymia: Psychological Poverty or Psychological Richness? A Rorschach Study
Djaouida Petot (France)
The Rorschach Experience and Play Activities
Pamela Pressley Abraham (United States)

Volume 22, 1997

Speaking Rorschach: Our Method Stands Tall
Irving B. Weiner (United States)
Cultural Norms for TAT Narratives in Psychological Practice and Research: Illustrative Studies
David Ephraim, Ingrid Söchting, and James E. Marcia (Venezuela and Canada)
Location Tables, Form Quality, and Popular Responses in a Spanish Sample of 470 Subjects
Fátima Miralles Sangro (Spain)
Personality Factors in Genocide: The Rorschachs of Nazi War Criminals
Barry Ritzler (United States)
Rorschach and Hemispheric Specialization
Latife Yazigi (Brazil)
Hemipsheric Differences in the Processing of Ambiguity: Tachistoscopic Studies with Inkblots
Marianne Regard and Theodor Landis (Switzerland)
Rorschach Research and the Psychodiagnosis of Antisocial and Psychopathic Personalities
Carl B. Gacono and J. Reid Meloy (United States)
Borderline Personality Disorder: Content and Formal Analysis of the Rorschach
Franco Burla, Stefano Ferracuti, and Renato Lazzari (Italy)
Perversion: Affect and Thought
Pedro Pérez García, A. Tomayo Lacalle, M. L. Plumed Martin, and N. Briones del Dedo (Spain)
The Skull as a Symbol of Death in One Man's Rorschach
Kari S. Carstairs (England)
Rorschach Findings and Neuropsychological Comparison of First-Episode Psychotic Depression with First-Episode Nonpsychotic Depression and Schizophrenia: A Preliminary Report
Tuula Ilonen, Carl-Erik Mattlar, and Raimo K. R. Salokangas (Finland and Sweden)

Volume 23, 1999

The Rorschach Test in the Detection of Suicidal Potential
Alicia Martha Passalacqua (Argentina)

Rorschach and MMPI Evaluation of Depressive Components in Neurologically Affected Patients
Concepcion Sendín and Jesús De Felipe Oroquieta (Spain)
Examiner Effect on Number of Rorschach Responses at Current and Later Occasions
Harald Janson (Sweden)
Study of the Impact of a Gastroplasty on the Self-Image Through the Rorschach
Eric Marsden, Aude Michel, and Christian Mormont (Belgium)
Mania and Thought Disorders in a Ten-Year-Old Boy
Djaouida Petot (France)
The Adolf Eichmann Case: Contradictions, New Data and Integration
Alberto A. Peralta (USA)
Subtypes of Antisocial Personality Disorder and the Implications for Forensic Research: Issues in Personality Disorder Assessment
Hilda C. P. Morana (Brazil)
Methodological and Epistemological Issues Raised by the Use of the Rorschach Comprehensive System in Cross-Cultural Research
Vijé Franchi and Anne Andronikof-Sanglade (France)

Volume 24, 2000

Science and Ideology
Anne Andronikof (France)
Rorschach's Idea of a "Movement" Response in the Light of Recent Philosophy and Psychology of Perception
Helge Malmgren (Sweden)
The SCZI Index and the Normative Sample of Barcelona (1993)
Vera Campo (Spain)
Rorschach Content and Coping Type
Theresia Gabriel and Elfriede Opgenoorth (Austria)
Fantasmatic Dynamics of the Family: A Projective Approach and Psychosis
Isabelle Orgiazzi-Billon-Galland (France)
The Study of Some Personality Traits in Theological Students Using the Rorschach Test
Maria Célia Esgaib Kayatt Lacoski and Vera Nice Assumpção do Nascimento (Brazil)
A Comparative Study of Elective Abortion and Childbirth among Young Women in Quebec
Aïcha N. Dembri and Jocelyn Aubut (Canada)
Some Rorschach Variables from a Normative Study with 10-Year-Old Portuguese Children
Danilo R. Silva and Rui Campos (Portugal)
The Rorschach Comprehensive System Scoring Conceptualized by a Phenomenological Metalanguage
Jan Ivanouw (Denmark)
Rorschach Applications in Treatment Planning
John E. Exner, Jr. (USA)

Volume 25, 2002

Editorial Note
Anne Andronikof
Special Section: Rorschach Trauma Assessment
Guest Editor: David Ephraim
Introduction
David Ephraim (Venezuela/Canada)
Deciphering the Broken Narrative of Trauma: Signs of Traumatic Dissociation on the Rorschach
Judith G. Armstrong (USA)
Transgenerational Transmission of Trauma in Children of Holocaust Survivors: A Case Study
Ety Berant (Israel)
Rorschach Trauma Assessment of Survivors of Torture and State Violence
David Ephraim (Venezuela/Canada)
Rorschach Psychodiagnosis of Psychic Trauma in Sexually Abused Children
Maria Cristina Gravenhorst (Argentina)
Use of the Rorschach in the Assessment of War-Related Stress in Military Personnel
Patrick Sloan, Linda Arsenault, and Mark Hilsenroth (USA)

Other Topics
The Effect of Color on Productivity on Card X of the Rorschach
Danilo R. Silva (Portugal)
Chimeric Rorschach: A Research on Hemispheric Specialization
Latife Yazigi, Cristiane Seixas Duarte, Jacqueline Santoantonio, Andrés Eduardo Aguirre Antúnez, Antonio Carlos Pachecoe, Silva Neto, and Paulo Santana (Brasil)
Defying the Odds and Rorschach Space Responses: An Empirical Contribution
Uriel Last (Israel)
Rorschach Characteristics of Depressive Children with Suicidal Ideation
Djaouida Petot (France)
Cognitive Deficits in Patients with First-Episode Psychosis as Identified by Exner's Schizophrenia Index in Finland and Spain
Outi Kalla, Jarl Wahlström, Jukka Aaltonen, Juha Holma, Pentti Tuimala, and Carl-Erik Mattlar (Finland)

Volume 26, 2004

Editorial Note
Anne Andronikof
Special Section: Cross-Cultural Issues
Guest Editor: Carl-Erik Mattlar

Rorschachiana: Contents of Previous Volumes

Introduction
Carl-Erik Mattlar (Sweden)
Reaction to Tragic Loss of Sociocultural Environment in the Adivasi Tribes: A Rorschach Study
Hélène Salaün de Kertanguy and Anne Andronikof (France)
Comparison between the Original Rorschach Plates and the Parisi-Pes Parallel Series in Argentina
Alicia Martha Passalacqua and Lelia Sandra Pestana (Argentina)
The Impact of Education and/or Socioeconomic Conditions on Rorschach Data in a Brazilian Nonpatient Sample
Regina Sonia Gattas Fernandes do Nascimento (Brasil)
Rorschach Characteristics and Comparison of First-Episode Psychotic Patients in Finland and Spain
Outi Kalla, Jarl Wahlström, Jukka Aaltonen, Juha Holma, Pentti Tuimala, and Carl-Erik Mattlar (Finland)
Are We Entitled to Use the Rorschach Workshop's Norms When Interpreting the Comprehensive System in Finland?
Carl-Erik Mattlar (Sweden)

Other Topics
Differences in Comprehensive System Rorschach Variables between Groups Differing in Therapy Suitability
Marianne Nygren (Sweden)
Family Violence, Immigration Law, and the Rorschach
F. Barton Evans (USA)
The Rorschach Comprehensive System is Reliable, Valid, and Cost-Effective
Carl-Erik Mattlar (Sweden)